Lecture Notes in Computer Scien

Commenced Publication in 1973
Founding and Former Series Editors:
Gerhard Goos, Juris Hartmanis, and Jan van Leeuwen

Pascal Van Hentenryck (Ed.)

Practical Aspects of Declarative Languages

8th International Symposium, PADL 2006
Charleston, SC, USA, January 9-10, 2006
Proceedings

 Springer

Volume Editor

Pascal Van Hentenryck
Brown University
Dept. of Computer Science
P.O. Box 1910, Providence, RI 02912, USA
E-mail: pvh@cs.brown.edu

Library of Congress Control Number: 2005937161

CR Subject Classification (1998): D.3, D.1, F.3, D.2

LNCS Sublibrary: SL 2 – Programming and Software Engineering

ISSN	0302-9743
ISBN-10	3-540-30947-0 Springer Berlin Heidelberg New York
ISBN-13	978-3-540-30947-5 Springer Berlin Heidelberg New York

Springer is a part of Springer Science+Business Media

springer.com

© Springer-Verlag Berlin Heidelberg 2006
Printed in Germany

Typesetting: Camera-ready by author, data conversion by Scientific Publishing Services, Chennai, India
Printed on acid-free paper   SPIN: 11603023   06/3142   5 4 3 2 1 0

Preface

This volume contains the papers presented at the Eighth International Symposium on Practical Aspects of Declarative Languages (PADL 2006) held on January 9-10, 2006, in Charleston, South Carolina. Information about the conference can be found at http://www.cs.brown.edu/people/pvh/PADL06.html. As is now traditional, PADL 2006 was co-located with the 33rd Annual Symposium on Principles of Programming Languages that was held on January 11-13, 2006.

The PADL conference series is a forum for researchers and practioners to present original work emphasizing novel applications and implementation techniques for all forms of declarative concepts. Topics of interest include, but are not limited to:

- Innovative applications of declarative languages;
- Declarative domain-specific languages and applications;
- Practical applications of theoretical results;
- New language developments and their impact on applications;
- Evaluation of implementation techniques on practical applications;
- Novel implementation techniques relevant to applications;
- Novel uses of declarative languages in the classroom;
- Practical experiences.

This year, there were 36 submissions. Each submission was reviewed by at least three Programme Committee members. The committee decided to accept 15 papers. In addition, the programme also included three invited talks by Erik Meijer, David Roundy, and Philip Walder.

I would like to thank the Program Committee members who worked hard to produce high-quality reviews for the papers, as well as all the reviewers involved in the paper selection. It was a great pleasure to work with all of you. I also would like to thank Gopal Gupta for his availability and his expert advice in many aspects of the conference. We were also lucky to attract three outstanding invited speakers and I would like to take this opportunity to thank them again for accepting our invitation. Finally, thanks to Andrei Voronkov for his help with the EasyChair system that automates so many of the tedious tasks involved in chairing a conference.

October 2005   Pascal Van Hentenryck

Organization

Chairs

Gopal Gupta
General Chair
Department of Computer Science
University of Texas at Dallas
Dallas, TX, USA
Email: gupta@utdallas.edu

Pascal Van Hentenryck
Programme Chair
Department of Computer Science
Brown University
Providence, RI, USA
Email: pvh@cs.brown.edu

Programme Committee

Kenichi Asai
Daniel Damian
Mireille Ducasse
Matthew Flatt
Gopal Gupta
Manuel Hermenegildo
Paul Hudak
Narendra Jussien
Laurent Michel
Gopalan Nadathur
Enrico Pontelli
Peter Van Roy
Vitor Santos-Costa
Christian Schulte
Peter Stuckey
David S. Warren
Roland Yap

Additional Reviewers

Ajay Bansal
Ralph Becket

Nicolas Beldiceanu
Stefano Bistarelli
Francisco Bueno
Daniel Cabeza
Hadrien Cambazard
Manuel Carro
Mike Codish
Raphael Collet
Jesus Correas
Tristan Denmat
Wlodek Drabent
Greg Duck
Ines Dutra
Kevin Glynn
Yves Jaradin
Srividya Kona
Ricardo Lopes
Ajay Mallya
Boriss Mejias
Jose Morales
Yoann Padioleau
Luis Quesada
Emad Saad
Benjamin Sigonneau
Luke Simon
Tran Cao Son
Fred Spiessens
Qian Wang

Table of Contents

Using CHRs to Generate Functional Test Cases for the Java Card Virtual Machine*

Sandrine-Dominique Gouraud and Arnaud Gotlieb

IRISA/CNRS UMR 6074,
Campus Universitaire de Beaulieu,
35042 Rennes Cedex, France
Phone: +33 (0)2 99 84 75 76 – Fax: +33 (0) 2 99 84 71 71
gouraud@lri.fr, gotlieb@irisa.fr

Abstract. Automated functional testing consists in deriving test cases from the specification model of a program to detect faults within an implementation. In our work, we investigate using Constraint Handling Rules (CHRs) to automate the test cases generation process of functional testing. Our case study is a formal model of the Java Card Virtual Machine (JCVM) written in a sub-language of the Coq proof assistant. In this paper we define an automated translation from this formal model into CHRs and propose to generate test cases for each bytecode definition of the JCVM. The originality of our approach resides in the use of CHRs to faithfully model the formally specified operational semantics of the JCVM. The approach has been implemented in Eclipse Prolog and a full set of test cases have been generated for testing the JCVM.

Keywords: CHR, Software testing, Java Card Virtual Machine.

1 Introduction

The increasing complexity of computer programs ensures that automated software testing will continue to play a prevalent role in software validation. In this context, automated functional testing consists in 1) generating test cases from a specification model, 2) executing an implementation using the generated test cases and then 3) checking the computed results with the help of an oracle. In automated functional testing, oracles are generated from the model to provide the expected results. Several models have been used to generate test cases: algebraic specifications [1], B machineries [2] or finite state machines [3], just to name a few.

In our work, we investigate using Constraint Handling Rules (CHRs) to automate the test cases and oracles generation process of functional testing. Our

---

* This work is supported by the Réseau National des Technologies Logicielles as part of the CASTLES project (www-sop.inria.fr/everest/projects/castles/). This project aims at defining a certification environment for the JavaCard platform. The project involves two academic partners: the Everest and Lande teams of INRIA and two industrial partners: Oberthur Card Systems and Alliance Qualit Logicielle.

P. Van Hentenryck (Ed.): PADL 2006, LNCS 3819, pp. 1–15, 2006.

specification model is written in a sub-language of Coq: the Jakarta Specification Language (JSL) [4]. Coq is the INRIA's proof assistant [5] based on the calculus of inductive constructions that allows to mechanically prove high-order theorems. Recently, Coq and JSL were used to derive certified Byte Code Verifiers by abstraction from the specification of a Java Card Virtual Machine [4,6]. The Java Card Virtual Machine (JCVM) carries out all the instructions (or bytecodes) supported by Java Card (new, push, pop, invokestatic, invokevirtual, etc.). In this paper, we present how to generate test cases and oracles for each JSL byte code specification. Our idea is to benefit from the high declarativity of CHRs to express the test purpose as well as the JSL specification rules into a single framework. Then, by using traditional CHR propagation and labelling, we generate test cases and oracles as solutions of the underlying constraint system. The approach has been implemented with the CHR library of Eclipse Prolog [7] and a full set of test cases have been generated for testing the JCVM.

This paper is organised as follows: Section 2 introduces JSL and its execution model; Section 3 recalls some background on CHRs; Section 4 introduces the translation rules used to convert a formal specification written in JSL into CHRs; Section 5 presents our algorithm to generate functional test cases and oracles for testing an implementation of the JCVM; Section 6 describes some related works, and finally Section 7 concludes the paper with some research perspectives.

2   The Jakarta Specification Language

The Jakarta Specification Language (JSL), as introduced in [8], is a first order language with a polymorphic type system. JSL functions are formally defined with conditional rewriting rules.

2.1   Syntax

JSL expressions are first order terms with equality (==), built from term variables and from constant symbols. A constant symbol is either a constructor symbol introduced by data types definitions or a function symbol introduced by function definitions.

Let $\mathcal{C}$ be a set of constructor symbols, $\mathcal{F}$ be a set of function symbols and $\mathcal{V}$ be a set of term variables. The JSL expressions set is the term set $\mathcal{E}$ defined by: $\mathcal{E} ::= \mathcal{V} | \mathcal{E} == \mathcal{E} | \mathcal{C}\mathcal{E}^* | \mathcal{F}\mathcal{E}^*$. Let var be the function defined on $\mathcal{E} \to \mathcal{V}^*$ which returns the set of variables of a JSL expression.

Each function symbol is defined by a set of conditional rewriting rules. This unusual format for rewriting is close to functional language with pattern-matching and proof assistant. These (oriented) conditional rewriting rules are of the form $l_1 \to r_1, \ldots, l_n \to r_n \Rightarrow g \to d$ where:

- $g = f v_1 \ldots v_m$ where $\forall i, v_i \in \mathcal{V}$ and $\forall i, j, v_i \neq v_j$
- l_i is either a variable or a function which does not introduce new variables: for $1 \leq i \leq n$, $var(l_i) \subseteq var(g) \cup var(r_1) \cup \ldots \cup var(r_{i-1})$

- r_i should be a value called *pattern* (built from variables and constructors), should contain only fresh variables and should be linear[1]:
  for $1 \leq i, j \leq n$ and $i \neq j$, $var(r_i) \cap var(g) = \emptyset$ and
  $var(r_i) \cap var(r_j) = \emptyset$
- d is an expression and $var(d) \subseteq var(g) \cup var(r_1) \ldots \cup var(r_n)$

The rule means if for all i, l_i can be rewritten into r_i then g is rewritten into d. Thereafter, these rules are called JSL rules. JSL allows the definition of partial or non-deterministic functions.

*Example 1 (JSL def. of **plus** extracted from the JCVM formal model).*
data nat $= 0 \mid S$ nat.
function **plus** :=
$\langle plus\_r1 \rangle \quad n \rightarrow 0 \quad \Rightarrow (plus\,n\,m) \rightarrow m;$
$\langle plus\_r2 \rangle \quad n \rightarrow (S\,p) \Rightarrow (plus\,n\,m) \rightarrow (S\,(plus\,p\,m)).$

2.2   Execution Model of JSL

Let $e_{|p}$ denote the subterm of e at position p then expression $e[p \leftarrow d]$ denotes the term e where $e_{|p}$ is replaced by term d.

Let $\mathcal{R}$ be a set of rewriting rules, then an expression e is rewritten into e' if there exists a rule $l_1 \rightarrow r_1, \ldots, l_n \rightarrow r_n \Rightarrow g \rightarrow d$ in $\mathcal{R}$, a position p and a substitution θ such as:

- $e_{|p} = \theta g$ and $e' = e[p \leftarrow \theta d]$
- $\{\theta l_i \rightarrow^* \theta r_i\}_{\forall 1 \leq i \leq n}$ where $\rightarrow^*$ is the transitive cloture of $\rightarrow$

Note that nothing prevents JSL specifications to be non-terminating or non-confluent. However, the formal model of the JCVM we are using as a case study has been proved terminating and confluent within the Coq proof assistant [4,6].

Example 2 (Rewriting of $(plus\,0\,(plus(S\,0)\,0))$).
$(plus\,0\,(plus\,(S\,0)\,0)) \rightarrow_{r1} (plus\,(S\,0)\,0) \rightarrow_{r2} (S\,(plus\,0\,0)) \rightarrow_{r1} (S\,0)$

3   Background on Constraint Handling Rules

This section is inspired of Thom Frühwirth's survey and book [9,10]. The Constraint Handling Rules (CHRs) language is a committed-choice language, which consists of multi-headed guarded rules that rewrite constraints into simpler ones until they are solved. This language extends a host language with constraint solving capabilities. Implementations of CHRs are available in Eclipse Prolog [7], Sicstus Prolog, HAL [11], etc.

---

[1] All the variables are required to be distinct.

3.1   Syntax

The CHR language is based on **simplification** where constraints are replaced by simpler ones while logical equivalence is preserved and **propagation** where new constraints which are logically redundant are added to cause further simpli-fication. A constraint is either a built-in (predefined) first-order predicate or a CHR (user-defined) constraint defined by a finite set of CHR rules. Simplification rules are of the form H <=> G | B and propagation rules are of the form H ==> G | B where H denotes a possibly multi-head CHR constraint, the guard G is a conjunction of constraints and the body B is a conjunction of built-in and CHR constraints. Each time a CHR constraint is woken, its guard must either succeed or fail. If the guard succeeds, one commits to it and then the body is executed. Constraints in the guards are usually restricted to be built-in constraints. When other constraints are used in the guards (called *deep guards*), special attention must be paid to the way guards are evaluated. Section 4.2 discusses the use of *deep guards* in our framework.

Example 3 (CHRs that can be used to define the plus *constraint).*
R1 @ plus(A,B,R) <=> A=0 | R=B.
R2 @ plus(A,B,R) <=> A=s(C) | plus(C,B,D), R=s(D).
C @ plus(A,B,R) ==> plus(B,A,R).
The construction ...@ gives names to CHRs.

3.2   Semantics

Given a constraint theory (CT) (with true, false and an equality constraint $=$) which determines the meaning of built-in constraints, the declarative interpreta-tion of a CHR program is given by a conjunction of universally quantified logical formula. There is a formula for each rule.

If $\bar{x}$ denotes the variables occurring in the head H and $\bar{y}$ (resp. $\bar{z}$) the variables occurring in the guard (resp. body) of the rule, then

  – a simplification CHR is interpreted as $\forall \bar{x}(\exists \bar{y}G \rightarrow (H \leftrightarrow \exists \bar{z}B))$
  – a propagation CHR is interpreted as $\forall \bar{x}(\exists \bar{y}G \rightarrow (H \rightarrow \exists \bar{z}B))$

The operational semantics of CHR programs is given by a transition system where a state $< G, C >$ consists of two components: the goal store G and the constraint store C. An initial state is of the form $< G, true >$. A final state $< G, C >$ is successful when no transition is applicable whereas it is failed when $C = false$ (the constraint store is contradictory).

Solve.   If C is a built-in constraint and $CT \models (C \wedge D) \leftrightarrow D'$
      Then $< C \wedge G, D > \mapsto < G, D' >$
Simplify.   If $F <=> D|H$ and $CT \models \forall(C \rightarrow \exists \bar{x}(F = E \wedge D)$
      Then $< E \wedge G, C > \mapsto < H \wedge G, (F = E) \wedge D \wedge C >$
Propagate.   If $F => D|H$ and $CT \models \forall(C \rightarrow \exists \bar{x}(F = E \wedge D)$
      Then $< E \wedge G, C > \mapsto < E \wedge H \wedge G, (F = E) \wedge D \wedge C >$

Rules are applied fairly (every rule that is applicable is applied eventually). Propagation rule is applied at most once on the same constraints in order to avoid trivial non-termination. However, CHR programs can be non-confluent and non-terminating.

Example 4 (Several examples of the CHR solving process).

```
                plus(s(0),s(0),R)
⟼Simplify_R2  plus(0,s(0),R1), R=s(R1)
⟼Simplify_R1  R1=s(0), R=s(R1)
⟼Solve        R=s(s(0))
```

The following example exploits the propagation rule of **plus**. Without this rule, the term plus(M,s(0),s(s(0))) would be delayed.

```
                plus(M,s(0),s(s(0)))
⟼Propagate_C  plus(M,s(0),s(s(0))), plus(s(0),M,s(s(0)))
⟼Simplify_R2  plus(M,s(0),s(s(0))), plus(0,M,s(0))
⟼Simplify_R1  plus(M,s(0),s(s(0))), M=s(0)
⟼Solve        plus(s(0),s(0),s(s(0))), M=s(0)
⟼Simplify_R2  plus(0,s(0),s(0)), M=s(0)
⟼Simplify_R1  s(0)=s(0), M=s(0)
⟼Solve        M=s(0)
```

The following example shows the deduction of a relation $(M = N)$:

```
                plus(M,0,N)
⟼Propagate_C  plus(M,0,N), plus(0,M,N)
⟼Simplify_R1  plus(M,0,N), M=N
⟼Solve        plus(M,0,M), M=N
```

4 JSL to CHR Translation Method

Our approach is based on the syntactical translation of JSL specifications into CHRs. The translation method is described under the form of judgements.

4.1 Translation Method

There are three kinds of judgements: judgements for JSL expressions, judgements for JSL rewriting rules (main operator $\longrightarrow$) and judgements for JSL functions (main operator $\Rightarrow$).

The judgement $e \rightsquigarrow t \lhd \{C\}$ states that JSL expression e is translated into term t under the conjunction of constraints C.

$$\frac{variable(v)}{v \rightsquigarrow v \lhd \{\mathtt{true}\}} \qquad \frac{constant(c)}{c \rightsquigarrow c \lhd \{\mathtt{true}\}}$$

$$\frac{e_1 \rightsquigarrow t_1 \lhd \{c_1\} \ \ldots \ e_n \rightsquigarrow t_n \lhd \{c_n\}}{c\, e_1 \ldots e_n \rightsquigarrow c(t_1, \ldots, t_n) \lhd \{c_1, \ldots, c_n\}}$$

$$\frac{e_1 \rightsquigarrow t_1 \lhd \{c_1\} \ \ldots \ e_n \rightsquigarrow t_n \lhd \{c_n\}}{f\, e_1 \ldots e_n \rightsquigarrow r \lhd \{c_1, \ldots, c_n, f(t_1, \ldots, t_n, r)\}}$$

The judgement $(e \to p) \rightsquigarrow \{C\}$ states that the JSL rewriting rule $e \to p$ is translated into the conjunction of constraints $\{C\}$.

$$\overline{(v \to p) \rightsquigarrow \{v = p\}}$$

$$\frac{e_1 \rightsquigarrow t_1 \lhd \{c_1\} \ \ldots \ e_n \rightsquigarrow t_n \lhd \{c_n\} \quad p \rightsquigarrow p \lhd \{\texttt{true}\}}{(f\, e_1 \ldots e_n \to p) \rightsquigarrow \{c_1, \ldots, c_n, f(t_1, \ldots, t_n, p)\}}$$

The judgement $(l_1 \to r_1, \ldots, l_n \to r_n \Rightarrow g \to d) \rightsquigarrow g' \Leftrightarrow \texttt{guard|body}$ states that the JSL function rule $l_1 \to r_1, \ldots, l_n \to r_n \Rightarrow g \to d$ is translated into the CHR $g' \Leftrightarrow \texttt{guard|body}$ where g' is a CHR constraint associated to the expression g, guard is the conjunction of constraints corresponding to the translation of the rules $l_i \to r_i$, and body is a conjunction of constraints corresponding to the translation of the expression d.

$$\frac{l_1 \to r_1 \rightsquigarrow g_1 \quad \ldots \quad l_n \to r_n \rightsquigarrow g_n \qquad\qquad e \rightsquigarrow t \lhd \{B\}}{\begin{array}{c}(l_1 \to r_1, \ldots, l_n \to r_n \Rightarrow f\, v_1 \ldots v_k \to e) \\ \rightsquigarrow f(v_1, \ldots, v_k, r) \Leftrightarrow g_1, \ldots, g_n | B, r = t.\end{array}}$$

Note that non-determinism, confluence and termination are preserved by the translation as the operational semantics of CHRs extends the execution model of JSL functions.

4.2   Deep Guards

In the translation method, we considered that CHR guards could be built over prolog goals and CHR calls. This approach, which is referred to as deep guards, has received much attention by the past. See [9,12] for a detailed presentation of deep guards. Smolka recalls in [13] that "deep guards constitute the central mechanism to combine processes and (encapsulated) search for problem-solving". Deep guards are used in several systems such as AKL, Eclipse Prolog [7,9], Oz [12] or HAL [11].

Deep guards rely on how guard entailment is tested in conditional constraints and CHRs. Technically, a guard entailment test is called an "ask constraint" whereas a constraint added to the constraint store is called a "tell constraint" and both operations are clearly distinct. For example, if the constraint store contains $X = p(Z), Y = p(a)$ then a tell constraint $X = Y$ where = denotes Prolog unification, will result in the store $X = p(a), Y = p(a), Z = a$ whereas the corresponding ask constraint will leave the store unchanged and will suspend until the constraint $Z = a$ would be entailed or disentailed.

The current approach to deal with deep guards that contain Prolog goals (but not CHR calls) consists in considering guards as tell constraints and checking at runtime that no guard variable is modified. This approach is based on the fact that the only way of constraining terms in the Herbrand Universe is unification ($=$) and that the corresponding ask constraint of unification is well-known: this is the "equality of terms" test ($==$). For example, if $X = Y$ is a tell constraint then $X == Y$ corresponds to its ask constraint. However, when Prolog goals are involved into the guards, the guard entailment test is no more decidable as non-terminating computations can arise. Note that CHR programs are not guaranteed to terminate (consider for example $p <=> true|p$). Even when non-terminating computations are avoided this approach can be very inefficient as possible long term computations in guards are executed every time a CHR constraint is woken. An approach for this problem consists in pre–computing the guard by executing the Prolog goal only once, and then testing entailment on the guard variables.

When CHRs are involved into the guards, the problem is more difficult as guards can set up constraints. In that case, considering guards as tell constraints is no longer correct as wrong deductions can be made. Our approach for this problem consists in suspending the guard entailment test until it could be decided. More precisely, the guard entailment test is delayed until all the guard variables become instantiated[2]. At worst, this instantiation arises during the labelling process. Of course, this approach leads to fewer deductions at propagation time but it remains manageable when we have to deal with deep guards containing CHR calls.

4.3   Implementation of the Translation Method

We implemented the translation method into a library called JSL2CHR.pl. Given a file containing JSL definitions, the library builds an abstract syntax tree by using a Definite Clause Grammar of JSL, and then automatically produces equivalent CHR rules. The library was used on the JSL specifications of the JCVM, which is composed of 310 functions. As a result, 1537 CHRs were generated.

5   Tests Generation for the JCVM

This section is devoted to the presentation of both the JCVM specification model and the test cases and oracle generation method. The experimental results we obtained by generating test cases for the JCVM are presented in Section 5.3.

5.1   The Java Card Virtual Machine

Unlike other smart cards, a Java Card includes a Java Virtual Machine implemented in its read-only memory part. The structure of a Java Card platform is given in Fig.1. It consists of several components, such as a runtime environment, an implementation of the Java Virtual Machine, the open and global platform applications, a set of packages implementing the standard SUN's Java Card API and a set of proprietary APIs. A Java Card program is called an applet and communicates with a card reader through APDU[3] buffers.

---

[2] This solution is close to the traditional techniques of coroutining in Prolog as implemented by `freeze` or `delay` built-in predicates.

[3] <u>A</u>pplication <u>P</u>rotocol <u>D</u>ata <u>U</u>nit is an ISO-normalised communication format between the card and the off-card applications.

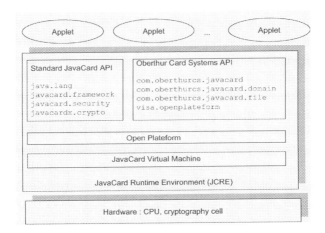

Fig. 1. A Java Card platform

All the components of a Java Card platform must be thoroughly tested before the Card would be released. But, in this paper, we concentrate only on the JCVM functional testing process. In the formal model given in [14], the JCVM is a state machine described by a small-step semantics: each bytecode is formalised as a state transformer.

States modelling. Each state contains all the elements manipulated by a program during its execution: values, objects and an execution environment for each called method. States are formalised as a record consisting of a heap (he) which contains the objects created during execution, a static heap (sh) which contains static fields of classes and a stack of frames (fr) which contain the execution environments of methods. States are tagged "Abnormal" if an exception (or an error) is raised, "Normal" otherwise.

Bytecodes modelling. The JCVM contains 185 distinct bytecodes which can be classified into the following classes[15]: arithmetic operations (`sadd`, `idiv`, `sshr`, ...), type verifications on objects (`instanceof`, ...), (conditional) branching (`ifcmp`, `goto`, ...), method calls (`invokestatic`, `invokevirtual`, ...), operations on local variables (`iload`, `sstore`, ...), operations on objects (`getfield`, `newarray`, ...), operations on operands stack (`ipush`, `pop`, ...) and flow modifiers (`sreturn`, `throw`, ...).

Most of the bytecodes have a similar execution scheme: to decompose the current state, to get components of the state, to perform tests in order to detect execution errors then to build the next state. In the JSL formal model of the JCVM, several bytecodes are specified with the similar JSL functions. They only distinguish by their type which is embodied in the JSL function definition as a parameter. As a result, the model contains only 45 distinct JSL functions associated to the bytecodes. Remaining functions are auxiliary functions that perform various computations. Some JSL functions calls other functions in their rewriting rules; this process is modelled by using deep guards in CHR, preserving so the operational semantics of the JCVM.

Example of a JSL bytecode specification. As an example, consider the JSL specification of bytecode *push*: given a primary type t, a value x and a JCVM state st, *push* updates the operand stack of the first execution method environment in st by adding the value x of type t:

$function$ **push** :=
$\langle push\_r1 \rangle\ (stack\_f\ st) \to Nil$
$\quad \Rightarrow (push\ t\ x\ st) \to (abortCode\ State\_error\ st);$
$\langle push\_r2 \rangle\ (stack\_f\ st) \to (Cons\ h\ lf)$
$\quad \Rightarrow (push\ t\ x\ st) \to (update\_frame(result\_push\ t\ x\ h)\ st).$

push uses the auxiliary function **stack_f** that returns the stack of frames (environments for executing methods) of a given state.

$function$ **stack_f** :=
$\langle stack\_f\_r1 \rangle\ st \to (Jcvm\_state\ sh\ he\ fr) \Rightarrow (stack\_f\ st) \to fr.$

Example of CHR generated for a bytecode. The following CHRs were produced by the library JSL2CHR.pl:

```
stack_f_r1 @ stack_f(St,R) <=> St=jcvm_state(Sh,He,Fr)
  | R=Fr.
push_r1 @ push(T,X,St,R) <=> stack_f(St,nil)
  | abortCode(state_error(St),Ra), R=Ra.
push_r2 @ push(T,X,St,R) <=> stack_f(St,cons(H,Lf))
  | result_push(T,X,H,Res), update_frame(Res,St,Ru), R=Ru.
```

In this example, the JSL function **stack_f** was translated into a CHR although it is only an accessor. As a consequence we get a deep guard in the definition of CHR push. This could be easily optimised by identifying the accessors into the JSL specification with the help of the user. However, we would like the approach to remain fully automated hence we did not realized this improvement and maintained the deep guards.

5.2   Test Cases and Oracles Generation Method

Our approach is inspired of classical functional testing where test cases are generated according to some coverage criteria. We proposed to generate test cases that ensure each CHR would be covered at least once during the selection. We call this criterion *All_rules*. Note that this approach is based on two usual assumptions, namely the correctness of the formal specification and the uniformity hypothesis[1]. The uniformity hypothesis says that if a rule provides a correct answer for a single test case then it will provide correct answers for all the test cases that activate the rule. Of course, this assumption is strong and nothing can prevent it to be violated but recall that testing can only detect faults within an implementation and cannot prove the correctness of the implementation (as stated by Prof. E. Dijkstra).

Abstract test cases. In the JSL formal model of the JCVM, a test case consists of a fully instantiated state of the VM and the valuation of several input parameters. However, it happens that several values of the state or several parameter values remain useless when testing a selected bytecode. To deal with these situations, the notion of abstract test case is used. In our case, an abstract test case represents a class of test cases that activate a given JSL function or equivalently a given CHR. The process which consists to instantiate an abstract test case to actually test an implementation is called concretization [2] and can be delayed until the test-execution time. For each CHR automatically generated, the goal is to find a minimal substitution of the variables (an abstract test case) that activate it. Covering a CHR consists in finding input values such as its guard would be satisfied. Hence, a constrained search process over the guards and the possible substitutions is performed. Before going to more details into this process, consider the CHRs of bytecode *push*. To activate *push_r1*, the states stack St must be empty whereas to activate *push_r2*, St must be rewritten into *cons H Lf* (i.e. to posses at least one frame). Note that H, Lf, T and X are not constrained and do not require to be instantiated in the abstract test case. However, a randomised labelling can be used and to generate the two following concrete test cases, written under the form of JSL expressions[4]:
$(Bool, POS(XI(XO(XH))), Jcvm\_state(Nil, Nil, Nil))$ and
$(Byte, NEG(XH), Jcvm\_state(Nil, Nil, Cons(Frame(Nil, Nil, S(S(0)),$
$Package(0, S(0), Nil), True, S(0)), Nil)))$.

A constrained search process over the guards. As usual in constraint programming, we would like to see the constraints playing an active role by exploiting the relations before labelling (test-and-generate approach). Note that this contrasts with classical functional testing techniques that usually instantiate first the variables and then check if they satisfy the requirements (generate-and-test approach).

Consider a CHR $r : H \Leftrightarrow G|B$ where $G = p_1, \ldots, p_n$. Satisfying the guard G requires to satisfy at least one guard of the CHRs that define each predicate p_i of G, i.e. finding a valuation such as p_i is simplified either in $true$ or in a consistent conjunction of equalities. When p_i himself is a CHR call (deep guards), then its guard and body are also required to be consistent with the rest of the constraints. According to the *All_rules* testing criterion, the constraint store takes the following form:

$$\bigwedge_i \left(\bigvee_j (guard(p_i, j) \wedge body(p_i, j)) \right)$$

where $guard(p_i, j)$ (resp. $body(p_i, j)$) denotes the guard (resp. body) of the jth rule defining p_i. Any solution of this constraint store can be interpreted as a test case that activates the CHR under test. Finding a solution to this constraint

---

[4] *Jcvm_state, Frame, Package, XI, X0, XH, POS, Byte, NEG, Bool* and *True* are JSL constructor symbols given in the JCVM formal model.

store leads to explore a possibly infinite search tree, as recursive or mutually recursive CHR are allowed. However, a simple occur-check test permits to avoid such problems. In this work, we followed a heuristic which consists to select first the guard with the easier guard to satisfy. A guard was considered easier to satisfy than another when it contains a smaller number of deep guards. The idea behind this heuristic is to avoid the complex case during the generation. This approach is debatable as these complex cases may contain the more subtle faults. See section 5.3 for a discussion on possible improvements. Note that the constraint store consistency is checked before going into a next branch, hence constraints allows pruning the search tree before making a choice. Note also that the test case generation process requires only to find a single solution and not all solutions, hence a breath-first search could be performed to avoid infinite derivations.

Oracles generation. As the CHR specification of the JCVM is executable and the formal model is supposed to be correct, oracles can be generated just by interpreting the CHR program with generated test cases. For example, the following request gives us the oracle for the test case generated for $push\_r1$:

```
?- push(bool,pOS(xI(xO(xH))),jcvm_state(nil,nil,nil)),R).
R=abnormal(jCVMError(eCode(state_error)),jcvm_state(nil,nil,nil))
```

Providentially, oracles can also be derived for abstract test cases. For example, oracle for abstract test case of $push\_r1$ is computed by the following request:

```
?- push(T,X,jcvm_state(Sh,He,nil)),R).
R=abnormal(jCVMError(eCode(state_error)),jcvm_state(Sh,He,nil))
```

When delayed goals are present, a labelling process must be launched to avoid suspension. For example, the following request obtained by using the generated abstract test cases for $push\_r2$:

```
?- push(T,X,jcvm_state(Sh,He,cons(H,Lf))),R).
T=T, X=X, Sh=Sh, He=He, H=H, Lf=Lf, R=R
Delayed goals: push(T,X,jcvm_state(Sh,He,cons(H,Lf)),R)
```

requires R to be unified to $cons(\_X, \_S)$ to wake up the suspended goal. The labelling process can be based on deterministic or randomised[16] labelling strategies. In software testing approaches, random selection is usually preferred as it improves the flaws detection capacity. The simplest approach consists in generating terms based on a uniform distribution. Lot of works have been carried out to address the problem of uniform generation of terms and are related to the random generation of combinatorial structures [17]. In a previous work [18], we proposed a uniform random test cases generation technique based on combinatorial structures designs.

5.3   Experimental Results

As previously said, the library JSL2CHR.pl generated 1537 CHRs that specify 45 JCVM bytecodes. The library generates a CHR program that is compiled by using the *ech* library of Eclipse Prolog [7]. We present the experimental results we obtained by generating abstract test cases for covering all the 443 CHRs

Table 1. Memory and CPU runtime measures for each bytecode

Name	#tc	global stack (bytes)	local stack (bytes)	trail stack (bytes)	runtime (ms)
aload	1	33976048	148	1307064	0
arraylength	1	33849512	148	1299504	0
astore	1	33945864	148	1306660	0
invokestatic	1	33849512	148	1299504	0
nop	1	33945864	148	1306660	0
aconstnull	2	33854760	424	1300336	0
goto	2	33951112	424	1307492	0
jsr	2	33951112	424	1307492	0
push	2	33951112	424	1307492	0
conv	3	34055304	1076	1315924	10
dup	3	33972696	992	1310252	0
getfield	3	33876344	992	1303096	10
getfield_this	3	33876344	992	1303096	0
neg	3	34055304	1076	1315924	11
new	3	33971904	1020	1309932	11
pop	3	33972152	992	1310156	0
pop2	3	34074480	1076	1317828	0
putfield	3	33885840	1076	1303944	0
putfield_this	3	33876344	992	1303096	0
dup2	4	34122280	1884	1322772	10
swap	4	34029448	1884	1315948	11
ifnull	5	34023088	2216	1315392	10
ifnonnull	5	33926736	2216	1308236	10
icmp	6	34409440	3480	1343428	50
if_acmp_cond	6	34012528	3624	1316892	20
const	7	33968512	1512	1309716	0
invokespecial	7	34027448	4020	1317168	20
if_cond	8	34047496	3772	1319316	10
ret	8	34059064	3940	1320780	11
invokevirtual	9	34432272	7632	1349576	60
arith	11	33948080	836	1306660	0
athrow	11	34596760	7648	1364512	90
invokeinterface	11	35007240	12104	1394104	120
newarray	13	34073536	7604	1325612	20
return	13	34889544	11448	1386532	91
if_scmp_cond	14	34349752	11004	1351220	49
inc	18	34305392	9568	1344628	29
lookupswitch	18	34117768	9548	1332008	29
tableswitch	18	34117768	9548	1332008	31
load	19	34263232	11672	1343060	30
store	25	34752536	20108	1390876	81
checkcast	30	35053520	21384	1419380	280
getstatic	33	34408808	20652	1360596	60
putstatic	34	34944800	28660	1416196	120
instanceof	62	36468800	46964	1555588	580

associated to the bytecodes of the JCVM. These results were obtained on an Intel Pentium M at 2GHz with 1GB of RAM under Linux Redhat 2.6 The full process of generation of the abstract test cases for the 45 bytecodes (443 test cases) took 3.4s of CPU time and 47 Mbytes as the global stack size, 0.3 Mbytes as the local stack size and 2.6 Mbytes as the trail stack size. The detailed results for each bytecode are given in Tab.1, ordered by increasing number of abstract test cases (second column). Tab.1 contains the stack sizes as well as the CPU time (excluding time spent in garbage collection and system calls) required for the generation.

Analysis and discussion. The approach ensures the coverage of each rule of the JSL bytecodes in a very short period of CPU time. The global and trail stacks remain stable whereas the local stack size increases with the number of test cases. A possible explanation is that some CHRs exit non-deterministically and allocation of variables cannot be undone in this case. We implemented a heuristic which consists to favour the CHRs that contain the smallest number of deep guards. This heuristic behaves well as shown by the short CPU time required for the bytecodes that are specified with a lot of CHRs (`instanceof` is specified with 62 CHRs and only 0.6s of CPU time is required to generate the 62 abstract test cases). However, most of the time, this heuristic leads to generate test cases that put the JCVM into an abnormal state. In fact, in the JSL specification of the JCVM the abnormal states can often be reached by corrupting an input parameter. As a consequence, they are easy to reach. Although this heuristic is suitable to reach our test purpose (covering *All_rules*) and corresponds to some specific testing criterion such as *Test_all_corrupting_input* , it is debatable because it does not represent the general behaviour. Other approaches, which could lead to better test cases, need to be studied and evaluated. For example, selecting first the guard that contains the greatest number of deep guards could lead to build test cases that activate interesting parts of the specification. Finally, in these experiments, we only generated abstract test cases and did not evaluate the time required in the concretization step. Although, this step does not introduce research problems, considering it would allow to get a more accurate picture of test case and oracle generation with CHR. Thus, we could evaluate the efficiency of our approach and compare it to existing techniques.

6   Related Work

Bernot and al. [1] pioneered the use of Logic Programming to construct a test set from a formal specification. Starting from an algebraic specification, the test cases were selected using Horn clauses Logic. More recently, Gotlieb and al. [19] proposed to generate test sets for structural testing of C programs by using Constraint Logic Programming over finite domains. Given the source code of a program, a semantically-equivalent constraint logic program was built and questioned to find test data that cover a selected testing criterion. Legeard and al.[2] proposed a method for functional boundary testing from B and Z formal specifications based on set constraint solving techniques (CLP($\mathcal{S}$)). They applied the approach to the transaction mechanism of Java Card that was formally specified in B. Test cases were only derived to activate the boundary states of the specification of the transaction mechanism. Only Lötzbeyer and Pretschner [20,21] proposed a software testing technique that uses CHR constraint solving. In this work, models are finite state automata describing the behaviour of the system under test and test cases are composed of sequence of input/output events. CHR is used to define new constraint solvers and permits to generate complex data types. Our work distinguishes by the systematic translation of formal specifications into CHRs. Our approach does not restrict the form of guards in CHR and appears so as more declarative to generate test cases.

7   Conclusion

In this paper, we have proposed to use the CHRs to generate functional test cases for a JCVM implementation. A JSL formal specification of the JCVM has been automatically translated into a CHR program and a test cases and oracles generation process has been proposed. The method permits to generate 443 test cases to test the 45 bytecodes formally specified. This result shows that the proposed approach scales up to a real-world example.

However, as discussed previously, other approaches need to be explored and evaluated. In particular, the coverage criterion *All_rules* initially selected appears as being too restrictive and other testing criteria could be advantageously used. Moreover, the test concretization step need to be studied in order to compare the efficiency of our approach against existing methods.

Finally, the key point of the approach resides in the use of deep guards, although their treatment needs to be evaluated both from the analytic and the experimental points of view.

Acknowledgements

We wish to acknowledge E. Coquery for fruitful discussions on CHR, and G. Dufay and G. Barthe who gave us the JSL formal model of the JCVM.

References

1. Bernot, G., Gaudel, M.C., Marre, B.: Software testing based on formal specifications : a theory and a tool. Software Engineering Journal **6** (1991) 387–405
2. Bernard, E., Legeard, B., Luck, X., Peureux, F.: Generation of test sequences from formal specifications: GSM 11-11 standard case study. International Journal of Software Practice and Experience **34** (2004) 915–948
3. Grieskamp, W., Gurevich, Y., Schulte, W., Veanes, M.: Generating finite state machines from abstract state machines. In: ISSTA '02: Proceedings of the 2002 ACM SIGSOFT international symposium on Software testing and analysis, New York, NY, USA, ACM Press (2002) 112–122

4. Barthe, G., Dufay, G., Huisman, M., Sousa, S.: Jakarta: a toolset for reasoning about JavaCard. In: Proceedings of E-smart 2001. Volume 2140 of LNCS., In I. Attali and T. Jensen Eds. Springer-Verlag (2001) 2–18
5. http://coq.inria.fr/.
6. Barthe, G., Dufay, G., Jakubiec, L., Serpette, B., de Sousa, S.M.: A Formal Executable Semantics of the JavaCard Platform. In: Proceedings of ESOP'01. Volume 2028 of LNCS., D. Sands Eds. Springer-Verlag (2001) 302–319
7. Brisset, P., Sakkout, H., Fruhwirth, T., Gervet, C., Harvey, e.a.:   ECLiPSe Constraint Library Manual. International Computers Limited and Imperial College London, UK. (2005) Release 5.8.
8. de Sousa, S.M.: Outils et techniques pour la vérification formelle de la plate-forme JavaCard. PhD thesis, Université de Nice (2003)
9. Frühwirth, T.: Theory and Practice of Constraint Handling Rules. Logic Programming 37 (1998) Special Issue on Constraint Logic Programming, In P. Stuckey and K. Marriott Eds.
10. Frühwirth, T., Abdennadher, S.: Essentials of Constraint Programming. Cognitive Technologies. Springer Verlag (2003) ISBN 3-540-67623-6.
11. Duck, G., Stuckey, P., de la Banda, M.G., Holzbaur, C.:   Extending arbitrary solvers with constraint handling rules. In: Proceedings of the 5th ACM SIGPLAN International Conference on Principles and Practice of Declaritive Programming (PPDP03). (79-90) 2003
12. Schulte, C.: Programming deep concurrent constraint combinators. In Pontelli, E., Costa, V.S., eds.: Second International Workshop on Practical Aspects of Declarative Languages. Volume 1753 of LNCS., Springer-Verlag (2000) 215–229
13. Podelski, A., Smolka, G.: Situated Simplification. In Montanari, U., ed.: Proceedings of the 1st Conference on Principles and Practice of Constraint Programming. Volume 976 of LNCS., Springer-Verlag (1995) 328–344
14. Barthe, G., Dufay, G., Jakubiec, L., Serpette, B., de Sousa, S.M., Yu, S.W.: Formalization of the JavaCard Virtual Machine in Coq. In: Proceedings of FTfJP'00 (ECOOP Workshop on Formal Techniques for Java Programs), S. Drossopoulou and al, Eds (2000) 50–56
15. Dufay, G.: Vérification formelle de la plate-forme Java Card. PhD thesis, Université de Nice-Sophia Antipolis (2003)
16. Gouraud, S.D., Denise, A., Gaudel, M.C., Marre, B.: A New Way of Automating Statistical Testing Methods. In: Sixteenth IEEE International Conference on Automated Software Engineering (ASE). (2001) 5–12
17. Flajolet, P., Zimmermann, P., Van Cutsem, B.: A calculus for the random generation of labelled combinatorial structures. Theoretical Computer Science 132 (1994) 1–35
18. Denise, A., Gaudel, M.C., Gouraud, S.D.: A Generic Method for Statistical Testing. In: Fifteenth IEEE International Symposium on Software Reliability Engineering. (2004) 25–34
19. Gotlieb, A., Botella, B., Rueher, M.: A CLP Framework for Computing Structural Test Data. In: Constraints Stream, First International Conference on Computational Logic. Number 1891 in LNAI, Springer-Verlag (2000) 399–413
20. Pretschner, A., Lötzbeyer, H.: Model Based Testing with Constraint Logic Programming: First Results and Challenges. In: Proceedings 2nd ICSE Intl. Workshop on Automated Program Analysis, Testing and Verification. (2001)
21. Lötzbeyer, H., Pretschner, A.:   AutoFocus on Constraint Logic Programming. In: Proceedings of (Constraint) Logic Programming and Software Engineering (LPSE'2000). (2000)

Generic Cut Actions for External Prolog Predicates

Tiago Soares, Ricardo Rocha, and Michel Ferreira

DCC-FC & LIACC,
University of Porto, 4150-180 Porto, Portugal
Tel: (+351) 226078830, Fax: (+351) 226003654
{tiagosoares, ricroc, michel}@ncc.up.pt

Abstract. An interesting feature of current Prolog systems is the ability to define external Prolog predicates that can be written in other languages. However, an important drawback of these interfaces is the fact that they lack some important features necessary to improve both the efficiency and the transparent integration of the Prolog system and the external predicates. Such an example is the *cut operation*. This operation is used quite often in Prolog programs, both for efficiency and semantic preservation. However, its use after a call to an externally defined predicate can have undesired effects. For example, if we have a pending connection to another application, or if we have memory blocks allocated by an external predicate, when a cut operation occurs, we may not be able to perform generic destruct actions, such as closing the pending connection or freeing the unnecessary memory. In this work, we propose an extension of the interface architecture that allows to associate generic user-defined functions with external predicates, in such a way that the Prolog engine transparently executes them when a cut operation occurs. We describe the implementation details of our proposal in the context of the Yap Prolog system.

Keywords: Prolog Systems Implementation, External Modules, Pruning.

1 Introduction

Logic programming provides a high-level, declarative approach to programming. Arguably, Prolog is the most popular logic programming language. Throughout its history, Prolog has demonstrated the potential of logic programming in application areas such as Artificial Intelligence, Natural Language Processing, Knowledge Based Systems, Database Management, or Expert Systems.

Prolog's popularity was sparked by the success of the WAM [1] execution model that has proved to be highly efficient for common computer architectures. The success obtained with the WAM led to further improvements and extensions. Such an example is the foreign-interface to other languages. An interesting feature of this interface is the ability to define external Prolog predicates that can be written in other languages. These predicates can then be used to combine

P. Van Hentenryck (Ed.): PADL 2006, LNCS 3819, pp. 16–30, 2006.

Prolog with existing programs or libraries, thereby forming coupled systems; or to implement certain critical operations that can speed up the execution. Since most language implementations are linkable to C, a widely implemented interface by most Prolog systems is a foreign-interface to the C language.

However, an important drawback of these interfaces is the fact that they lack some important features necessary to improve both the efficiency and the transparent integration of the Prolog system and the external predicates. Consider, for example, the *cut operation*. This operation is used quite often in Prolog programs, both for efficiency and semantic preservation. However, its use after a call to an externally defined predicate can have undesired effects. For example, if we have a pending connection to another application, or if we have memory blocks allocated by the external predicate, when a cut operation occurs we may not be able to perform generic destruct actions, such as closing the pending connection or freeing the unnecessary memory.

In this work we focus on the transparent use of the cut operation over external Prolog predicates. The motivation for this work appeared from the undesired effects of the cut operation in the context of our previous work [2] on coupling the Yap Prolog system [3] with the MySQL RDBMS [4], in order to obtain a deductive database system that takes advantage of the YapTab [5] tabling mechanism in a similar manner to the XSB system [6]. The effect of the cut operation in this context is well-known and can be so significant that systems such as XSB clearly state in the programmers' manual that cut operations should be used very carefully with relationally defined predicates [7]:

> "*The XSB-ODBC interface is limited to using 100 open cursors. When XSB systems use database accesses in a complicated manner, management of open cursors can be a problem due to the tuple-at-a-time access of databases from Prolog, and due to leakage of cursors through cuts and throws.*"

To solve the problem between cuts and external predicates we propose an extension of the interface architecture that allows to associate generic user-defined functions with external predicates, in such a way that the Prolog engine transparently executes them when a cut operation occurs. With this functionality we can thus use these generic functions to avoid the kind of problems discussed above.

The idea of handling cuts transparently by setting actions to be executed on cut is not completely new. Systems like Ciao Prolog [8] and SWI Prolog [9] also provide support for external predicates with the possibility to set actions to be executed on cut. Our approach innovates because it uses the choice point data structure to easily detect when a cut operation occurs on externally defined predicates, and thus from the user's point of view, pruning standard predicates or externally defined predicates is equivalent. We describe the implementation details of our approach in the context of the Yap Prolog system and we use the coupling interface between Yap and MySQL as a working example. As we shall see, our implementation requires minor changes to the Yap engine and interface. Despite the fact that we have chosen this particular system, we believe that our approach can be easily incorporated in other Prolog systems that are also based on the WAM execution model.

The remainder of the paper is organized as follows. First, we briefly describe the cut semantics of Prolog and the problem arising from its use to prune external predicates. Next, we present the C language interface of Yap and its implementation details. Then we describe the needed extension of the interface architecture in order to deal with pruning for external predicates. At the end we discuss some experimental results on the specific case of relational database interfaces and outline some conclusions.

2   Pruning External Predicates

Cut is a system built-in predicate that is represented by the symbol '!'. Its execution results in pruning all the branches to the right of the *cut scope branch*. The cut scope branch starts at the current node and finishes at the node corresponding to the predicate containing the cut.

Figure 1 gives a general overview of cut semantics by illustrating the left to right execution of an example with cuts. The query goal a(X) leads the computation to the first alternative of predicate a/1, where !(a) means a cut with scope node a. If !(a) gets executed, all the right branches until the node corresponding to predicate a, inclusively, should be pruned. Predicate b(X) is then called and suppose that it succeeds with its first alternative. Next, !(a) gets executed and all the remaining alternatives for predicates a and b are pruned. As a consequence, the nodes for a and b can be removed.

Consider now the coupling interface between a logic system and a database system. Logic goals are usually translated into SQL queries, which are then sent to the database system. The database system receives the query, processes it,

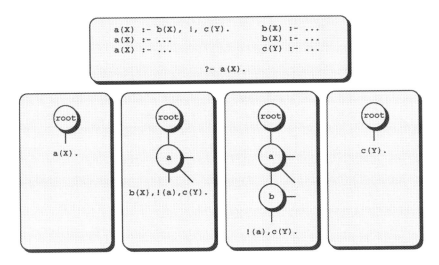

Fig. 1. Cut semantics

and sends the resulting tuples back to the logic system. The usual method of accessing the tuples in the result set is to use the Prolog backtracking mechanism, which iteratively increments the result set pointer (*cursor*) and fetches the current tuple. Using this tuple-at-a-time access, the deallocation of the data structure holding the result set, whether on the server or on the client side, is only performed when the last tuple in the result set has been reached.

The problem is when, during the tuple-at-a-time navigation, a cut operation occurs before reaching the last tuple. If this happens, the result set cannot be deallocated. This can cause a lack of cursors and, more important, a lack of memory due to a number of very large non-deallocated data structures. Consider the example described in Fig. 1 and assume now that predicate b/1 is a database predicate. The execution of b(X) will query the database for the corresponding relation and bind X with the first tuple that matches the query. Next, we execute !(a) and, as mentioned before, it will disable the action of backtracking for node b. The result set with the facts for b will remain in memory, although it will never be used.

3   The C Language Interface to Yap Prolog

Like other Prolog Systems, Yap provides an interface for writing predicates in other programming languages, such as C, as external modules. An important feature of this interface is how we can define predicates. Yap distinguishes two kinds of predicates: *deterministic predicates*, which either fail or succeed but are not backtrackable, and *backtrackable predicates*, which can succeed more than once.

Deterministic predicates are implemented as C functions with no arguments which should return zero if the predicate fails and a non-zero value otherwise. They are declared with a call to YAP_UserCPredicate(), where the first argument is the name of the predicate, the second the name of the C function implementing the predicate, and the third is the arity of the predicate.

For backtrackable predicates we need two C functions: one to be executed when the predicate is first called, and other to be executed on backtracking to provide (possibly) other solutions. Backtrackable predicates are declared with a call to YAP_UserBackCPredicate(). When returning the last solution, we should use YAP_cut_fail() to denote failure, and YAP_cut_succeed() to denote success. The reason for using YAP_cut_fail() and YAP_cut_succeed() instead of just returning a zero or non-zero value, is that otherwise, when backtracking, our function would be indefinitely called. For a more exhaustive description on how to interface C with Yap please refer to [10].

3.1   Writing Backtrackable Predicates in C

To explain how the C interface works for backtrackable predicates we will use a small example from the interface between Yap and MySQL. We present the db_row(+ResultSet,?ListOfArgs) predicate, which given a previously generated query result set, the ResultSet argument, fetches the tuples in the result set, tuple-at-a-time through backtracking, and, for each tuple, unifies the attribute values with the variables in the ListOfArgs argument. The code for the db_row/2 predicate is shown next in Fig. 2.

```c
#include "Yap/YapInterface.h"    // header file for the Yap interface to C

void init_predicates() {
  YAP_UserBackCPredicate("db_row", c_db_row, c_db_row, 2, 0);
}

int c_db_row(void) {                       // db_row: ResultSet -> ListOfArgs
  int i, arity;
  YAP_Term arg_result_set, arg_list_args, head;
  MYSQL_ROW row;
  MYSQL_RES *result_set;

  arg_result_set = YAP_ARG1;
  arg_list_args = YAP_ARG2;
  result_set = (MYSQL_RES *) YAP_IntOfTerm(arg_result_set);
  arity = mysql_num_fields(result_set);
  if ((row = mysql_fetch_row(result_set)) != NULL) {     // get next tuple
    for (i = 0; i < arity; i++) {
      head = YAP_HeadOfTerm(arg_list_args);
      arg_list_args = YAP_TailOfTerm(arg_list_args);
      YAP_Unify(head, YAP_MkAtomTerm(YAP_LookupAtom(row[i])));
    }
    return TRUE;
  } else {                                 // no more tuples
    mysql_free_result(result_set);
    YAP_cut_fail();
    return FALSE;
  }
}
```

Fig. 2. The C code for the db_row/2 predicate

Figure 2 shows some of the key aspects about the Yap interface. The include statement makes available the macros for interfacing with the Yap engine. The init_predicates() procedure tells Yap, by calling YAP_UserBackCPredicate(), the predicate defined in the module. The function c_db_row() is the implementation in C of the desired predicate. We can define a function for the first time the predicate is called and another for calls via backtracking. In this example the same function is used for both calls. Note that this function has no arguments even though the predicate being defined has two. In fact the arguments of a Prolog predicate written in C are accessed through the macros YAP_ARG1, ..., YAP_ARG16 or with YAP_A(N) where N is the argument number.

The c_db_row() function starts by converting the first argument (YAP_ARG1) to the corresponding pointer to the query result set (MYSQL_RES *). The conversion is done by the YAP_IntOfTerm() macro. It then fetches a tuple from this result set, through mysql_fetch_row(), and checks if the last tuple as been already reached. If not, it calls YAP_Unify() to unify the values in each attribute of the tuple (row[i]) with the respective elements in arg_list_args and returns TRUE.

On the other hand, if the last tuple has been already reached, it deallocates the result set, as mentioned before, calls YAP_cut_fail() and returns FALSE.

For simplicity of presentation, we omitted type checking procedures over MySQL attributes that must be done to convert each attribute to the appropriate term in Yap. For some predicates it is also useful to preserve some data structures across backtracking. This can be done by calling YAP_PRESERVE_DATA() to associate such space and by calling YAP_PRESERVED_DATA() to get access to it later. With these two macros we can easily share information between backtracking steps. This example does not need this preservation, as the cursor is maintained in the result set structure.

3.2 The Yap Implementation of Backtrackable Predicates

In Yap a backtrackable predicate is compiled using two WAM-like instructions, try_userc and retry_userc, as follows:

```
try_userc c_first arity extra_space
retry_userc c_back arity extra_space
```

Both instructions have three arguments: the c_first and c_back arguments are pointers to the C functions associated with the backtrackable predicate, arity is the arity of the predicate, and extra_space is the memory space used by the YAP_PRESERVE_DATA() and YAP_PRESERVED_DATA() macros.

When Yap executes a try_userc instruction it uses the choice point stack to reserve as much memory as given by the extra_space argument, next it allocates and initializes a new choice point (see Fig. 3), and then it executes the C function pointed by the c_first argument. Later, if the computation backtracks to such choice point, the retry_userc instruction gets loaded from the CP_AP choice point field and the C function pointed by the c_back argument is then executed.

In order to repeatedly execute the same c_back function when backtracking to this choice point, the retry_userc instruction maintains the CP_AP field pointing to itself. This is the reason why we should use YAP_cut_succeed() or YAP_cut_fail() when returning the last solution for the predicate, as otherwise

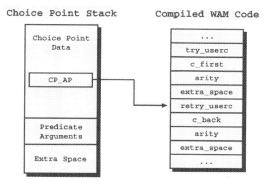

Fig. 3. The Yap implementation of backtrackable predicates

the choice point will remain in the choice point stack and the c_back function will be indefinitely called.

The execution of the YAP_PRESERVE_DATA() and the YAP_PRESERVED_DATA() macros in the C functions corresponds to calculate the starting position of the reserved space associated with the extra_space argument. For both functions, this is the address of the current choice point pointer plus its size and the arity of the predicate.

4   Generic Cut Actions for External Predicates

In this section, we discuss how we can solve the problem of pruning external predicates. We discuss two different approaches: a first approach where the user explicitly calls special predicates that perform the required action; and a second approach, which is our original proposal, where the system transparently executes a generic cut action when a cut operation occurs. To support our discussion, we will consider again the coupling interface between Yap and MySQL. However and as we shall see, our approach can be generalised to handle not only database predicates, but also any external predicate that requires a generic action over a cut.

4.1   Handling Cuts Explicitly

In this approach the user has to explicitly call a special predicate to be executed when a cut operation is performed over external predicates. For instance, for the interface between Yap and MySQL, the idea is as follows: before executing a cut operation that potentially prunes over databases predicates, the user must explicitly call a predicate that releases beforehand the result sets for the predicates to be pruned.

If we consider again the example from Fig. 1 and assume that b(X) is a database predicate, we might think of a simple solution: every time a database predicate is first called, we store the pointer for its result set in an auxiliary stack frame (we can extend the c_db_row() function to implement that). Then we could implement a new C predicate, db_free_result/0 for example, that deallocates the result set in the top of the stack. Having this, we could adapt the code for the first clause of predicate a/1 to:

```
a(X) :- b(X), db_free_result, !, c(X).
```

To use this approach, the user must be careful to always include a call to db_free_result/0 before a cut operator. A problem with this db_free_result/0 predicate occurs if we call more than one database predicate before a cut. Consider the following definition for the predicate a/1, where b1/1 and b2/1 are database predicates.

```
a(X) :- b1(X), b2(Y), db_free_result, !, c(X).
```

The db_free_result/0 will only deallocate the result set for b2/1, leaving the result set for b1/1 pending. A possible solution for this problem is to *mark* beforehand the range of predicates to consider. We can thus implement a new C predicate, db_cut_mark/0 for example, that *marks* where to cut to, and change the db_free_result/0 predicate to free all the result sets within the mark left by the last db_cut_mark/0 predicate.

```
a(X) :- db_cut_mark, b1(X), b2(Y), db_free_result, !, c(X).
```

A more intelligent and transparent solution is implemented in Ciao Prolog system [8]. The user still has to explicitly call a special predicate, the '!!'/0 predicate, which will execute the cut goal specified using a special primitive det_try(Goal,OnCutGoal,OnFailGoal). For our db_row/2 example this would be det_try(db_row(ResultSet,_),db_free_result(ResultSet),fail), and now if a db_row/2 choice point is pruned using a '!!', the associated result set is deallocated by db_free_result/1.

This solution solves the problem of cursor leaks and memory deallocation when pruning database predicates. However, because it relies on calling special predicates, the transparency in the use of relationally defined predicates is lost. Moreover, if the user happens to mistakenly use a '!' instead of a '!!', incorrect behaviour may happen the next time a '!!' is used [8].

4.2 Handling Cuts Transparently

We next present our approach to handle cuts transparently. As we shall see, this requires minor changes to the Yap engine and interface. First, we extended the procedure used to declare backtrackable predicates, YAP_UserBackCPredicate(), to include an extra C function. Remember that for backtrackable predicates we used two C functions: one to be executed when the predicate is first called, and another to be executed upon backtracking. The extra function is where the user should declare the function to be executed in case of a cut, which for database predicates will involve the deallocation of the result set. Declaring and implementing this extra function is the only thing the user needs to do to take advantage of our approach. Thus, from the user's point of view, pruning standard predicates or relationally defined predicates is then equivalent.

With this extra C function, the compiled code for a backtrackable predicate now includes a new WAM-like instruction, cut_userc, which is used to store the pointer to the extra C function, the c_cut argument.

```
try_userc c_first arity extra_space
retry_userc c_back arity extra_space
cut_userc c_cut arity extra_space
```

When now Yap executes a try_userc instruction, it also allocates space for a cut frame data structure (see Fig. 4). This data structure includes two fields: CF_inst is a pointer to the cut_userc instruction in the compiled code for the predicate and CF_previous is a pointer to the previous cut frame on stack. A top cut frame global variable, TOP_CF, always points to the youngest cut frame on stack. Frames form a linked list through the CF_previous field.

By putting the cut frame data structure below the associated choice point, we can easily detect the external predicates being pruned when a cut operation

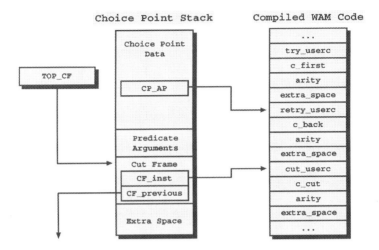

Fig. 4. The Yap support for generic cut actions

occurs. To do so, we extended the implementation of the cut operation to start by executing a new `userc_cut_check()` procedure (see Fig. 5). Remember that a cut operation receives as argument the choice point to cut to. Thus, starting from the `TOP_CF` variable and going through the cut frames, we can check if a cut frame will be pruned. If so, we load the `cut_userc` instruction stored in the corresponding `CF_inst` field in order to execute the cut function pointed by the `c_cut` argument. The `userc_cut_check()` procedure is like a handler in other programming languages that throws an exception, that is, executes the `cut_userc` instruction for the cut frames being pruned, when it encounters an abnormal condition that it can not handle itself, in this case, a cut operation over an externally defined predicate.

```
void userc_cut_check(choiceptr cp_to_cut_to) {
  while (TOP_CF < cp_to_cut_to) {
    execute_cut_userc(TOP_CF->CF_inst);
    TOP_CF = TOP_CF->CF_previous;
  }
  return;
}
```

Fig. 5. The pseudo-code for the `userc_cut_check()` procedure

The process described above is done before executing the original code for the cut instruction, that is, before updating the global registry B (pointer to the current choice point on stack). This is important to prevent the following situation. If the cut function executes a `YapCallProlog()` macro to call the Prolog engine from C, this might have the side-effect of allocating new choice points on stack. Thus, if we had updated the B register beforehand, we will potentially overwrite the cut frames stored in the pruned choice points and avoid the possibility of executing the corresponding cut functions.

As a final remark, note that we can also call the YAP_PRESERVED_DATA() macro from the cut function to access the data store in the extra space. We thus need to access the extra space from the cut frames. This is why we store the cut frames above the extra space. The starting address of the extra space is thus obtained by adding its size to the pointer of the current cut frame.

To show how the extended interface can be used to handle cuts transparently, we next present in Fig. 6 the code for generalising the db_row/2 predicate to perform the cursor closing upon a cut.

```
void init_predicates() {
  YAP_UserBackCPredicate("db_row", c_db_row_first, c_db_row,
                         c_db_row_cut, 2, sizeof(MYSQL_RES *));
}

int c_db_row_first(void) {
  MYSQL_RES **extra_space;
  ...                               // the same as for the c_db_row function
  result_set = (MYSQL_RES *) YAP_IntOfTerm(arg_result_set);
  YAP_PRESERVE_DATA(extra_space, MYSQL_RES *);  // initialize extra space
  *extra_space = result_set;        // store the pointer to the result set
  ...                               // the same as for the c_db_row function
}

int c_db_row(void) {
  ...                                           // the same as before
}

void c_db_row_cut(void) {
  MYSQL_RES **extra_space, *result_set;

  YAP_PRESERVED_DATA(extra_space, MYSQL_RES *);
  result_set = *extra_space;         // get the pointer to the result set
  mysql_free_result(result_set);
  return;
}
```

Fig. 6. Extending the db_row/2 predicate to handle cuts transparently

First, we need to define the function to be executed when a cut operation occurs. An important observation is that this function will be called from the cut instruction, and thus it will not be able to access the Prolog arguments, YAP_ARG1 and YAP_ARG2, as described for the c_db_row() function. However, we need to access the pointer to the corresponding result set in order to deallocate it. To solve this, we can use the YAP_PRESERVE_DATA() macro to preserve the pointer to the result set. As this only needs to be done when the predicate is first called, we defined a different function for this case. The YAP_UserBackCPredicate() macro was thus changed to include a cut function, c_db_row_cut(), and to use a different function when the predicate is first called, c_db_row_first(). The c_db_row() function is the same as before (see Fig. 2). The last argument of the YAP_UserBackCPredicate() macro defines the size of the extra space for the YAP_PRESERVE_DATA() and YAP_PRESERVED_DATA() macros.

The c_db_row_first() function is an extension of the c_db_row() function. The only difference is that it uses the YAP_PRESERVE_DATA() macro to store the pointer to the given result set in the extra space for the current choice point. On the other hand, the c_db_row_cut() function uses the YAP_PRESERVED_DATA() macro to be able to deallocate the result set when a cut operation occurs. With these two small extensions, the db_row/2 predicate is now protected against cuts and can be safely pruned by further cut operations.

5   Experimental Results

In this section we evaluate the performance of our generic cut action mechanism on the problem we have been addressing of relational queries result sets deallocation. As we mentioned in the introduction, the XSB manual recommends the careful use of *cut* with relationally defined predicates and recommends the following solution:

> "When XSB systems use database accesses in a complicated manner, management of open cursors can be a problem due to the tuple-at-a-time access of databases from Prolog, and due to leakage of cursors through cuts and throws. **Often, it is more efficient to call the database through set-at-a-time predicates such as findall/3, and then to backtrack through the returned information.**"

Using this solution it is clear that a *cut* operation will provide the correct pruning over database tuples, as tuples are now stored on the WAM heap, but at the sacrifice of execution time, as we will show.

The existing literature also lacks a comparative performance evaluation of the coupling interfaces between a logic system and a relational database system and, in this section, we also try to contribute to the benchmarking of such systems. We compare the performance of XSB 2.7.1, Ciao 1.10 and Yap 4.5.7, accessing a relational database. Yap has an ODBC interface and a native interface to MySQL. XSB has an ODBC interface and Ciao has a native interface to MySQL. We used MySQL Server 4.1.11, both for the native and ODBC interfaces, running on the same machine, an AMD Athlon 1000 with 512 Mbytes of RAM.

This performance evaluation is directed to the cut treatment on the different systems. For this purpose, we created a relation in MySQL using the following SQL declaration:

```
CREATE TABLE table1 (
    num1    INT NOT NULL,
    PRIMARY KEY (num1));
```

and populated it with $1,000$, $100,000$ and $1,000,000$ tuples. This relation was imported as the db_relation/1 predicate. To evaluate cut treatment over this predicate we created the two queries presented in Fig. 7.

Query 1 represents the typical backtracking search as is trivially implemented in Prolog. We want to find a particular value among the tuples of the database

```
query1 :- db_relation(Tuple),
          test(Tuple),
          !.

query2 :- findall(Element,db_relation(Element),List),
          member(Tuple,List),
          test(Tuple),
          !.

% test predicate for 1,000 tuples
test(500).

% test predicate for 100,000 tuples
test(50000).

% test predicate for 1,000,000 tuples
test(500000).
```

Fig. 7. Queries evaluated

relation, testing each one with the test/1 predicate, and execute a cut after finding it. On average we should go through half of the tuples, and so our test/1 predicate succeeds when this middle tuple has been reached.

Query 2 follows the approach recommended on the XSB manual. Tuples are stored in a Prolog list [11], which is kept on the WAM heap data structure and thus works properly with cuts. Backtracking goes through the elements of the list using the member/2 predicate. The same test/1 predicate is used. Note that, after running the SQL query on the database server, the result set is stored completely on the client side both in query 1 and query 2. The main difference between query 1 and query 2 is that the native result set structure is used in query 1, while in query 2 navigation is performed on a Prolog list structure.

Table 1 presents the execution time for query 1 and the difference in allocated memory at the end of the query, for Yap with (Yap$^+$) and without (Yap$^-$) our generic cut action mechanism. Table 2 presents the execution time and the difference in allocated memory for Yap$^+$, XSB and Ciao (for Ciao we used '!!' instead of '!') in both queries. We measured the execution time using walltime. The memory values are retrieved by consulting the status file of the system being tested in the /proc directory. All of the time results are in seconds, and the memory results are in Kbytes. Queries 1 and 2 are run for a $1,000, 100,000$ and $1,000,000$ tuples.

Table 1. Query 1 results for Yap with and without our generic cut action mechanism

Interface	System	Memory (Kb)			Running Time (s)		
		1K	100K	1M	1K	100K	1M
ODBC	Yap$^+$	0	72	72	0.005	0.481	4.677
	Yap$^-$	0	3324	31628	0.005	0.474	4.625
MySQL	Yap$^+$	0	60	60	0.004	0.404	4.153
	Yap$^-$	0	3316	31616	0.005	0.423	4.564

There is one straightforward observation that can be made from Table 1. As expected, memory comparison for query 1 translates the fact that Yap⁻ cannot deallocate the result set pruned by a cut. As a result, memory size will grow proportionally to the size of the result sets and to the number of queries pruned.

Table 2. Queries results for Yap, XSB and Ciao

Interface	System	Query	Memory (Kb)			Running Time (s)		
			1K	100K	1M	1K	100K	1M
ODBC	Yap⁺	Query 1	0	72	72	0.005	0.481	4.677
		Query 2	0	8040	73512	0.008	0.720	7.046
	XSB	Query 1	0	3284	31584	0.008	0.735	7.068
		Query 2	0	4088	39548	0.012	1.191	11.967
MySQL	Yap⁺	Query 1	0	60	60	0.004	0.404	4.153
		Query 2	0	8028	73500	0.006	0.640	6.474
	Ciao	Query 1 (!!)	176	204	204	0.015	1.645	16.467
		Query 2 (!!)	36	13708	n.a.	0.036	3.820	n.a.

Regarding Table 2 there are some interesting comparisons that can be made. According to the approach suggested on the XSB manual to deal with cuts, query 2 can be seen to be around 1.5 to 2 times slower than query 1 for all interface/system combinations. These results thus confirm our observation that this approach sacrifices the execution time. Memory results for query 2 are not so relevant because at the end of query 2 no memory is left pending. The results obtained in Table 2 simply reflect the fact that, during evaluation, the execution stacks were expanded to be able to store the huge Prolog list constructed by the findall/3 predicate. For Ciao we were not able to run query 2 for the list term with 1,000,000 tuples.

For query 1, we can compare Yap with XSB interfacing MySQL through an equivalent ODBC driver and Yap with Ciao interfacing MySQL through the MySQL C API. In terms of memory comparison for query 1, the results obtained for XSB translate the fact that it cannot deallocate the result set pruned by a cut (remember that for Ciao we used '!!' to correctly deal with cuts). In terms of execution time for query 1, Yap is a little faster than XSB and around 4 times faster than Ciao. This is probably due to the fact that Ciao negotiates the connection with MySQL server at each Prolog goal, which causes important slow-downs.

We should mention that in order to use the '!!' approach of Ciao we modified the Ciao source code to use the special primitive det_try/3 as described in subsection 4.1 to correctly deallocate the pending result sets when a '!!' occurs. By default, Ciao uses a different approach to deal with pending results sets. It uses the *tuple-at-a-time* functionality of the MySQL C API and negotiates the connection with MySQL server at each Prolog goal.

MySQL offers two alternatives for sending tuples to the client program that generated the query: **(i)** store the set of tuples on a data structure on the database server side and send each tuple *tuple-at-a-time* to the client program; or **(ii)** store the set of tuples on a data structure on the client side sending the *set of tuples at once*. Note that with a tuple-at-a-time transfer between server and client, the problem of pruned result sets also happens, though leaving the allocated result set in the MySQL Server process and not in the Prolog process. However, with the negotiation of connections at the goal level, Ciao can overcome this problem, by closing connection with MySQL and therefore deallocating result sets, but at the price of execution time, as is clear from Table 2.

6   Concluding Remarks

We discussed the problem of pruning externally defined Prolog predicates and we proposed a completely transparent approach where the Prolog engine executes a user-defined function when a cut operation occurs. We implemented our proposal in the context of the Yap Prolog system with minor changes to the Yap engine and interface. Our approach is applicable to any predicate that requires a generic action over a cut.

We evaluated the performance of our generic cut action mechanism on the problem we have been addressing of relational queries result sets deallocation, using the Yap, XSB and Ciao Prolog systems interfacing MySQL for two queries where a cut was executed over a large database extensional predicate. We observed that, when using a typical backtracking search mechanism without support for deallocation of result sets over a cut, this can cause memory to grow arbitrarily due to the very large number of non-deallocated data structures. Alternatively, if we follow an approach like the one recommended on the XSB manual to avoid this problem or if we maintain the result sets on the MySQL server as in Ciao, we observed that we need to sacrifice the execution time.

Acknowledgements

This work has been partially supported by MYDDAS (POSC/EIA/59154/2004) and by funds granted to LIACC through the Programa de Financiamento Plurianual, Fundação para a Ciência e Tecnologia and Programa POSC.

References

1. Warren, D.H.D.: An Abstract Prolog Instruction Set. Technical Note 309, SRI International (1983)
2. Ferreira, M., Rocha, R., Silva, S.: Comparing Alternative Approaches for Coupling Logic Programming with Relational Databases. In: Colloquium on Implementation of Constraint and LOgic Programming Systems. (2004) 71–82
3. Santos Costa, V.: Optimising Bytecode Emulation for Prolog. In: Principles and Practice of Declarative Programming. Number 1702 in LNCS, Springer-Verlag (1999) 261–267
4. Widenius, M., Axmark, D.: MySQL Reference Manual: Documentation from the Source. O'Reilly Community Press (2002)

5. Rocha, R., Silva, F., Santos Costa, V.: YapTab: A Tabling Engine Designed to Support Parallelism. In: Conference on Tabulation in Parsing and Deduction. (2000) 77–87

6. Sagonas, K., Swift, T., Warren, D.S.: XSB as an Efficient Deductive Database Engine. In: ACM SIGMOD International Conference on the Management of Data, ACM Press (1994) 442–453

7. Sagonas, K., Warren, D.S., Swift, T., Rao, P., Dawson, S., Freire, J., Johnson, E., Cui, B., Kifer, M., Demoen, B., Castro, L.F.: (XSB Programmers' Manual) Available from http://xsb.sourceforge.net.

8. Bueno, F., Cabeza, D., Carro, M., Hermenegildo, M., Lpez, P., Puebla, G.: (Ciao Prolog System Manual) Available from http://clip.dia.fi.upm.es/Software/Ciao+.

9. Wielemaker, J.: (SWI-Prolog Reference Manual) Available from http://www.swi-prolog.org+.

10. Santos Costa, V., Damas, L., Reis, R., Azevedo, R.: (YAP User's Manual) Available from http://www.ncc.up.pt/~vsc/Yap.

11. Draxler, C.: Accessing Relational and NF^2 Databases Through Database Set Predicates. In: UK Annual Conference on Logic Programming. Workshops in Computing, Springer Verlag (1992) 156–173

Controlling Search Space Materialization in a Practical Declarative Debugger

Ian MacLarty[1] and Zoltan Somogyi[1,2]

[1] Department of Computer Science and Software Engineering,
University of Melbourne, Australia
[2] NICTA Victoria Laboratory
{maclarty, zs}@csse.unimelb.edu.au

Abstract. While the idea of declarative debugging has been around for a quarter of a century, the technology still hasn't been adopted by working programmers, even by those working in declarative languages. The reason is that making declarative debuggers practical requires solutions to a whole host of problems. In this paper we address one of these problems, which is that retaining a complete record of every step of the execution of a program is infeasible unless the program's runtime is very short, yet this record forms the space searched by the declarative debugger. Most parts of this search space therefore have to be stored in an implicit form. Each time the search algorithm visits a previously unexplored region of the search space, it must decide how big a part of the search space to rematerialize (which it does by reexecuting a call in the program). If it materializes too much, the machine may start to thrash or even run out of memory and swap space. If it materializes too little, then materializing all the parts of the search space required by a debugging session will require too many reexecutions of (parts of) the program, which will take too long. We present a simple algorithm, the *ideal depth strategy*, for steering the ideal middle course: minimizing reexecutions while limiting memory consumption to what is feasible. We show that this algorithm performs well even when used on quite long running programs.

1 Introduction

The aim of the Mercury project is to bring the benefits of declarative programming languages to the software industry. Mercury is designed explicitly to support teams of programmers working on large application programs. It has a modern module system, detects a large fraction of program errors at compile time, and has an implementation that is both efficient and portable. To ensure that programmers can actually enjoy the benefits claimed for logic programs, Mercury has no non-logical constructs that could destroy the declarative semantics that gives logic programs their power.

As part of the project, we have built a declarative debugger for Mercury. We have ample motivation to make this declarative debugger work well because many parts of the Mercury implementation (including the compiler and most

P. Van Hentenryck (Ed.): PADL 2006, LNCS 3819, pp. 31–44, 2006.

of the declarative debugger itself) are written in Mercury. Using the Mercury declarative debugger to debug the Mercury implementation requires us to confront and solve all the problems that would face anyone attempting to use a declarative debugger to debug large, long-running programs. In previous work, we addressed some usability issues such as how to support the browsing of large (possibly multi-megabyte) terms [3], and implemented search strategies that are effective even for very large search spaces [4].

The problem we address in this paper is how to manage the storage of very large search spaces in the first place. The problem exists because the space searched by a declarative debugger is equivalent to a complete record of every step of the execution of a program, and given today's CPU speeds, describing the actions of a program that runs for just a second or two requires gigabytes of storage. This makes storing the record in its entirety clearly infeasible. We must store only a part, and recreate the other parts on demand. But how should the system decide exactly what parts of the record to materialize when? We give some algorithms for making that decision in sections 4 and 5, together with some experimental evaluation. But first, section 2 introduces the Mercury declarative debugger, and section 3 gives our general approach. We assume familiarity with standard logic programming terminology.

2   Background: The Mercury Declarative Debugger

When the Mercury compiler is asked to generate debuggable code (with a flag similar to gcc's -g), it includes callbacks to the runtime system at significant events in the program. These events fall into two categories: interface events and internal events. Interface events record transfers of control between invocations of predicates and functions. While Mercury supports functions as well as predicates, the distinctions between them are only syntactic, so we call each predicate or function a *procedure*. (Strictly speaking, it is possible for a predicate or function to have multiple modes of usage, and a procedure corresponds to just one mode of a predicate or function, but this distinction is not relevant to this paper.) There are five kinds of interface events, the first four of which correspond to the four ports of the Byrd box model [2]:

call   A call event occurs just after a procedure has been called, and control has just reached the start of the body of the procedure.

exit   An exit event occurs when a procedure call has succeeded, and control is about to return to its caller.

redo   A redo event occurs when all computations to the right of a procedure call have failed, and control is about to return to this call to try to find alternative solutions.

fail   A fail event occurs when a call has run out of alternatives, and control is about to return to the rightmost computation to its left that has remaining alternatives which could lead to success.

excp   An exception event occurs when control leaves a procedure call because that call has thrown an exception.

There are also internal events which record decisions about the flow of control, but these are not important for this paper. The precise set of internal events is not important for this paper.

When a Mercury program that was compiled with debugging enabled is run under the Mercury debugger mdb, the runtime system gives the debugger control at each of these events. The debugger can then decide to interact with the user, i.e. to prompt for and accept commands, before giving control back to the program being debugged [13]. The mdb command set provides all the usual debugger facilities, e.g. for inspecting the values of variables and setting breakpoints. It also allows the *retry* of the current call or any of its ancestors. The retry resets the program to the state it had at the time of the call event of the selected procedure invocation. This is possible because in Mercury there are no global variables that the call could have modified, and we have I/O tabling [12,10] to simulate the undoing of any interaction of the call with the outside world.

Retry capability is very useful in its own right, but it is also crucial in the implementation of declarative debugging. Users can give the command to initiate declarative debugging when execution is at an exit event that computed a wrong solution, when execution is at the fail event of a call that did not compute all the solutions it was expected to compute, or when execution is at the excp event of a call that was not expected to throw that exception. In all three cases, the Mercury declarative debugger uses the retry mechanism to reexecute the affected call, but this time the code executed by the runtime system at each event has the task of building a record of all the events of the call. We call this record the *annotated trace* [1]. When execution arrives at the event at which declarative debugging was initiated, the annotated trace is complete, and the system invokes the declarative debugging algorithm.

That algorithm searches a tree called the *evaluation dependency tree* or EDT [7]. Each node in the EDT corresponds to an exit, fail or excp event in the trace. Each of these nodes also makes an assertion: that the solution represented by an exit event is correct, that the set of solutions returned before a fail event is complete, or that the exception thrown at an excp event was expected to be thrown. The children of a given node N in the EDT are the exit, fail and excp events generated by child calls made by the procedure invocation represented by node N which could have affected the correctness of the assertion made by N. The declarative debugger searches the EDT for a incorrect node whose children are all correct: such nodes represent bugs.

The declarative debugger constructs the EDT from the annotated trace on demand. The reason why we don't build the EDT directly is that we need to build different EDT fragments for negated goals than for non-negated goals, and the condition of an if-then-else is a negated goal only if the condition fails. We therefore wouldn't know what kind of EDT to build until it is too late. Building a more general data structure such as the annotated trace allows us to avoid this problem [1].

Besides the heap space used by the program under normal conditions, there are two additional memory costs when the annotated trace is being built. One cost is that each node in the annotated trace consumes a few words of memory; the number of words depends on the node type. The other cost comes about because some of our search algorithms need to know the values of procedure arguments. We therefore include copies of the call's input arguments in each `call` node and copies of the call's output arguments in each `exit` node. The copied values may be (and usually are) pointers to the heap. These references prevent the garbage collector from recovering the heap cells reachable through those pointers. This doesn't add to memory consumption *directly*, but the indirect effect on memory requirements is very significant. The exact amount of heap memory retained by e.g. a specific `call` node is impossible to predict, but on average, the amount of heap memory retained by n events is usually linear in n. This is because (1) Mercury programs can only execute straight line code between events, so the amount of memory allocated between two events is bounded for any given program, and the average doesn't even vary very much between programs; and (2) the rate of recovery of heap cells must roughly match the rate of their allocation if the program is not to run out of memory. The memory overhead imposed by collecting the annotated trace is thus broadly linear in the number of nodes and the ratio can be measured for any particular program run. This allows us to control the memory overhead of the annotated trace by controlling the number of nodes in the annotated trace.

3   Rematerialization on Demand

To generate an annotated trace for a call, the call must be reexecuted and the resulting events collected. Not all the events need be collected though. We may collect a subset of the events generated by the call and ask the declarative debugger to try to find a bug in one of these. If the declarative debugger needs to explore events not collected the first time around, then the missing events can always be added by reexecuting the appropriate call. (Reexecuting a deeper call will require less time.)

On each reexecution of a call we require the set of events gathered during that run to form an EDT. For each node in the EDT derived from a generated portion of the annotated trace, we require that either all the children of the node are present in the annotated trace, or none of them are present. If none of them are present then we mark the node as an *implicit root*. An implicit root is the root of a subtree in the EDT whose nodes have not been materialized in the annotated trace.

If the declarative debugger needs to search the nodes in an implicit subtree, the call corresponding to the `exit`, `fail` or `excp` event at the implicit root must be reexecuted. To do this we use the debugger's retry capability to rewind the state of the program to a point just before the `call` event corresponding to the `exit`, `fail` or `excp` event at the root of the implicit subtree. We then proceed to reexecute the program from that point, gathering events into the annotated trace, until we arrive at the `exit`, `fail` or `excp` event at the implicit root.

The first version of the algorithm we use to decide which events should be added to the annotated trace on a given run is depicted in figure 1 (this algo-

build_annotated_trace(*call_number*, *end_event*, *depth_limit*) returns *trace* is

trace := NULL
inside := false
Rewind execution to a call before or equal to *call_number*
For each executed event *e* loop
      If *e* is a call or redo event for call *call_number*
          inside := true
      If *inside*
          If depth(*e*) < *depth_limit*
              trace := create_annotated_node(*e*, *trace*)
          Else if depth(*e*) = *depth_limit* and *e* is an interface event
              trace := create_annotated_node(*e*, *trace*)
              If *e* is an exit, fail or excp event
                  trace := mark_as_implicit_root(*e*, *trace*)
      If *e* is an exit, fail or excp event for call *call_number*
          inside := false
Until the event number of *e* is *end_event*

Fig. 1. Algorithm for building the annotated trace to a predefined depth limit

Fig. 2. The EDT corresponding to the whole annotated trace (left), and the EDT fragments corresponding to the parts of the trace materialized on demand (right)

rithm is from [1]). Here the *depth_limit* parameter controls the depth of each generated portion of the annotated trace, or more precisely, the depth of the EDT represented by the generated portion of the annotated trace. The depth function returns the depth of an event relative to the root of the portion of the EDT currently being materialized. Initially *end_event* will be the event where the user started the declarative debugging session. On subsequent invocations *end_event* will be the event at the root of an implicit subtree we wish to materialize. *call_number* is the call sequence number of the call corresponding to the event at the root of the implicit subtree.

The manipulation of *inside* ensures that we collect events only from inside the call tree of the selected call. Of the events that pass this test, the algorithm includes in the annotated trace all events *above* the depth limit, only interface events *at* the depth limit, and no events *below* the depth limit. Given a large EDT such as the one on the left in figure 2, successive invocations of this algorithm materialize annotated traces that yield EDT fragments whose relationship is shown by the triangles on the right of that figure.

When the event with event number *end_event* is executed, the new annotated trace fragment is complete. If this is the first, topmost fragment, the declarative

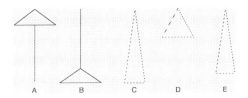

Fig. 3. The shape of the trees for "bigsmall" and "smallbig", and their approximations

debugger starts running the search algorithm on it, converting nodes in the annotated trace into nodes of the EDT on demand. If the search algorithm wants to explore a part of the search space beneath an implicit root, it will invoke `build_annotated_trace` again. When it returns, the debugger will link the new fragment into the EDT at the point of the implicit root. Our representation scheme allows the declarative debugger to view the EDT as a single whole tree whose nodes are materialized on demand, not as something stitched together from several fragments.

4   Ineffective Heuristics

The simplest way to control the space-time trade-off is to give a fixed value for *depth_limit* in figure 1. The problem with this solution is that it is impossible for the declarative debugger implementor to give a value for *depth_limit* that yields acceptable results in most cases, let alone all cases. This is because the EDTs of different programs have greatly different average branching factors. It is possible for a given depth setting to cause the declarative debugger to try to collect infeasibly many events for one program, while collecting only a handful of events for another program, requiring a huge number of reexecutions of the program to construct the required parts of the EDT.

A practical algorithm must therefore make *depth_limit* a function of the shape of the implicit tree we wish to materialize. Initially nothing is known about the shape of the search space. We therefore initially give `build_annotated_trace` a small fixed depth limit (currently five), but make it record information in each node at the bottom edge of the first fragment about the implicit subtree rooted there. This allows us to give better depth limits to the invocations that build lower fragments. Our ideal depth limit is one which will cause no more than a specified number of nodes, *node_limit*, to be included in the new trace fragment, since (statistically) this also bounds the memory required by the new fragment. For now, *node_limit* is a parameter; later, we will look at what values of this parameter are sensible.

Average branching factor. It is easy to modify the code in figure 1 to detect when execution enters and leaves an implicit subtree, to record the maximum depth of each subtree (d_{max}) and the numbers of calls (C) and events (E) in each subtree, and to record this data in the root of each implicit subtree. While this info doesn't tell us about the implicit EDT directly, it tells us about a related tree we call the *weighted call tree*. We can think of the annotated trace as a weighted tree where each node corresponds to a `call` event, and the weight of a node is the number of events that have the same call sequence number as the node, including internal events. Since the sum of the weights of all the nodes equals the number of annotated trace nodes represented in the tree, this tree is useful for modeling memory consumption.

For a weighted call tree with a constant branching factor b, the same weight for each node w, and maximum depth d_{max}, the number of events represented by the tree, N, is given by $N = w \sum_{i=0}^{d_{max}-1} b^i$. In this case, $N = E$, and we can compute the average w as E/C. This makes it easy to solve for b by applying e.g. Newton's method to the monotonic function $f(b) = w \sum_{i=0}^{d_{max}-1} b^i - N$ to find b where $f(b) = 0$. This gives us the average branching factor of the implicit subtree. Assuming the branching factors of most nodes are close to this average, we can calculate the depth limit we need to collect about *node_limit* nodes by calculating the root of the monotonic function $g(d) = w \sum_{i=0}^{d_{max}-1} b^i - node\_limit$.

Unfortunately, our benchmarking shows the assumption is often very far from the truth. We used four synthetic benchmark programs: fib, stick, bigsmall and smallbig, and one real one: the Mercury compiler mmc. For now, we ran all five on data that yielded 1 to 25 million events. Our benchmark machine was a PC with a 2.4 GHz Intel Pentium IV with 512 Mb of RAM running SuSe Linux 8.1. The behavior of the heuristic is ok on the test program whose tree is a thin (predictable) stick and isn't *too* bad for Fibonacci, though for fib it collects 10 to 60 times as many nodes as intended due to the difference between the average branching factor 1.55 and the actual branching factor of 2 for all non-leaf nodes. However things are worse for the other benchmarks. Many programs contain components with characteristics similar to bigsmall or smallbig, whose tree shapes are shown in trees A and B respectively in figure 3. For small-big, there didn't appear to be any correspondence at all between *node_limit* and the average number of nodes actually constructed per reexecution. With *node_limit* = 20 000, we got about 150 000; with *node_limit* = 100 000, we got about 35 000. Since the tree suddenly gets exponentially large in the bottom few layers, the computed average branching factor needs to be only a little bit too optimistic for the number of nodes constructed to explode. How optimistic the approximation is depends on how close to the widening point of the tree the relevant approximation is taken from. That in turn depends on the depths used for the fragments above in an essentially unpredictable manner. For bigsmall, the computed *depth_limit* is so bad that trying to collect only 100 nodes ran our test machine out of memory, and the same thing happens with mmc with *node_limit* = 2 000.

Biased branching factor. The problem with bigsmall arises because the approximation tree (C in figure 3) is way too deep and narrow: it doesn't have the same shape as the actual tree, even though it has the same maximum depth and number of nodes. Based on this, the heuristic believes that most nodes are near the bottom and thus it is safe to collect many levels at the top, but those levels contain far more events than expected.

Even though smallbig and bigsmall have very different shapes, they are approximated by the same tree, tree C in figure 3. We could fix this by approximating each implicit tree with a constant-branching-factor tree of the same *average* depth. The smallbig and bigsmall examples would then be approximated by trees D and E respectively in figure 3.

Calculating the average depth of an implicit tree is almost as simple as calculating the maximum depth; we now solve for β in $N = w \sum_{i=0}^{d_{ave}-1} \beta^i$ where d_{ave} is the average depth of the nodes in the tree. This approach does perform better. For stick and fib, the numbers of nodes collected are much closer than the number asked for by *node_limit*, though there are still some significant deviations. However, the new estimates are still far from perfect. The bigsmall and mmc tests still collect far too many nodes, though with this heuristic they run out only with *node_limit* = 2 000 for bigsmall and *node_limit* = 200 000 for mmc. The smallbig tests still suffers from exactly the same problem as before: the numbers of nodes collected still bears little relationship to *node_limit*, though the chaotic pattern is different.

5   An Effective Strategy

Clearly, approximating an implicit subtree using a tree with a constant branching factor is not a useful approach, since realistic programs do not behave this way. Real programs call all sorts of different predicates. Some are simple recursive predicates which produce stick-like trees; some have long conjunctions in their bodies which produce wide trees with large branching factors. We need a heuristic that works with both these shapes and everything in between. The heuristics of the previous section were also flawed in that their estimates of *depth_limit* could inherently fail in either direction: they could try to collect too many levels as well as too few. While trying to collect too few levels is relatively benign, requiring only a small increase in the number of reexecutions, our benchmarking shows that trying to collect even a few too many levels can require far more memory than is available. We therefore want a heuristic that guarantees that no more than *node_limit* nodes will be added to the annotated trace. The ideal value for *depth_limit* is the highest value that has this property.

Our *ideal depth strategy*, whose algorithm is shown in figure 4, is designed to compute this value directly. When processing events we don't link into the new trace fragment, we don't just record their maximum or average depth; we build a more detailed record. The algorithm does this by building an array *counts* that records the number of events at each depth in the tree below the current depth limit for any given implicit subtree. The `calculate_ideal_depth` function scans this array, incrementing the depth and computing the cumulative number of events at or above the current depth until it gets to a depth at which this total exceeds *node_limit*, then returns one less than this depth as *ideal_depth*. (If the subtree contains fewer than *node_limit* nodes, then there is no such depth, and we return a depth that causes all those nodes be included in the fragment.) We attach the ideal depth of each subtree to the node that acts as the root of that subtree. We specify *depth_limit* = 5 for the first invocation of

```
build_annotated_trace(call_number, end_event, node_limit, depth_limit)
returns trace is


trace := NULL
inside := false
Initialise the counts array to size ⌊node_limit/2⌋, all zeros
Rewind execution to a call before or equal to call_number
For each executed event e loop
        If e is a call or redo event for call call_number
                inside := true
        If inside
                If depth(e) < depth_limit
                        trace := create_annotated_node(e, trace)
                Else if depth(e) = depth_limit and e is an interface event
                        trace := create_annotated_node(e, trace)
                        If e is an exit, fail or excp event
                                ideal_depth := calculate_ideal_depth(counts, node_limit)
                                trace := mark_as_implicit_root(e, ideal_depth, trace)
                                Reset counts to all zeros
                Else
                        depth_in_implicit_subtree := depth(e) - depth_limit
                        If depth_in_implicit_subtree ≤ ⌊node_limit/2⌋
                                Add 1 to counts[depth_in_implicit_subtree]
        If e is an exit, fail or excp event for call call_number
                inside := false
Until the event number of e is end_event
```

Fig. 4. Algorithm for building the annotated trace using the ideal depth strategy

build_annotated_trace, as before. However, later invocations, whose task is to build an annotated trace fragment from an implicit root at the bottom edge of a previous fragment, will be given as *depth_limit* the recorded ideal depth for the subtree at that node. This guarantees that we collect as many nodes as we can without going over *node_limit*.

Since when we materialize the subtree at an implicit root we will wish to collect at most *node_limit* events, it suffices to counts events down to a depth of ⌊*node_limit*/2⌋. This is because the minimum number of events at each depth is two (a call event and its corresponding exit, fail or excp event). We can reuse the same array to calculate the ideal depth for all the implicit subtrees encountered during a particular run. Reserving ⌊*node_limit*/2⌋ words of memory for this purpose is not a problem, since we are clearly willing to have the new fragment occupy space linear in *node_limit*. The array just increases the constant factor slightly.

Materializing the subtree of a predicate that may succeed more than once requires a slight variation on our algorithm. Suppose a predicate succeeds twice, producing a call/exit pair and a redo/exit pair. The subtree rooted at the second exit node can contain events both from between the call/exit pair and from between the subsequent redo/exit pair (consider a child call whose

Table 1. bigsmall: ideal depth strategy

$node\_limit$	$exec\_count$	$total\_created$	$\frac{total\_created}{exec\_count}$	T_U	T_R	RSS	VSZ
100	1124	102 910	91	35.36	51.60	41	49
500	210	101 826	484	10.63	13.67	41	49
1 000	105	102 188	973	7.81	9.40	41	49
5 000	23	112 432	4 888	5.66	6.17	41	49
10 000	12	116 280	9 690	5.45	5.81	41	49
50 000	4	173 876	43 469	5.56	5.80	51	65
100 000	2	165 514	82 757	5.85	6.10	50	57
500 000	1	262 130	262 130	7.28	7.53	59	74
1 000 000	1	524 124	524 124	9.65	9.93	90	99

Table 2. Mercury compiler compiling small module, ideal depth strategy

$node\_limit$	$exec\_count$	$total\_created$	$\frac{total\_created}{exec\_count}$	T_U	T_R	RSS	VSZ
1 000	83	59 460	716	19.27	21.14	98	126
5 000	42	173 383	4 128	18.76	19.89	106	134
10 000	31	265 019	8 549	18.93	19.83	115	142
50 000	11	507 947	46 177	18.39	18.93	150	176
100 000	7	640 189	91 455	19.48	19.98	157	184
500 000	2	911 521	455 760	19.52	19.97	200	226
1 000 000	1	913 087	913 087	24.19	24.70	246	268

Table 3. Mercury compiler compiling large module, ideal depth strategy

$node\_limit$	$exec\_count$	$total\_created$	$\frac{total\_created}{exec\_count}$	T_U	T_R	RSS	VSZ
1 000	56	26 921	480	274.48	277.48	205	233
5 000	31	86 131	2 778	225.00	226.96	201	225
10 000	25	162 232	6 489	214.26	215.92	206	233
50 000	15	583 876	38 925	186.18	187.54	254	284
100 000	13	1 034 614	79 585	186.63	188.03	311	334
500 000	7	2 969 020	424 145	174.98	190.41	477	542
1 000 000	6	5 130 084	855 014	193.08	684.92	443	866

result is used in both solutions). The algorithm in figure 4 resets *counts* at each
`exit` event, which means the ideal depth limit stored at the second `exit` will
be too big because it is based only on the events between the `redo` and second
`exit`. To fix this, we can reexecute the call in question using a modified version
of the algorithm in figure 4 which doesn't reset the *counts* array and doesn't
construct any trace nodes. (Since most calls can succeed at most once, this extra
reexecution will be required only rarely.) The usual `calculate_ideal_depth`
function at the second `exit` node will then compute the right ideal depth.

Table 1 gives experimental results for the most problematic of our small programs, bigsmall. Tables 2 and 3 do the same for the Mercury compiler. Table 2
shows the compilation of a small module, while table 3 shows the compilation
of a large 6 000+ line source file, a process that generates more than 200 million

events. Each test simulates a declarative debugging session using the divide-and-query search strategy [11]. The search starts at the top node of tree (the exit node of main), and since our testing harness automatically answers 'no' to all questions, it ends at a leaf node. (For our largest test, finding this "bug" required 22 questions.) This is the kind of search that puts the most stress on our algorithm since it requires the most reexecutions of the program.

In each table, the only parameter is *node_limit*, the upper bound on the number of nodes that we want to collect for the annotated trace fragment built by each reexecution. We do not include the initial or final reexecutions in the shown measurements, since the initial reexecution uses a small constant depth limit (since nothing is known about the tree at this time) and the size of the fragment built by the final reexecution is limited by the size of the subtree, not *node_limit*. *total_created* is the total actual number of annotated trace nodes which were produced during the complete debugging session (except for the first and last reexecutions). *exec_count* is the number of reexecutions required to locate the bug (again minus the first and last reexecutions). *total_created/exec_count* gives the actual average number of nodes collected per reexecution, which we would like to be less than *node_limit* but otherwise as close to it as possible. The T_U and T_R columns show the user CPU time and the real (wall clock) time required for the tests in seconds; the times were averaged over ten runs. The last two columns show (in megabytes) the total resident set size (RSS) and the total virtual size (VSZ) of the process (including swap space) at the time when the bug is located, which is when they are at their maximum. All this data is available, in more detail and for more values of *node_limit*, for all our benchmarks and all our heuristics in [3], though we have improved our system since that earlier work.

The results show that the extra calculation required to compute the ideal depth limit (instead of estimating it) is well worth it. For all our benchmarks, including the ones not in the tables, we get more than acceptable performance for a wide range of *node_limit* values, with values in the 10 000-100 000 range generally performing best. Having *node_limit* much lower wastes time in too many reexecutions; having *node_limit* much higher runs the risk of running out of memory. (The last row of table 3 shows the start of thrashing.) We have found *node_limit* = 20 000 to work well for all the programs we have tried. For example, when the Mercury compiler is invoked on that 6 000 line source file, our algorithm needs about three and a half minutes to materialize all the fragments needed to find the "bug" in a leaf node. During this time, the search algorithm asked the oracle 22 questions. If it were the user answering these questions, there would be on average about an 8 to 10 second delay between his/her answer and the next question. Given that the user will certainly take much more than 10 seconds to answer each query, the overhead of search space materialization is not the bottleneck in the search for the bug.

With *node_limit* = 50 000, the sizes of fragments tend to be in the 5-25 Mb range, both for the compiler and some other programs we have looked at. When the cumulative sizes of the fragments materialized so far starts to exceed the available memory, it would be relatively straightforward to release the memory of the least recently used fragment. The EDT nodes constructed from it would remain, and if the search algorithm ever needs the other nodes from that fragment, it could construct the fragment again.

On any given reexecution of part of the program, most events end up being ignored. It is therefore important to optimize the handling of these events. This is why the we use a simple depth cutoff as the criterion for inclusion in a new fragment. Other criteria may lead to fragments that have a higher proportion of nodes useful to the search algorithm (whichever one is being used), but this is unlikely to compensate for the sharply greater cost of evaluating the test of any nontrivial criterion.

6   Related Work

Nilsson and Fritzson [6,5] also propose constructing the program trace piece by piece. They introduce the concept of the *query distance* to a node. This is the number of questions required to get to the node using a top-down, left-to-right search.

They optimistically materialize nodes and then uses the query distance to decide which nodes should be discarded if memory usage becomes too high. Nodes with higher query distances are the first to be discarded.

This works well for top-down search, since most of the time the next question will be in a materialized fragment of the EDT. This technique doesn't work with the Mercury declarative debugger because it can use multiple search strategies (including a version of Shapiro's divide-and-query [11] algorithm and a search strategy similar to Pereira's rational debugger [8]). With these search strategies [4] the query distance ceases to become a useful heuristic for deciding which nodes to throw away.

Modifying the notion of the query distance to work for different search strategies is not a viable option, since it is unclear how the modified query distance could be efficiently calculated for search strategies like divide-and-query. Also, a node may have a small query distance for one search strategy and a large query distance for another strategy. Since the user may switch search strategies mid-session, the query distance heuristic doesn't help to decide whether to keep such a node.

There is also a penalty to be paid for first creating a node in the EDT and then disposing of that node later when resources become tight (mostly due to the extra work garbage collection must do). Using our method we are able to know *ahead of time* how much of the EDT can be viably generated in a single reexecution, so no nodes are created only to be destroyed later.

Plaisted [9] proposed an efficient method for deciding which nodes in the EDT to materialize. Unfortunately the method only works with the divide-and-query search strategy, and generates questions that are hard for users to answer.

7   Conclusion

During our work on the Mercury declarative debugger we found that we needed a new algorithm to control the resources consumed by the annotated trace, because none of the techniques in the current literature were adequate in the presence of multiple search strategies.

We first tried two variations on a method that tries to guess the shape of the subtree to be constructed from information about its branching factor. These methods don't work, because their implicit assumption that most nodes have similar branching factors is much too far from the truth.

Analyzing the cause of the failure led us to the ideal depth strategy. While this strategy uses a bit more memory, it allows us to calculate *exactly* how much of the search space we can viably materialize each time the search algorithm visits a previously unexplored part of the search space. We have found this algorithm to work very well in practice, so well that users of the Mercury declarative debugger spend much more time answering questions than waiting for rematerialization, even when debugging long running, real programs. Our algorithm thus helps programmers find bugs more quickly.

The techniques we presented are certainly not specific to Mercury. They can be applied to any declarative debugger with a tree that must be searched and an execution replay mechanism that can rebuild previously unmaterialized parts of the tree.

We would like to thank the Australian Research Council and Microsoft for their support.

References

1. Mark Brown and Zoltan Somogyi. Annotated event traces for declarative debugging. Available from http://www.cs.mu.oz.au/mercury/, 2003.
2. Lawrence Byrd. Understanding the control flow of Prolog programs. In *Proceedings of the 1980 Logic Programming Workshop*, pages 127–138, Debrecen, Hungary, July 1980.
3. Ian MacLarty. Practical declarative debugging of Mercury programs. MSc thesis, University of Melbourne, July 2005.
4. Ian MacLarty, Zoltan Somogyi, and Mark Brown. Divide-and-query and subterm dependency tracking in the Mercury declarative debugger. In *Proceedings of AADEBUG 2005*, Monterey, California, September 2005.
5. Henrik Nilsson. Tracing piece by piece: affordable debugging for lazy functional languages. In *Proceedings of ICFP '99*, pages 36–47, Paris, France, September 1999.
6. Henrik Nilsson and Peter Fritzson. Algorithmic debugging for lazy functional languages. *Journal of Functional Programming*, 4(3):337–370, July 1994.
7. Henrik Nilsson and Jan Sparud. The evaluation dependence tree as a basis for lazy functional debugging. *Automated Software Engineering*, 4(2):121–150, April 1997.
8. Luis Moniz Pereira. Rational debugging in logic programming. In *Proceedings of ICLP '86*, pages 203–210, London, England, June 1986.
9. D. A. Plaisted. An efficient bug location algorithm. In *Proceedings of ICLP '84*, pages 151–158, Uppsala, Sweden, July 1984.
10. M. Ronsse, K. de Bosschere, and J.C. de Kergommeaux. Execution replay and debugging. In *Proceedings of AADEBUG 2000*, Munich, Germany, 2000.
11. Ehud Y. Shapiro. *Algorithmic program debugging*. MIT Press, 1983.

12. Zoltan Somogyi. Idempotent I/O for safe time travel. In *Proceedings of the AADE-BUG 2003*, Ghent, Belgium, September 2003.
13. Zoltan Somogyi and Fergus Henderson. The implementation technology of the Mercury debugger. In *Proceedings of WPLE '99*, pages 35–49, Las Cruces, New Mexico, November 1999.

Automatic Verification of a Model Checker by Reflection

Bow-Yaw Wang[*]

Institute of Information Science,
Academia Sinica,
128 Sec 2 Academia Rd,
Taipei 115, Taiwan
TEL: +886-2-2788-3799x1717 FAX: +886-2-2782-4814
bywang@iis.sinica.edu.tw

Abstract. Intuitively, reflection is the feature that can represent and reason meta-level entities at the object level. In this paper, we use a reflective language to implement a local model checker and analyze the implementation. The implementation is greatly simplified by reflection. Further, we show the feature can be applied to verify the concise implementation rather easily. The simplicity of our approach suggests that reflection may be useful in the implementation and verification of other explicit-state model checking algorithms.

Keywords: Reflection, Rewriting Logic, Model Checking, Logic Programming.

1 Introduction

Model checking has become a popular technique to improve system quality during the past decade. Thanks to its success in hardware verification, many model checkers are being developed in research laboratories and sold by companies. But building a model checker requires sophisticated programming and algorithm-developing skills. A typical model checker may contain tens, even hundreds, of thousands of lines of C code. Since model checkers have been deployed in the design of many critical systems, one wonders whether there is a way to ensure the quality of these verification tools.

In this paper, we use rewriting logic [15] as the formalism to verify a working model checker. Following the framework proposed in [23,10,21], we implement a model checker in Maude, a logic programming language based on rewriting logic [6]. Unlike other model checkers which use different languages in their implementation and model specification, the Maude language is also used as the modeling language of our model checker.

The key to use Maude as the algorithm implementation *and* the model specification language is reflection. Intuitively, reflection is the feature that can represent and reason about meta-level entities at the object level. In the framework

---

[*] This research was partly supported by NSC 94-2213-E-001 -003 -.

P. Van Hentenryck (Ed.): PADL 2006, LNCS 3819, pp. 45–59, 2006.

of [23,10,21], model specifications reside in the meta level. The model checking algorithm inspects meta-level specifications by reflection. Hence, we can implement a model checking algorithm in Maude. It is unnecessary to have different languages in different levels. Additionally model simulation can be performed by reflection. This simplifies our implementation in Maude significantly.

Furthermore, we can verify our implementation by another application of reflection. While verifying our model checker, the implementation becomes an entity in the meta level. We are able to use other object-level model checkers to analyze our implementation. Specifically, we verify our model checker by two different model checkers — the abstract model checking algorithm and the Maude built-in LTL model checker in [10].

The advantages of our approach are its simplicity and clarity. With the reflective language Maude, the model checking paradigm is modeled as two levels of computation. Using the same principle, it is straightforward to model the verification of model checkers as another level of computation. We feel the same task would be too complicated to achieve had the concept of reflection not been introduced in the framework. Reflection in declarative languages is not only of theoretical endeavor, but also of practical interests.

1.1 Related Work

Model checking algorithms have been formally verified by proof assistants [19,13]. In these work, the semantics and algorithms are formalized in the meta logic of proof assistants. Verifying model checking algorithms amounts to proving that the outcomes of algorithms agree with the semantics in the meta logic. In principle, it is possible to verify systems that can be formalized in the meta logic. But intensive human intervention is required.

An LTL model checker is available in recent releases of Maude [10]. The performance of the built-in LTL model checker is comparable to the model checker SPIN [11]. But the implementation is written in C++. It is difficult for verification tool developers to modify and improve the internal model checker.

The inconvenience is resolved in [21] where a proof-theoretic μ-calculus model checking algorithm [9,20,24] is presented. The μ-calculus model checking algorithm is implemented in an older version of Maude, and requires extension to core Maude system for technical reasons. Subsequently, it is less efficient than what we present in this paper.

In [2,7], reflection is used for reasoning families of membership equational theories. Metatheorems about families of theories are represented and proved as theorems at object level by reflection. The idea is realized in the theorem prover ITP for membership equational theories [5].

1.2 Outline

The paper is organized as follows. Section 2 provides necessary technical backgrounds. An abstract μ-calculus model checking algorithm is presented in Section 3. It is followed by its concrete implementation in Section 4. We use the concrete implementation in Section 4 to verify properties of Peterson's algorithm in Section 5. The μ-calculus model checker is then verified by two different algorithms in Section 6. Finally, we discuss future work and conclude the paper in Section 7.

2 Preliminaries

We briefly review μ-calculus model checking and rewriting logic. For a more detailed exposition, the reader is referred to [12,9,20,24,8,4,10].

2.1 μ-Calculus

A μ-calculus formula φ is constructed by the following rules [12]:

- propositional variables: $X, Y, Z, \ldots$;
- atomic propositions (AP): $p, q, r, \ldots$;
- Boolean operators: $\neg\varphi$, $\varphi \vee \varphi'$;
- modal existential next-state operator: $\langle \bar{\ell} \rangle \varphi$, where $\bar{\ell}$ is a set of transition labels;
- greatest fixed-point operator: $\nu X.\varphi$, where the bound variable X occurs positively in φ.

As usual, we use derived operators such as $\varphi \wedge \varphi' (\equiv \neg(\neg\varphi \vee \neg\varphi'))$, $[\bar{\ell}]\varphi(\equiv \neg\langle\bar{\ell}\rangle\neg\varphi)$ and $\mu X.\varphi(\equiv \neg\nu X.\neg\varphi[\neg X/X])$.

The semantics of μ-calculus formulae is defined over a *Kripke structure* $K = (S, Labl, \rightarrow, s_0, P)$ where S is the set of states, $Labl$ the set of transition labels, $\rightarrow \subseteq S \times Labl \times S$ the transition relation, $s_0 \in S$ the initial state, and $P \in S \rightarrow 2^{AP}$ the labeling function which maps each state to a set of atomic propositions satisfied in the state. For clarity, we write $s \xrightarrow{a} t$ for $(s, a, t) \in \rightarrow$. A *valuation* ρ is a function mapping propositional variables to subsets of S. Let $R \subseteq S$. We write $\rho[X \mapsto R]$ for the valuation mapping X to R and Y to $\rho(Y)$ for $X \neq Y$. Given the valuation ρ, the semantic function $[\![\varphi]\!]\rho$ for a μ-calculus formula φ computes the set of states satisfying φ under the valuation ρ:

- $[\![X]\!]\rho = \rho(X)$;
- $[\![p]\!]\rho = \{s \in S : p \in P(s)\}$;
- $[\![\neg\varphi]\!]\rho = S \setminus [\![\varphi]\!]\rho$;
- $[\![\varphi \vee \varphi']\!]\rho = [\![\varphi]\!]\rho \cup [\![\varphi']\!]\rho$;
- $[\![\langle\bar{\ell}\rangle\varphi]\!]\rho = \{s \in S : \exists a \in \{\bar{\ell}\}, t \in S.s \xrightarrow{a} t \text{ and } t \in [\![\varphi]\!]\rho\}$;
- $[\![\nu X.\varphi]\!]\rho = \bigcup\{R \subseteq S : R \subseteq [\![\varphi]\!](\rho[X \mapsto R])\}$.

For any μ-calculus formula φ and Kripke structure $K = (S, L, \rightarrow, s_0, P)$, we write $K, s \models \varphi$ when $s \in [\![\varphi]\!]\emptyset$. The μ-calculus model checking problem is to determine whether $K, s_0 \models \varphi$.

In order to solve the μ-calculus model checking problem, various algorithms have been developed (see, for example, [3]). In tableau-based local model checking algorithms [9,20], the problem is solved by constructing proofs of the judgment $K, s \vdash \varphi$. The tableau-based algorithms were then simplified to a set of reduction rules in [24]. The following extension to the greatest fixed point operator, $\nu X\{\bar{r}\}\varphi$ where $\bar{r}$ is a set of states, is introduced in [24]:

$$[\![\nu X\{\bar{r}\}\varphi]\!]\rho = \bigcup \{R \subseteq S : R \subseteq \{\bar{r}\} \cup [\![\varphi]\!](\rho[X \mapsto R])\}.$$

Note that $\nu X\{\}\varphi \equiv \nu X.\varphi$. Any fixed-point operator can be translated to its extended form syntactically. Intuitively, the formula $\nu X\{\bar{r}\}\varphi$ records previously visited states in $\{\bar{r}\}$, which is handy for co-inductive proofs. The extension reduces the side condition of tableau-based algorithms to membership checking and allows the proof search to be performed by rewriting. Given a Kripke structure $K = (S, Labl, \rightarrow, s_0, P)$ and a μ-calculus formula φ, the following rules reduce $K, s \vdash \varphi$ to Boolean values true or false [24]:

- $(K, s \vdash p) =$ true if $p \in P(s)$;
- $(K, s \vdash p) =$ false if $p \notin P(s)$;
- $(K, s \vdash$ false$) =$ false;
- $(K, s \vdash \neg\varphi) = \neg b$ where $(K, s \vdash \varphi) = b$;
- $(K, s \vdash \varphi \vee \varphi') = b_0 \vee b_1$ where $(K, s \vdash \varphi) = b_0$ and $(K, s \vdash \varphi') = b_1$;
- $(K, s \vdash \langle\bar{\ell}\rangle\varphi) =$ true if $(K, t \vdash \varphi) =$ true for some t and a such that $a \in \{\bar{\ell}\}$ and $s \xrightarrow{a} t$;
- $(K, s \vdash \nu X\{\bar{r}\}\varphi) =$ true if $s \in \{\bar{r}\}$;
- $(K, s \vdash \nu X\{\bar{r}\}\varphi) = (K, s \vdash \varphi[\nu X\{s, \bar{r}\}\varphi/X])$ if $s \notin \{\bar{r}\}$.

Let K be a finite Kripke structure and φ a μ-calculus formula. It is shown that $(K, s \vdash \varphi) =$ true if and only if $K, s \models \varphi$ [24].

2.2   Rewriting Logic

Since its introduction in [15], rewriting logic has been used as a unified formalism for modeling concurrency [15,16,14] and as a logical framework [1]. It is not hard to see that rewriting logic is capable of property and model specification [23,10,21]. In the following, we will briefly review rewriting logic and its verification framework as proposed in [10].

In rewriting logic, a *term* is constructed by function and constant symbols. Each term belongs to one or several *sorts*. *Equations* specify equivalent terms. *Rewriting rules* specify how to transform a term into another. A rewrite theory consists of equations and rewriting rules for terms. If a rewrite theory does not contain any rewriting rules, we also call it an *equational theory*.

We follow the syntax of Maude in our presentation. Maude is a term rewriting system based on rewriting logic. In Maude, function and constant symbols are declared by the keyword **op**. Sorts are declared by the keyword **sort**. Equations are specified by **eq** *lhs* = *rhs*; conditional equations are specified by **ceq** *lhs* = *rhs* **if** *cond*. Similarly, rewriting rules and conditional rewriting rules are defined by **rl** [*l*] : *lhs* $\Rightarrow$ *rhs* and **crl** [*l*] : *lhs* $\Rightarrow$ *rhs* **if** *cond* respectively, where *l* is the label of the rule. The left-hand side of equations and rewriting rules allows pattern matching. Since there may be several ways to match a term, applying a rewriting rule to a given term may yield multiple results. All results obtained by any of these applications are admissible in rewriting logic.

For any term t, we write $[t]$ for its equivalence class defined by the equations in a rewrite theory. Let $\mathcal{R}$ be a rewrite theory and t, t' two terms in $\mathcal{R}$. We write

$$\mathcal{R} \vdash_l [t] \rightarrow [t']$$

if there is a rule labeled l in $\mathcal{R}$ that rewrites t to t'.

In rewriting logic, there is a universal theory $\mathcal{U}$ such that any rewrite theory $\mathcal{R}$ and a term t can be represented as meta-level terms $\underline{\mathcal{R}}$ and $\underline{t}$ in $\mathcal{U}$ respectively. Furthermore, we have

$$\mathcal{R} \vdash_l [t] \rightarrow [t'] \Leftrightarrow \mathcal{U} \vdash_{l,n} [\underline{\mathcal{R}}, \underline{t}] \rightarrow [\underline{\mathcal{R}}, \underline{t'}]$$

if t' is the n-th result obtained by applying the rewriting rule labeled l to t in $\mathcal{R}$. By the universal theory $\mathcal{U}$, we can manipulate meta-level terms at the object level. We call the feature that can represent and reason meta-level terms at the object level as *reflection*.

3   An Abstract μ-Calculus Model Checker

We begin with the representation of μ-calculus formulae. A μ-calculus formula is represented by a term of sort MuFormula. Figure 1 shows the symbols in MuFormula terms. In addition to the sort MuFormula, the sort MuVariable is declared to be used in fixed points. The underlines (_) denote the positions of parameters. For instance, the declaration _ $\wedge$ _ specifies that the symbol $\wedge$ is an infix operator. For modal operators, transition labels are quoted identifiers corresponding to rewriting rule labels. Hence the set of transition labels $\bar{\ell}$ in $\langle \bar{\ell} \rangle \varphi$ and $[\bar{\ell}] \varphi$ is denoted by the built-in sort QidList in $\langle \_ \rangle \_$ and $[\_] \_$ respectively. Finally, the state set $\bar{r}$ in the fixed point operators $\mu X \{\bar{r}\} \varphi$ and $\nu X \{\bar{r}\} \varphi$ is represented as a set of meta-level terms. We define the sort TermSet for the representation of meta-level term sets. The symbols Mu_ _ _ and Nu_ _ _ form terms of sort MuFormula from a MuVariable term, a TermSet term, and a MuFormula term.

sorts MuVariable MuFormula

ops False True : $\rightarrow$ MuFormula
op $\neg$ _ : MuFormula $\rightarrow$ MuFormula
op _ $\vee$ _ : MuFormula MuFormula $\rightarrow$ MuFormula
op _ $\wedge$ _ : MuFormula MuFormula $\rightarrow$ MuFormula
op $\langle \_ \rangle \_$: QidList MuFormula $\rightarrow$ MuFormula
op $[\_] \_$: QidList MuFormula $\rightarrow$ MuFormula
op Nu_ _ _ : MuVariable TermSet MuFormula $\rightarrow$ MuFormula
op Mu_ _ _ : MuVariable TermSet MuFormula $\rightarrow$ MuFormula

Fig. 1. Symbols for μ-Calculus Terms

$$\textbf{eq True} = \neg \textsf{ False}$$
$$\textbf{eq} \ \neg \ \neg \ f = f$$
$$\textbf{eq} \ f \wedge g = \neg \ (\neg \ f \vee \neg \ g)$$
$$\textbf{eq} \ [\ L\ ]\ f = \neg \ (\langle\ L\ \rangle \ \neg \ f)$$
$$\textbf{eq Mu} \ X \ TS \ f = \neg \ (\textsf{Nu} \ X \ TS \ \textsf{subst} \ (\neg \ f, X, \neg \ X))$$

Fig. 2. Equations for Derived Operators

To reduce the number of rules in our model checker, Figure 2 provides a set of equations for derived constant and function symbols. These equations follow directly from the corresponding logical equivalence relations. For the greatest fixed point, the substitution of μ-calculus formula is needed. The function subst (f, Z, g) replaces free occurrences of the variable Z in f by g (Figure 3). If f is the term False or an atomic proposition, subst leaves it unchanged. If f is a MuVariable term not equal to Z, the MuVariable term is returned; otherwise, it is replaced by g. For negative, disjunctive, and existential modal operators, subst invokes itself recursively. Finally, if f is a fixed point formula, subst substitutes the variable Z if Z is not bound. Note that we do not need rules for derived operators.

$$\textbf{eq subst (False}, Z, g) = \textsf{False}$$
$$\textbf{eq subst} \ (p, Z, g) = p$$
$$\textbf{ceq subst} \ (X, Z, g) = X \ \textbf{if} \ X \neq Z$$
$$\textbf{ceq subst} \ (X, Z, g) = g \ \textbf{if} \ X = Z$$
$$\textbf{eq subst} \ (\neg \ f, Z, g) = \neg \ \textsf{subst} \ (f, Z, g)$$
$$\textbf{eq subst} \ (f_0 \vee f_1), Z, g) = \textsf{subst} \ (f_0, Z, g) \vee \textsf{subst} \ (f_1, Z, g)$$
$$\textbf{eq subst} \ (\langle\ L\ \rangle \ f, Z, g) = \langle\ L\ \rangle \ \textsf{subst} \ (f, Z, g)$$
$$\textbf{ceq subst} \ (\textsf{Nu} \ X \ TS \ f, Z, g) = \textsf{Nu} \ X \ TS \ (\textsf{subst} \ (f, Z, g)) \ \textbf{if} \ X \neq Z$$
$$\textbf{ceq subst} \ (\textsf{Nu} \ X \ TS \ f, Z, g) = \textsf{Nu} \ X \ TS \ f \ \textbf{if} \ X = Z$$

Fig. 3. Definition of *subst*

We represent Winskel's reduction rules as rewriting rules for entailment terms.[1] Let K be a quoted identifier denoting the name of a rewrite theory, $\underline{s}$ a meta-level term representing a state, and f a MuFormula term. The entailment term $K \ \underline{s} \vdash f$ is of sort Bool. The idea is to rewrite the entailment term to false or true for any Kripke structure specified by the rewrite theory named K. It is crucial to use a meta-level term $\underline{s}$ in entailment terms. The rules of the rewrite theory $\mathcal{K}$ would rewrite the state s had we used the object-level term s in entailment terms.[2]

It is straightforward to write the rules for Boolean operators in Maude.

$$\textbf{rl} \ [\textit{ff}] : K \ \underline{s} \vdash \textsf{False} \Rightarrow \textsf{false}$$
$$\textbf{rl} \ [\textit{neg}] : K \ \underline{s} \vdash \neg \ f \Rightarrow \textsf{not} \ (K \ \underline{s} \vdash f)$$
$$\textbf{rl} \ [\textit{disj}] : K \ \underline{s} \vdash f_0 \vee f_1 \Rightarrow (K \ \underline{s} \vdash f_0) \ \textsf{or-else} \ (K \ \underline{s} \vdash f_1)$$

---

[1] Equational theory would suffice for model checking, but we need rule labels for formal verification.

[2] The calligraphic $\mathcal{K}$ is the rewrite theory with the quoted name K.

```
eq exists (K, s, f, nil, N) = false
eq exists (K, s, f, l L, N) =
    if U ⊢_{l,N} [K, s] → [K, t] then
        (K t ⊢ f) or-else (exists (K, s, f, l L, N + 1))
    else
        exists (K, s, f, L, 0)
    fi
```

Fig. 4. Definition of exists

The rule *ff* rewrites the entailment term $K \ s \vdash$ False to the built-in Bool constant term false. Similarly, the rule *neg* rewrites $K \ s \vdash \neg f$ to not $(K \ s \vdash f)$. The built-in Bool operator not waits until $K \ s \vdash f$ rewrites to either false or true, and then rewrites the Bool constant term to its complementary term. The rule *disj* uses the built-in short-circuited Boolean operator or-else. Observe how the computation is performed by a sequence of rewrites in rewriting logic.

For the existential modal operator, we use the following rule:

$$\textbf{rl } [ex] : K \ s \vdash \langle L \rangle \ f \Rightarrow \text{exists } (K, s, f, L, 0)$$

The function exists (K, s, f, L, N) checks if it is possible to rewrite the entailment $K \ t \vdash f$ to true at an L-successor t of s, where N serves as a counter (Figure 4). The built-in QidList term nil represents the empty quoted identifier list. Notice the semantics differ from those in [10]. Our semantics do not have implicit self-loops. If there is no transition label, the function returns false.

On the other hand, the universal theory $\mathcal{U}$ finds the N-th rewriting result t by applying the rule l in $\mathcal{K}$. Then the function exists rewrites the new entailment term $K \ t \vdash f$. If it does not rewrite to true, the next successor of s will be checked by exists $(K, s, f, l L, N + 1)$. On the other hand, if there is no successor of the current label, we look for a successor by applying the next rule.

Observe how the universal theory $\mathcal{U}$ is used to find the successor t of the current state s. The distinction between the object and meta levels clarifies the relation between the model specification and the algorithm implementation. Furthermore, model simulation by reflection allows us to present the algorithm succinctly.

It is rather straightforward to write the greatest fixed point rules by substitution:

$$\textbf{crl } [nu] : K \ s \vdash \text{Nu } X \ TS \ f \Rightarrow \text{true}$$
$$\quad \text{if } s \text{ isIn } TS$$
$$\textbf{crl } [nu] : K \ s \vdash \text{Nu } X \ TS \ f \Rightarrow K \ s \vdash \text{subst } (f, X, \text{Nu } X \ (\{s\} \cup TS) \ f)$$
$$\quad \text{if not } (s \text{ isIn } TS)$$

The *nu* rules check whether the current state s has been visited. If so, it rewrites the entailment term to true. Otherwise, the current state is added to the meta-level term set TS and the new set is used in the unfolding of the fixed-point formula. The function _isIn_ checks whether a meta-level term is in a term set. Also, the symbol _U_ implements the union of term sets. Both can be easily defined in an equational theory.

4   Concrete Implementation

The rules shown in Section 3 use the pre-defined Maude equations for or-else. Since we cannot fully control internal strategies at object level, we do not know how or-else works internally. In this section, we will get rid of this uncertainty and provide a concrete implementation of the rules.

Consider the definition of exists in Figure 4. We would like the term $(K \underline{t} \vdash f)$ or-else (exists $(K, \underline{s}, f, l\, L, N+1)$) to rewrite $K \underline{t} \vdash f$ first, even though there are equational rules for exists in the other subterm. In order not to reduce the second subterm unintentionally, we will not construct a term with the function symbol exists until necessary.

> **sort** SuccResult
> **op** $\lfloor \_,\_,\_ \rfloor$: Term QidList Nat $\rightarrow$ SuccResult
> **op** none : $\rightarrow$ SuccResult
> **op** succ : Qid Term QidList Nat $\rightarrow$ SuccResult
> **eq** succ $(K, \underline{s}, \text{nil}, N)$ = none
> **eq** succ $(K, \underline{s}, l\, L, N)$ =
>   if $\mathcal{U} \vdash_{l,N} [\underline{K}, \underline{s}] \rightarrow [\underline{K}, \underline{t}]$ **then**
> $\lfloor \underline{t}, l\, L, N+1 \rfloor$
>   **else**
>   succ $(K, \underline{s}, L, 0)$
> **fi**

Fig. 5. Definition of succ

To realize the idea, we define a new function succ $(K, \underline{s}, L, N)$ which returns a SuccResult term $\lfloor \underline{t}, L', N' \rfloor$ if s has a successor t by applying the rules in L (Figure 5). If L is nil, it returns none. Otherwise, succ $(K, \underline{s}, l\, L, N)$ checks whether s has the N-th successor t by applying rule l. If so, it returns $\lfloor \underline{t}, l\, L, N+1 \rfloor$. If not, it returns another successor of s by applying the remaining rules in L.

> **op** wrapper : Bool Qid Term MuFormula SuccResult $\rightarrow$ Bool
> **eq** wrapper (true, $K, \underline{s}, f, R$) = true
> **eq** wrapper (false, $K, \underline{s}, f,$ none) = false
> **eq** wrapper (false, $K, \underline{s}, f, \lfloor \underline{t}, L, N \rfloor$) =
>   wrapper $(K \underline{t} \vdash f, K, \underline{s}, f, \text{succ}\, (K, \underline{s}, L, N))$

Fig. 6. Definition of wrapper

With the function succ, we can implement the rule ex by the wrapper function (Figure 6) as follows.

   rl [ex] : $K \underline{s} \vdash \langle\, L\, \rangle f \Rightarrow$ wrapper (false, $K, \underline{s}, f, \text{succ}\, (K, \underline{s}, L, 0)$)

To check whether s satisfies $\langle\, L\, \rangle f$, we compute the first successor of s by succ $(K, \underline{s}, L, 0)$ and pass the result to wrapper. The wrapper function will check whether the successor satisfies f and compute the next successor. Observe that wrapper does not have a subterm formed by wrapper.

sorts Mode Proc

op $\_\_$: Proc Proc $\rightarrow$ Proc
ops outCS reqCS inCS : $\rightarrow$ Mode
op $\lhd$ $\_,\_,\_$ $\rhd$: Nat Mode Bool $\rightarrow$ Proc

rl $[request0]$: $\lhd 0,$ outCS$, X \rhd$ $\lhd 1, N, Y \rhd \Rightarrow \lhd 0,$ reqCS$, Y \rhd$ $\lhd 1, N, Y \rhd$
rl $[request1]$: $\lhd 0, M, X \rhd$ $\lhd 1,$ outCS$, Y \rhd \Rightarrow \lhd 0, M, X \rhd$ $\lhd 1,$ reqCS, not $X \rhd$
crl $[enter0]$: $\lhd 0,$ reqCS$, X \rhd$ $\lhd 1, N, Y \rhd \Rightarrow \lhd 0,$ inCS$, X \rhd$ $\lhd 1, N, Y \rhd$
   if $N =$ outCS **or** $X \neq Y$
crl $[enter1]$: $\lhd 0, M, X \rhd$ $\lhd 1,$ reqCS$, Y \rhd \Rightarrow \lhd 0, M, X \rhd$ $\lhd 1,$ inCS$, Y \rhd$
   if $M =$ outCS **or** $X = Y$
rl $[leave]$: $\lhd i,$ inCS$, X \rhd$ $\lhd j, N, Y \rhd \Rightarrow \lhd i,$ outCS$, X \rhd$ $\lhd j, N, Y \rhd$

Fig. 7. Peterson's Algorithm

We can use wrapper to implement the rule *disj* as well. The idea is to form a SuccResult term without invoking succ.

   rl $[disj]$: $K \underline{s} \vdash f_0 \vee f_1 \Rightarrow$ wrapper $(K \underline{s} \vdash f_0, K, \underline{s}, f_1, \lfloor \underline{s}, \text{nil}, 0 \rfloor)$

Similarly, the *nu* rules can be simplified by wrapper:

rl $[nu]$: $K \underline{s} \vdash$ Nu X TS $f \Rightarrow$
   wrapper $(\underline{s}$ isIn $TS, K, \underline{s},$ subst $(f, X,$ Nu X $(\{ \underline{s} \} \cup TS)$ $f), \lfloor \underline{s}, \text{nil}, 0 \rfloor)$

5 Verification of Peterson's Algorithm

We verify Peterson's algorithm [18] by our model checker as an example. The mutual exclusion algorithm is shown in Figure 7. Let i be 0 or 1, M a Mode term (outCS, reqCS, or inCS), and X a Bool term, a process term of sort Proc is represented by $\lhd i, M, X \rhd$. The rules *request0*, *request1*, *enter0*, *enter1*, and *leave* implement the transitions of Peterson's algorithm by rewriting the composition of two process terms.

In the rule *request0*, process 0 moves from outCS to reqCS by setting its local Bool term to that of process 1. When process 0 is in reqCS, it moves to inCS if process 1 is in outCS or the two local Bool terms are not equal (the rule enter0). Finally, any process can move out of inCS by the rule leave.

Define the initial state term init to be $\lhd 0,$ outCS, false $\rhd$ $\lhd 1,$ outCS, true $\rhd$ and the QidList term labels to be ('*request0* '*request1* '*enter0* '*enter1* '*leave*). We are interested in verifying whether the two processes cannot be in the critical section at the same time. Hence, we check whether the entailment term **eq** prop0 = 'PETERSON init $\vdash$ Nu X {} ($\neg$ in-cs (0) $\vee \neg$ in-cs (1)) $\wedge$ [labels] X rewrites to true or not. The rules for the atomic proposition in-cs (i) is defined as follows.

   rl $[AP]$: 'PETERSON $\underline{s} \vdash$ in-cs (i) $\Rightarrow$ critical (s, i)

     eq critical ($\lhd 0, M, X \rhd$ $P, 0$) = ($M =$ inCS)
     eq critical ($\lhd 1, N, Y \rhd$ $P, 1$) = ($N =$ inCS)

Similarly, we can check if process 0 always enters the critical section first. The corresponding entailment term is the following:

eq prop1 = 'PETERSON <u>init</u> ⊢ Mu X {} (in-cs (0) ∨ (¬ in-cs (1) ∧ [labels] X))

Finally, we would like to check if process 0 can enter the critical section infinitely often.

eq prop2 = 'PETERSON <u>init</u> ⊢ Nu X {} Mu Y {} ⟨ labels ⟩ ((in-cs (0) ∧ X) ∨ Y)

The entailment terms prop0, prop1, and prop2 rewrite to true, false, and true in 0.5, ≪0.1, ≪0.1 seconds by Maude respectively.[3] The model checker contains 250 lines of Maude code. The concise implementation shows that reflection indeed helps in writing an explicit-state model checker. Since model simulation in explicit-state model checkers is implemented by the universal theory $\mathcal{U}$, programmers can pay more attention to the model checking algorithm. Additionally, the short implementation may be feasible for formal analysis. Theorem provers based on rewriting logic (such as ITP [5]) may be used to verify our implementation semi-automatically.

6   Model Checking μ-Calculus Model Checker

The correspondence between Winskel's rules and the concrete implementation is less obvious than that of abstract rules. Additionally, a typo or a missing case in the definitions of subst, succ, wrapper, and term sets may make our implementation incorrect, even if the correspondence is ensured. The verification of Peterson's algorithm in Section 5 only shows that our model checker has *one* intended behavior. It does not imply *all* internal rewriting strategies will produce the same result. Particularly, if our model checker could yield contradictory results or fail to rewrite an entailment term by different strategies, the user would be very confused.

These questions call for the analysis of our model checker. Since the abstract algorithm is known to be sound, we are more interested in the correctness of our particular implementation. Specifically, we would like to verify if the concrete implementation always rewrites the entailment terms prop0, prop1, and prop2 to true, false, and true respectively.

This problem can be formalized as follows. Define a Kripke structure $\mathcal{M}_0 = (E, RL, \Rightarrow, \text{prop0}, P)$ where E is the set of all entailment terms, RL the set of all rule labels, and

$$P(e) = \begin{cases} \{\text{ isTrue }\} & \text{if } e = \text{true} \\ \{\text{ isFalse }\} & \text{if } e = \text{false} \\ \emptyset & \text{otherwise} \end{cases}.$$

For any two entailment terms e and e', $e \overset{l}{\Rightarrow} e'$ if e rewrites to e' by applying the rule l in our model checker. To verify whether the term prop0 always rewrites to true, it amounts to checking whether $\mathcal{M}_0 \models \mu X.\ \text{isTrue} \vee [RL]X$. Similarly, we

---

[3] The experiments are conducted in a 2.8GHz Pentium 4 with 2GB memory running Fedora Core 4 Linux system.

can define two Kripke structures $\mathcal{M}_1$ and $\mathcal{M}_2$ with initial states prop1 and prop2 respectively, and check $\mathcal{M}_1 \models \mu X.$ isFalse $\vee [RL]X$ and $\mathcal{M}_2 \models \mu X.$ isTrue $\vee [RL]X$. Hence we can resolve the aforementioned questions if we solve these model checking problems.

With the help of reflection, these problems can be solved rather easily. Notice that the Kripke structures $\mathcal{M}_0$, $\mathcal{M}_1$, and $\mathcal{M}_2$ are infinite-state structures. There are countably infinite entailment terms in E. Fortunately, the number of reachable entailment terms is finite because our model checker always terminates. Since both the local model checking and the Maude LTL model checking algorithms explore the reachable states only, they can be used to solve these problems.

6.1   Checking with Abstract Local Model Checker

Let M be the quoted identifier of a model checking theory, e an entailment term, and f a MuFormula term. We define the abstract entailment term $M \underline{e} \Vdash f$ to be of sort Bool. It is easy to implement Winskel's reduction rules in an equational theory (Figure 8). However, specifying properties of a model checker exposes a subtle semantic issue. Consider the following entailment term:

$$\text{'PETERSON } \underline{\text{init}} \vdash \text{False.}$$

It rewrites to false trivially. However, $\underline{\text{init}}$ also satisfies $\mu X.$ isTrue $\vee [RL]X$. This is because our model checker always terminates after a finite number of rewrites. Subsequently, the property $[\, L \,]\, f$ will be true eventually for any QidList term L and MuFormula term f. In the example, the least fixed point rewrites to a disjunction after one unfolding. But the second disjunct rewrites to true because there is no successor.

Our solution is to add implicit self-loops to irreducible terms. If an entailment term has successors, we leave them unchanged. But if an entailment term does not have any successor, we make the entailment term to be its only successor. This can be done by the meta-exists function (Figure 9).

The function meta-exists checks if any successor has been found. If there is no label, it reduces to false if the entailment term $\underline{e}$ has other successors. Otherwise, meta-exists checks whether the current entailment term satisfies the MuFormula term f. Effectively, the entailment term $\underline{e}$ is its only successor when no successor can be found.

> **eq** $M \underline{e} \Vdash$ False $=$ false
> **eq** $M \underline{e} \Vdash \neg f = \neg (M \underline{e} \Vdash f)$
> **eq** $M \underline{e} \Vdash f_0 \vee f_1 = (M \underline{e} \Vdash f_0)$ or-else $(M \underline{e} \Vdash f_1)$
> **eq** $M \underline{e} \Vdash \langle\, L \,\rangle\, f =$ meta-exists $(M, \underline{e}, f, L, 0, \text{false})$
> **ceq** $M \underline{e} \Vdash$ Nu $X\, TS\, f =$ true
>   **if** $\underline{e}$ isIn TS
> **ceq** $M \underline{e} \Vdash$ Nu $X\, TS\, f = M \underline{e} \Vdash$ subst $(f, X,$ Nu $X\, (\{\, \underline{e}\, \}\, \text{U}\, TS)\, f)$
>   **if** not $(\underline{e}$ isIn $TS)$

Fig. 8. Abstract Local Model Checker

eq meta-exists $(M, \underline{e}, f, \text{nil}, N, hasSuccessor) =$
  if $hasSuccessor$ **then false else** $M \underline{e} \Vdash f$ **fi**
eq meta-exists $(M, \underline{e}, f, l\ L, N, hasSuccessor) =$
  if $\mathcal{U} \vdash_{l,N} [\underline{\mathcal{M}}, \underline{e}] \rightarrow [\underline{\mathcal{M}}, f]$ **then**
    $(M \underline{f} \Vdash f)$ or-else meta-exists $(M, \underline{e}, l\ L, N+1, \text{true})$
  else
    meta-exists $(M, \underline{e}, f, L, 0, hasSuccessor)$
  fi

Fig. 9. Definition of meta-exists

Let LOCAL-MODEL-CHECK be the name of our model checking rewrite theory and rules the QidList (*'AP 'ff 'neg 'disj 'ex 'nu*). To verify whether prop0 will always rewrite to true, we check whether the entailment term

eq meta-prop0 = 'LOCAL-MODEL-CHECK $\underline{\text{prop0}} \Vdash$ Nu X {} isTrue $\vee$ [rules] X

reduces to true where

$$\textbf{eq}\ M \underline{e} \Vdash \text{isTrue} = (\underline{e} = \underline{\text{true}}).$$

Similarly, we define entailment terms meta-prop1 and meta-prop2 as follows.
eq meta-prop1 = 'LOCAL-MODEL-CHECK $\underline{\text{prop1}} \Vdash$ Nu X {} isFalse $\vee$ [rules] X
eq meta-prop2 = 'LOCAL-MODEL-CHECK $\underline{\text{prop2}} \Vdash$ Nu X {} isTrue $\vee$ [rules] X
where

$$\textbf{eq}\ M \underline{e} \Vdash \text{isFalse} = (\underline{e} = \underline{\text{false}}).$$

Maude reduces meta-prop0, meta-prop1, and meta-prop2 to true in 341.5, 0.3, 6.5 seconds respectively. Hence the abstract model checker verifies that our model checker always rewrites prop0, prop1, and prop2 to true, false, and true respectively, independent of rewrite strategies.

6.2   Checking with Maude LTL Model Checker

Alternatively, we can use the built-in Maude LTL model checker to verify whether prop0, prop1, and prop2 rewrite to true, false, and true regardless of rewrite strategies. The Maude LTL model checker uses an automata-theoretic algorithm to verify LTL properties. It is implemented in C++ and integrated in Maude version 2 [10,6].

The Maude LTL model contains several equational theories. Related LTL symbols are defined in the theory $\mathcal{LTL}$. The sorts Prop and Formula defined in $\mathcal{LTL}$ are used for atomic proposition and LTL formula terms. We first define two atomic proposition terms:

$$\textbf{op}\ \text{isFalse isTrue} : \rightarrow \text{Prop}$$

To define the reduction rules for atomic proposition terms, we use the modeling term $\models$ defined in the theory $\mathcal{SATISFACTION}$:

$$\textbf{subsort}\ \text{Entailment} \prec \text{State}$$
$$\textbf{eq}\ e \models \text{isFalse} = (e = \text{false})$$
$$\textbf{eq}\ e \models \text{isTrue} = (e = \text{true}).$$

The term $\_\models\_$ takes a term of sort State (defined in $\mathcal{SATISFACTION}$) and a Prop term to form a Bool term. The equations for isFalse and isTrue tell the Maude LTL model checker how to reduce a modeling term to a Bool term.

The property "p holds eventually" is represented by the LTL term $\Diamond\ p$. Thus, the properties that we would like to verify are represented by $\Diamond$ isFalse and $\Diamond$ isTrue. Finally, we use the built-in function modelCheck to verify whether an initial entailment term rewrites to a Bool term eventually:

$$
\begin{aligned}
&\text{modelCheck (prop0, } \Diamond \text{ isTrue)}\\
&\text{modelCheck (prop1, } \Diamond \text{ isFalse)}\\
&\text{modelCheck (prop2, } \Diamond \text{ isTrue)}
\end{aligned}
$$

The Maude LTL model checker is able to verify these three properties in 2.9, $\ll 0.1$, 0.1 seconds respectively. The built-in model checker performs significantly better than our abstract model checker. Since the built-in model checker is implemented in C++, it is expected to run much faster than our abstract model checker. On the other hand, we are free to modify our abstract model checker for different purposes. For instance, the built-in LTL model checker may not terminate on structures with infinite reachable states. But a bounded local model checker for such structures has been implemented using the same framework in [22].

7   Conclusion and Future Work

Reflection has been used for formal metareasoning of membership equational theories [2] and semantics of specifications [7]. In this paper, we present a concise implementation of a local model checking algorithm in the reflective language Maude. We show how the implementation is simplified by exploiting reflection and then verify Peterson's algorithm with our implementation in Maude. In our model checker, the model behavior is explored by the reflective feature of the language. The universal theory is used as a model simulator and thus simplifies the implementation. Since model simulation is required in explicit-state model checking algorithms, we feel the technique can simplify the implementations of other explicit-state algorithms as well.

More interestingly, we are able to verify our implementation by applying reflection again. We define a Kripke structure of entailment terms characterizing the behavior of our model checker. Hence the verification of our model checkers can be formalized as model checking problems. We then use an abstract local model checker and the Maude LTL model checker to solve these problems. Reflection not only simplifies our implementation of an explicit-state model checking algorithm, but also allows us to model-check our model checker rather easily. To the best of our knowledge, this is the first work which proposes an automatic formal verification technique of model checkers by reflection. From the simplicity of our approach, we believe it will be of use to ensure the quality of other verification tools as well.

Currently, we are interested in applying our technique in other model checking algorithms. Particularly, the analysis of binary decision diagram-based or

SAT-based algorithms would be more useful to model checking community. We are investigating the theory developed in [17,25] and specifying a BDD-based algorithm in rewriting logic as the first step.

Acknowledgments. The author would like to thank anonymous reviewers for their constructive comments and suggestions in improving the paper.

References

1. Basin, D., Clavel, M., Meseguer, J.: Rewriting logic as a metalogical framework. In Kapoor, S., Prasad, S., eds.: The 20th Conference on Foundations of Software Technology and Theoretical Computer Science. Volume 1974 of LNCS., Springer-Verlag (2000) 55–80
2. Basin, D., Clavel, M., Meseguer, J.: Reflective metalogical frameworks. ACM Transactions on Computational Logic **5** (2004) 528–576
3. Clarke, E.M., Grumberg, O., Peled, D.A.: Model Checking. The MIT Press, Cambridge, Massachusetts (1999)
4. Clavel, M.: Reflection in general logics, rewriting logic, and Maude. In Kirchner, C., Kirchner, H., eds.: Proceedings Second International Workshop on Rewriting Logic and its Applications. Volume 15 of Electronic Notes in Theoretical Computer Science., Elsevier Science Publishers (1998) 317–328
5. Clavel, M.: The ITP Tool - An Inductive Theorem Prover Tool for Maude Membership Equational Specifications. (2004)
6. Clavel, M., Durán, F., Eker, S., Lincoln, P., Martí-Oliet, N., Meseguer, J., Talcott, C.: Maude 2.0 Manuel. version 1.0 edn. (2003)
7. Clavel, M., Martí-Oliet, N., Palomino, M.: Formalizing and proving semantic relations between specifications by reflection. In Stirling, ed.: Algebraic Methodology and Software Technology: 10th International Conference. Volume 3116 of LNCS. (2004) 72–86
8. Clavel, M., Meseguer, J.: Reflection and strategies in rewriting logic. In Meseguer, J., ed.: Proceedings First International Workshop on Rewriting Logic and its Applications. Volume 4 of Electronic Notes in Theoretical Computer Science., Elsevier Science Publishers (1996) 125–147
9. Cleaveland, R.: Tableau-based model checking in the propositional mu-calculus. Acta Informatica **27** (1989) 725–747
10. Eker, S., Meseguer, J., Sridharanarayanan, A.: The Maude LTL model checker. In: Proceedings of the Fourth International Workshop on Rewriting Logic. Volume 71 of Electronic Notes in Theoretical Computer Science., Elsevier Science Publishers (2002)
11. Holzmann, G.: The model checker SPIN. IEEE Transaction on Software Engineering **23** (1997) 279–295
12. Kozen, D.: Results on the propositional μ-calculus. Theoretical Computer Science **27** (1983) 333–354
13. Manolios, P. In: Mu-Calculus Model-Checking. Kluwer Academic Publishers (2000) 93–111
14. Martí-Oliet, N., Meseguer, J.: Rewriting logic: roadmap and bibliography. Theoretical Computer Science **285** (2002) 121–154
15. Meseguer, J.: Conditional rewriting logic as a unified model of concurrency. Theoretical Computer Science **96** (1992) 73–155

16. Meseguer, J.: Rewriting logic as a semantic framework for concurrency: A progress report. In Montanari, U., Sassone, V., eds.: CONCUR '96: Concurrency Theory, 7th International Conference. Volume 1119 of LNCS., Springer-Verlag (1996) 331–372

17. van de Pol, J., Zantema, H.: Binary decision diagrams by shared rewriting. In Nielsen, M., Rovan, B., eds.: Mathematical Foundations of Computer Science 2000, 25th International Symposium. Volume 1893 of LNCS., Springer-Verlag (2000) 609–618

18. Silberschatz, A., Galvin, P.B., Gagne, G.: Operating System Concepts. 7th edn. John Wiley & Sons, Inc. (2004)

19. Sprenger, C.: A verified model checker for the modal μ-calculus in coq. In Steffen, B., ed.: Tools and Algorithms for the Construction and Analysis of Systems. Volume 1384 of LNCS., Springer-Verlag (1998) 167–183

20. Stirling, C., Walker, D.: Local model checking in the modal mu-calculus. In Díaz, J., Orejas, F., eds.: Proceedings Int. Joint Conf. on Theory and Practice of Software Development. Volume 351 of LNCS. Springer-Verlag, Berlin (1989) 369–383

21. Wang, B.Y.: μ-calculus model checking in maude. In Martí-Oliet, N., ed.: 5th International Workshop on Rewriting Logic and its Applications. Volume 117 of Electronic Notes in Theoretical Computer Science., Elsevier Science Publishers (2004) 135–152

22. Wang, B.Y.: Automatic verification of a model checker in rewriting logic. Technical Report TR-IIS-05-009, Institute of Information Science, Academia Sinica (2005) http://www.iis.sinica.edu.tw/LIB/TechReport/tr2005/tr05009.pdf.

23. Wang, B.Y., Meseguer, J., Gunter, C.A.: Specification and formal analysis of a PLAN algorithm in Maude. In Hsiung, P.A., ed.: Proceedings International Workshop on Distributed System Validation and Verification. (2000) 49–56

24. Winskel, G.: A note on model checking the modal nu-calculus. Theoretical Computer Science **83** (1991) 157–167

25. Zantema, H., van de Pol, J.: A rewriting approach to binary decision diagrams. Journal of Logic and Algebraic Programming **49** (2001) 61–86

Probabilistic-Logical Modeling of Music

Jon Sneyers, Joost Vennekens, and Danny De Schreye

Department of Computer Science, K.U.Leuven,
Celestijnenlaan 200A, 3001 Heverlee, Belgium
Tel: +3216327552, Fax: +3216327996
{jon, joost, dannyd}@cs.kuleuven.be

Abstract. PRISM is a probabilistic-logical programming language based on Prolog. We present a PRISM-implementation of a general model for polyphonic music, based on Hidden Markov Models. Its probability parameters are automatically learned by running the built-in EM-algorithm of PRISM on training examples. We show how the model can be used as a classifier for music that guesses the composer of unknown fragments of music. Then we use it to automatically compose new music.

Keywords: PRISM, probabilistic-logical programming, music classification, automatic music composition.

1 Introduction

Music composers are bound to certain - mostly unwritten - rules, defining the musical genre of their work. In this paper we will construct a general model to describe such rules.

Many formalisms have been proposed to express strict, logical rules. A well-known example is the logic programming language Prolog. However, most musical genres are hard or impossible to describe as a set of strict rules. It seems to be inherent to music to be somewhat 'random' and 'organic'.

Because of this inherent randomness, we will work in a probabilistic context, in which we represent musical rules as probabilistic experiments with some unknown probability distribution. We use a variant of Hidden Markov Models, for which the probability distributions can be computed in an automated way from a set of examples.

Probabilistic-logical programming is an extension of logic programming which allows programmers to express both statistical and relational knowledge in a natural way. We will use this formalism to build our model.

Traditionally, two types of models for music are distinguished. *Synthetic* models are used to generate music (automatic composition). *Analytic* models are designed to analyze (e.g. to classify) music. Conklin [2] pointed out that a general model can be applied to both tasks. A statistical analytic model can (in principle) be sampled to generate music.

The goal of this paper is to provide empirical evidence for the feasibility of implementing such a dual-use model, while showing the expressiveness and power of probabilistic-logical formalisms.

P. Van Hentenryck (Ed.): PADL 2006, LNCS 3819, pp. 60–72, 2006.

The paper is organized as follows. In section 2 we introduce a new representation for music that we use in the application. Section 3 recalls the basics of the programming language PRISM and shows how to model Hidden Markov Models in this language. In Section 4 we describe the system and the top-level of its implementation in PRISM. We report on our experiments with the system in Section 5 and conclude in Section 6.

2   Music Representation

For simplicity, we will consider only three aspects of music: melody (note pitch and octave), rhythm (note duration) and polyphony (different voices sounding together). We will ignore aspects like volume, timbre of instruments, articulations like the accent, staccato, portato, legato, . . .

To represent a music score in a form which is suitable for both Prolog-like environments and Markov-like models, we will use the following notation, which we call the *Interwoven Voices List* (IVL) notation:

Definition 1. *An IVL of length n with v voices is a Prolog list term of the form*

$$[(D_0, V_0, N_0), (D_1, V_1, N_1), \ldots, (D_n, V_n, N_n)]$$

where D_i are positive integer numbers and V_i and N_i are Prolog lists of length v. The elements of V_i are atoms: either the atom new *or the atom* old. *The elements of N_i are either a positive integer number or the atom* r. *If for some i ($< n$) and j ($\leq v$), the jth element of N_i and N_{i+1} are different, then the jth element of V_{i+1} must be* new. *If for some i ($< n$) and j ($\leq v$), the jth element of both N_i and N_{i+1} is* r, *then the jth element of V_{i+1} must be* old.

We say an IVL of length n consists of n *phases*. D_i is the duration of the ith phase. The list N_i represents the notes that are played in every voice in the ith phase. If no note is played by some voice, we use the symbol r (rest). We assume every voice to play only one note at the same time – if not, we can split them into as many voices as necessary. Note numbers encode both the pitch (c, cis=des, d, . . . , a, ais=bes, b) and the octave of a note. For example, c4 is represented as 48, cis4 as 49, d4 as 50, c5 as 60. When in some voice a note is followed by the same note, there are two possibilities: two distinct notes are played, or one long note is played (covering more than one phase because of shorter notes in the other voices). The list V_i indicates for every voice whether a new note is played (new) or the note played in the previous phase is continued (old). Figure 1 illustrates the representation on a small example.

3   PRISM and HMM's

In this section we will briefly introduce the PRISM programming language [9,10] and how to use it for Hidden Markov Models [1].

A PRISM-program consists of a logical and a probabilistic part. The probabilistic part defines a probability distribution $P_{\mathcal{F}}$ on a set $\mathcal{F}$ of collections of

[(16,[new,new],[55,r]), (16,[old,new],[55,36]),
  (16,[new,new],[60,38]), (16,[old,new],[60,40]),
  (16,[new,new],[59,41]), (16,[old,new],[59,38]),
  (16,[new,new],[60,40]), (16,[old,new],[60,36]),
  (32,[new,new],[62,43]), (32,[old,new],[62,31])]

Fig. 1. The Interwoven Voice List (IVL) notation

ground facts. The logical part takes the form of a definite Horn clause program D, which serves to extend this distribution $P_{\mathcal{F}}$ to a distribution on the set of Herbrand interpretations of the program. More precisely, the probability of an interpretation I is defined as the sum of all probabilities $P_{\mathcal{F}}(F)$ of sets of facts $F \in \mathcal{F}$, for which the least Herbrand model of $(F \cup D)$ equals I.

The facts that can appear in such a set F are all of the special form msw (s,i,v), with s, i, and v ground terms. A term s in such an atom is called a m*ultivalued* sw*itch* and it represents a random variable, which can take on a value from a certain domain. A declaration values(t, $[v_1, \ldots, v_n]$), with t a term and all v_i ground terms, can be used to specify that the domain $dom(s)$ of s is $\langle v_1, \ldots, v_n \rangle$, for all switches s which are ground instantiations of the term t. For each switch s and each value v from $dom(s)$, the probability $P_s(v)$ of s taking on this particular value needs to be defined. This is done using a query set_sw(t, $[\alpha_1, \ldots, \alpha_n]$), with t a term, the α_i real numbers and n the number of values in $dom(s)$. The meaning of this is that $P_s(v_i) = \alpha_i$, with $dom(s) = \langle v_1, \ldots, v_n \rangle$, for each switch s which is a ground instantiation of t.

Each set $F \in \mathcal{F}$ is of the form $\{\text{msw}(\text{s}, \text{i}, v_s^i) \mid$ s is a switch, $\text{i} \in I\}$, where I is some set of ground terms used to distinguish consecutive trials involving the same switch and each $v_s^i \in dom(s)$. All such trials are assumed to be probabilistically independent, i.e., for every such set F:

$$P_{\mathcal{F}}(F) = \prod_{\text{msw}(\text{s},\text{i},\text{v}) \in F} P_s(v).$$

Recently, an alternative syntax has been proposed, where instead of msw (s,i,v)-atoms, msw(s,v)-atoms are now used. Programs in this new syntax should be read as though each occurrence of such an atom had an implicit extra argument i which distinguishes it from all other occurrences of this predicate in the program.

The PRISM system has several useful properties. Firstly, the semantics of its language is easy to understand and quite natural. Secondly, the system offers an efficient learning algorithm, based on the well-known EM algorithm, which is able to estimate the probabilistic parameters $P_s(v)$, based on a set of observations. The built-in learning algorithm is provably as efficient as special purpose versions of the EM algorithm, such as the Baum-Welch algorithm for Hidden Markov Models, the Inside-Outside algorithm for Probabilistic context-free grammars, and the EM algorithm using evidence propagation for singly-connected Bayesian networks, provided that the models are appropriately programmed in PRISM.

For example, consider the experiment of flipping a coin a number of times. We could model this as follows:

```
target(flipN, 2).
values(coin, [heads,tails]).
flipN(0, []).
flipN(N, [T|Ts]) :- N>0, msw(coin,T), N1 is N-1, flipN(N1,Ts).
```

Let us say the coin is fair, i.e. both outcomes are equally probable. We can use the set_sw built-in to set the probability distribution of the coin experiment accordingly: set_sw(coin, [0.5,0.5]). Now we can use sample(flipN(N,S)) to get a randomly generated sequence S of N coin flips.

Now let us assume we do not know the probability distribution of coin – maybe the coin has been tampered with – but we do have a sequence S2 of N2 coin flip outcomes. In this case, we can use learn(flipN(N2,S2)) to estimate the probabilities. In this toy example, the result will simply correspond to the relative frequencies. In the learning phase, for every training example, all its *explanations* are enumerated, i.e. all combinations of msw outcomes that lead to the training example. In the coin flipping example there is just one explanation for every sequence of coin flips, but in general there can be many explanations for a single observation.

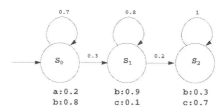

Fig. 2. A Hidden Markov Model

To illustrate how PRISM can be used to model HMMs, we consider the HMM in Figure 2. At each time point, this HMM probabilistically chooses both a successor state and an output symbol. Both these choices depend on the current state. To model this in PRISM, we need a switch *trans(s)*, representing the choice of a successor state, and a switch *out(s)*, representing the choice of an output symbol, for every state *s*.

```
values(trans(s0), [s0,s1]).
values(trans(s1), [s1,s2]).
values(trans(s2), [s2]).
values(out(s0), [a,b]).
values(out(s1), [b,c]).
values(out(s2), [b,c]).
```

Now, the state of the HMM at time T can be defined as follows:

```
state(s0,0).
state(Next, T) :- T > 0, TPrev is T - 1,
  state(Prev, TPrev), msw(trans(Prev), Next).
```

The output at time T can be defined as:

```
out(Char, T) :- state(State, T), msw(out(State), Char).
```

We can now define a predicate $hmm(S, T)$ to express that string S is generated after T steps, by simply gathering all the produced symbols into a list:

```
hmm([], 0).
hmm([Char | Chars], Time) :-
  Time > 0, TimePrev is Time - 1,
  out(Char, TimePrev), hmm(Chars, TimePrev).
```

The probabilities for the various switches can be set as follows:

```
:- set_sw(trans(s1), [0.8,0.2]), set_sw(trans(s2), [1]),
   set_sw(trans(s0), [0.7,0.3]), set_sw(out(s0), [0.2,0.8]),
   set_sw(out(s1), [0.9,0.1]), set_sw(out(s2), [0.3,0.7]).
```

Alternatively, these values can also be estimated on the basis of a set of hmm/1 observations, which are called *training examples*.

When the switch probabilities are set, the model can be sampled using the sample/1 built-in. For example, the query sample(hmm(L,10)) would result in unifying L to the length 10 list outputted by a random execution of the given HMM. The probability of an observed sequence can be computed using the prob/2 built-in.

4   Modeling IVL-Music in PRISM

Hidden Markov Models sequentially process data streams. For analytic music models, this approach makes sense: after all, this is how a human listener perceives music. However, if the model is also to be used as a synthetic music model, it forces a left-to-right composing strategy, which is not the way human composers usually work. Therefore, we will use *nested* HMMs, based on the intuition of global and local music structure. The global structure of a piece of music is captured by transitions between various Song States (SS). Within every such

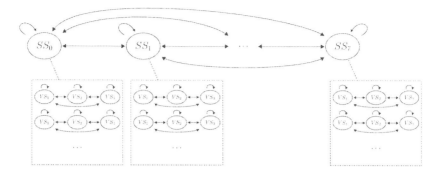

Fig. 3. Nested HMM structure

song state, there is one HMM for each voice, which captures the local structure
for that particular voice by transitions between various Voice States (VS). This
principle is illustrate in Figure 3.

A music fragment is encoded in facts of the form song(NV,L,BT,IVL), where
IVL is an IVL of length L with NV voices. For all examples, we manually determined the base tone (BT) to allow the model to transpose the notes. Doing this,
everything is learned modulo translations in pitch. All probabilities are learned
by performing the PRISM built-in EM algorithm on a set of song/4 facts.

We will now discuss the main predicates of the source code of our model. The
core of the model is a nested Hidden Markov Model. Every transition into the
next phase probabilistically selects one out of seven "song states", the probabilities depending on the current song state. For every voice, one out of three
"voice states" is chosen, the probabilities depending on the current song state
and the current voice state for that voice. All voice output (pitches, octaves,
old/new and rests) probabilities depend on the current song state and the current voice state for the relevant voice. Most song states restrict the domain for
output pitches to some harmonically relevant subdomain. The phase duration
probabilities depend only on the current song state.

Note that the number of song states s and the number of voice states v
can be chosen arbitrarily. The number of probability parameters to learn grows
linearly as sv grows, but the number of explanations (and hence the duration of
the learning phase) for a single training example IVL of length l with n voices
roughly corresponds to $(sv^n)^l$. Since the training fragments have to be long
enough to exhibit some musically meaningful properties, we are forced to use
small values for the other variables. We used the values $s = 7$ and $v = 3$, and for
training $n = 2$ and $l \approx 20$, because larger values quickly became computationally
infeasible. However, they are probably too low to capture sufficient detail. The
quality of the model can be improved by using more states, although it will also
become more likely to obtain insufficiently generalizing parameter values in the
training phase. The domains of the different probabilistic experiments are given
below:

```
values(tr_ss(_PrevS),[1,2,3,4,5,6,7]).  % song state transitions
values(tr_vs(_S,_PrevV),[a,b,c]). % voice state transitions
values(out_D(_S),[8,16,32,48,64,96,128]).  % durations
values(out_V(_S,_V),[old,new]).    % old or new note
values(out_rest(_S,_V),[rest,note]).        % rest or real note
values(out_octave(_S,_V),[-2,-1,0,1,2]).   % relative octave
values(out_modnote(1,_V),[0, 4, 7 ]).       % c e g
values(out_modnote(2,_V),[0, 2, 4, 5, 7, 9, 11]). % c d e f g a b
values(out_modnote(3,_V),[0, 2, 4, 6, 7, 9, 11]). % c d e fis g a b
values(out_modnote(4,_V),[0, 2, 4, 5, 7, 9, 10]). % c d e f g a bes
values(out_modnote(5,_V),[0, 3, 4, 5, 7, 8, 10]). % c es f g as bes
values(out_modnote(6,_V),[0, 2, 3, 5, 9, 10]).   % c d es f a bes
values(out_modnote(7,_V),[0,1,2,3,4,5,6,7,8,9,10,11]). % all pitches
```

The main loop of the program is a nested HMM: after every output observation, a state transition is made.

```
song(NV,L,BT,IVL):-
    initlist(NV,4,O_prev), initlist(NV,a,VoiceState),
    hmm(NV,1,L,1,VoiceState,BT,IVL,_,O_prev).

% length L; NV voices; base tone BT; current phase (D,V,N)
hmm(NV,T,L,SongState,VoiceState,BT,[(D,V,N)|Y],N_prev,O_prev) :-
    T < L, T > 1, T1 is T+1,
    observe(NV,SongState,VoiceState,BT,D,V,N,N_prev,O_prev),
    tr_voicestates(NV,SongState,VoiceState,VS_Next),
    msw(tr_ss(SongState),SS_Next),
    octaves(BT,N,O_prev,N_octave),
    hmm(NV,T1,L,SS_Next,VS_Next,BT,Y,N,N_octave).
```

The observe/9 predicate checks one IVL phase (D, V, N). First the phase length D is checked. Then the list elements of V and N are checked one by one.

```
observe(NV,SongState,VoiceState,BT,D,V,N,N_prev,O_prev) :-
    msw(out_D(SongState),D),
    nlist(NV,SongState,VoiceState,BT,N,V,N_prev,O_prev).
```

For every note, it is first determined whether it is a rest or a "real" note. The note value of the "real" note is checked in check_real_note. When it is identical to the previous note, we check whether it is new or old. Note that these experiments depend on both the song state (which is shared by all voices in given IVL phase) and the voice state of the corresponding voice.

```
nlist(NV,SongState,[VoiceState|RVS],BT,[N|RN],V,[PN|RPN],PrO) :-
    NV > 0, NV1 is NV-1, V=[ON|RON], PrO=[PO|RPO],
    check_note(SongState,VoiceState,BT,N,PO),  % check note itself
    check_new(SongState,VoiceState,N,PN,ON),   % check old/new
```

```
        nlist(NV1,SongState,RVS,BT,RN,RPN,RON,RPO).
nlist(0,_,[],_,[],[],[],[]).

check_note(SongState,VoiceState,BT,Note,PrevOct) :-
        msw(out_rest(SongState,VoiceState),X),
        check_note(SongState,VoiceState,BT,Note,PrevOct,X).

check_note(_,_,_,r,_,rest).
check_note(SongState,VoiceState,BT,Note,PrevOct,note) :-
        check_real_note(SongState,VoiceState,BT,Note,PrevOct).

check_new(SongState,VoiceState,X,X,OldNew) :-
        number(X), msw(out_V(SongState,VoiceState),OldNew).
check_new(_,_,r,r,old).
check_new(_,_,A,B,new) :- A \= B.
```

In check_real_note, we check the pitch and the relative octave, i.e. the difference compared to the octave of the previous note (of that voice).

Note that thus far, the program can be used both for analysis and generation, i.e. we can call the song(NV,L,BT,IVL) predicate with instantiated or partially uninstantiated arguments. However, when we are checking the note values, we will need two clauses for check_real_note, one for analysis/training and one for synthesis/sampling. When sampling, sanity_check is called to avoid too high or too low notes: it enforces the octave to stay in the range 2-6.

```
check_real_note(SongState,VoiceState,BT,Note,PrevOct) :-
        number(Note),                    % training
        Pitch is (Note-BT) mod 12,
        OctDiff is ((Note-BT) // 12) - PrevOct,
        msw(out_modnote(SongState,VoiceState),Pitch),
        msw(out_octave(SongState,VoiceState),OctDiff).

check_real_note(SongState,VoiceState,BT,Note,PrevOct) :-
        var(Note),                       % sampling
        msw(out_modnote(SongState,VoiceState),Pitch),
        msw(out_octave(SongState,VoiceState),OctDiff),
        NewOctave is PrevOct + OctDiff,
        sanity_check(NewOctave,SaneNewOctave),
        Note is BT + Pitch + 12*SaneNewOctave.
```

5   Experimental Results

5.1   Classification

Pollastri and Simoncelli [7] have used HMMs for classification of melodies by composer. In a similar way, we will use our model to classify fragments of polyphonic music. To keep things simple, we will consider only two composers: Bach and Mozart.

id	P_B	P_M	guess:	reality
b01	-129 >	-655	Bach	
b02	-119 >	-585	Bach	BMV 784
b03	-119 >	$-\infty$	Bach	(Bach)
b04	-116 >	$-\infty$	Bach	2 voices
b05	-121 >	$-\infty$	Bach	
m01	-297 <	-136	Mozart	KV 487
m02	-124 <	-114	Mozart	number 7
m03	-302 <	-120	Mozart	(Mozart)
m04	-203 <	-155	Mozart	2 voices
m05	-152 <	-116	Mozart	
b06	-144 >	-236	Bach	
b07	-189 >	-422	Bach	
b08	-178 >	-216	Bach	BMV 798
b09	-158 >	-317	Bach	
b10	-156 >	-608	Bach	(Bach)
b11	-166 >	-234	Bach	
b12	-174 >	-492	Bach	
b13	-161 >	-166	Bach	3 voices
b14	-153 >	-464	Bach	
b15	-171 >	-176	Bach	
m06	$-\infty$ <	-553	Mozart	
m07	$-\infty$ <	-230	Mozart	
m08	-431 <	-234	Mozart	KV 229
m09	-283 <	-165	Mozart	
m10	-424 <	-189	Mozart	(Mozart)
m11	-324 <	-119	Mozart	
m12	-429 <	-175	Mozart	
m13	-397 <	-169	Mozart	3 voices
m14	-330 <	-179	Mozart	
m15	-381 <	-175	Mozart	

(a) all information

id	P_B	P_M	guess:	reality
b01	-132 >	-140	Bach	
b02	-118 >	-125	Bach	BMV 784
b03	-121 >	-142	Bach	(Bach)
b04	-122 >	-140	Bach	2 voices
b05	-121 >	-143	Bach	
m01	-110 <	-103	Mozart	KV 487
m02	-100 >	-102	**Bach**	number 7
m03	-120 <	-110	Mozart	(Mozart)
m04	-102 <	-100	Mozart	2 voices
m05	-99 >	-101	**Bach**	
b06	-144 >	-162	Bach	
b07	-152 >	-158	Bach	
b08	-161 >	-171	Bach	BMV 798
b09	-162 >	-168	Bach	
b10	-155 >	-156	Bach	(Bach)
b11	-165 >	-169	Bach	
b12	-168 >	-172	Bach	
b13	-156 >	-167	Bach	3 voices
b14	-156 >	-166	Bach	
b15	-147 >	-154	Bach	
m06	-256 <	-178	Mozart	
m07	-177 <	-149	Mozart	
m08	-237 <	-167	Mozart	KV 229
m09	-153.7 <	-153.6	Mozart	
m10	-179 >	-182	**Bach**	(Mozart)
m11	-162 <	-109	Mozart	
m12	-174 <	-168	Mozart	
m13	-187 <	-155	Mozart	3 voices
m14	-156 >	-169	**Bach**	
m15	-185 <	-167	Mozart	

(b) ignoring durations

Fig. 4. Classification results

Using the built-in EM algorithm of PRISM, we train two instances of the model, M_B and M_M, the former using fragments from works of Bach, the latter using fragments of Mozart. To classify a new, unknown fragment we compute the probabilities of it being the output of M_B or M_M. The fragment is classified as being work of the composer for which the probability is highest.

plus .1em The computational complexity of this method is dominated by the training phase – which took something in the order of tens of minutes on a Pentium 4 machine with 1 gigabyte of RAM. Computing the probability of an unknown fragment took only one or two seconds. This is an interesting property of this approach, since training the model has to be done only once for every classification category, after which any number of fragments can be classified in reasonable time.

The experiments were originally performed in PRISM 1.6. In the preparation for this paper, we repeated some experiments using PRISM 1.8.1, with comparable results. For training M_B, 72 fragments from Bachs *Inventions* (BWV 772,773,775,779) were used. We used 50 fragments from Mozarts *duets for horn* (KV 487, numbers 1, 2, 5, 8, 9, 10 and 12) to train M_M. Together, this amounts to 1428 IVL phases for M_B and 948 IVL phases for M_M. All training examples have two voices.

Figure 4(a) gives an overview of the classification results for 30 other fragments. The numbers P_B and P_M are the log-probabilities of the fragment being the output of M_B and M_M, respectively. If $P_B > P_M$, the fragment is classified as "composed by Bach", otherwise it is classified as "composed by Mozart". For all 30 fragments, the classification was correct. This is a remarkable result, since 20 of these fragments were chosen from totally different work compared to the fragments used for training the models, and they have three voices, not two like the training examples.

In the fragments we used, it has to be noted that the phase durations D_i are most often 16th notes in pieces of Bach, while in pieces of Mozart the 8th note is more prominent. As a result, the correct classification may be mostly based on the typical durations of the IVL phases. We want of course to find out whether the trained models (implicitly) contain more musical style properties than just the notational tempo. To check whether our classification method still works without the strong duration differences, we could preprocess the training and testing data, scaling it to a common tempo. Instead, we repeated the experiment, adapting our model so that it does not consider the phase duration information at all. By not considering the durations, only the melody and polyphony information can be used to classify the fragments. In figure 4(b), the results are given for this new classification method, which does not take into account the phase durations. Of the 30 fragments, 26 were classified correctly. This is of course significantly better than random guessing.

5.2   Music Generation

We have also used our model to generate music: first we have trained the model using one of the training sets, then we sample the model using the `sample/1` built-in. Input parameters are the first notes, the base tone and the length (number of IVL phases). We arbitrarily chose (respectively) *c3* and *e4* of duration one eight, base tone 0 (*c*), and 30 phases. Two typical examples of the resulting output are given in Figure 5, and can be downloaded at [11].

Although the output does not even come close to a human-composed piece, it seems to contain musical style elements of the training examples. It cannot directly be used to generate acceptable full songs, but it might be an interesting source of inspiration for human composers.

We expect that using more refined models (e.g. with more HMM states and adding the concept of time signature to avoid excessive syncopation) and using larger sets of training examples, the style of the generated music would be increasingly indistinguishable from the style of the original training examples.

(a) Trained with fragments of Bach

(b) Trained with fragments of Mozart

Fig. 5. Sample of the model trained with fragments of Bach and Mozart

6   Conclusion

We have presented a simple, yet general model for music. It can handle any number of voices. The probability parameters can automatically be adjusted for any musical genre given sufficiently many training examples of the genre.

The classification method presented in section 5.1 seems to be a promising approach, given the outcome of the experiments. Experiments on a larger scale, involving more composers and larger datasets, have to be performed to get an accurate idea of the scope of its practical applicability.

In its current form, the model described in this paper cannot be used for fully automatic music composition. However, its output might be an interesting source of inspiration for human composers. In particular, in the context of computer assisted composition, our system could perform a very useful role by suggesting fragments or polyphones to the composer.

The main contribution of our work, however, lies in demonstrating the feasibility of using probabilistic-logical programming as an elegant tool for developing applications in the computer music domain. As we argued in the introduction, two aspects seem important in modelling music applications: logical rules (or, alternatively, constraints) and probabilities. It is interesting to observe that these two aspects have been considered separately by different researchers in the past as a basis for developing music systems.

Constraints and constraint processing have been successfully applied in a number of applications (see e.g. [12,8,4] and related work at IRCAM). The approach is natural, since music is governed by many constraints. However, there are even more 'weak' constraints involved in the application. These are more naturally expressed by probabilistic rules or HMMs. Another group of researchers has focussed on probabilities and HMMs as a basis for developing music analysis and synthesis applications (e.g. [7,6]). An important disadvantage of that approach is that it is not very flexible: it is hard to incorporate expert knowledge in such models or to experiment with variants of HMMs.

Our work combines these two aspects. In this respect, it is somewhat similar to the work of D. Cope [3], whose Experiments in Musical Intelligence system intelligently recombines randomly chosen parts of existing work to satisfy certain musical constraints. However, in contrast to this system, we have chosen to follow a declarative approach, in which we describe a general model of a piece of music, rather than develop specific algorithms to derive new music from old.

As far as we know, our work is the first application of a declarative language based on probabilistic logic to this problem. Our experiments show that the development of the applications in such a language is particularly elegant and that it provides a functionality of analysis and synthesis using the same model (and program). In developing the application, it feels as if PRISM was designed for this purpose.

Future work. An important musical concept, ignored in our model, is the meter, which distinguishes the stronger and more important notes from the decorative intermediate notes. One approach to incorporate this concept in the model is to change the representation: instead of using one flat list, a list of lists could be used where each sublist contains one bar. The model could then be refined, e.g. by handling the first note of every bar in a different way or by adding a higher level HMM state which has a transition after every bar instead of after every phase. It might also be useful to abandon the rather naive representation of a piece of music as a list of notes and move to a more structured representation such as, e.g., that used in [5].

As mentioned before, the results presented here should be validated with a more thorough experimental evaluation. The main difficulty will be to collect and prepare a large dataset.

References

1. Yoshua Bengio. Markovian models for sequential data. *Neural Computing Surveys*, 2:129–162, 1999.
2. Darell Conklin. Music Generation from Statistical Models. In *Proceedings of the AISB 2003 Symposium on Artificial Intelligence and Creativity in the Arts and Sciences*, pages 30–35, Aberystwyth, Wales, 2003.
3. David Cope. *The Algorithmic Composer*. Madison, WI: A-R Editions, 2000.
4. Martin Henz, Stefan Lauer, and Detlev Zimmermann. COMPOzE—Intention-based Music Composition through Constraint Programming. In *ICTAI '96: Proceedings of the 8th International Conference on Tools with Artificial Intelligence (ICTAI '96)*, page 118, Washington, DC, USA, 1996. IEEE Computer Society.
5. Paul Hudak, Tom Makucevich, Syam Gadde, and Bo Whong. Haskore music notation - an algebra of music. *Journal of Functional Programming*, 6(3):465–483, 1996.
6. Yuval Marom. Improvising Jazz using Markov chains. Honours Thesis, University of Western Australia, 1997.

7. Emanuele Pollastri and Giuliano Simoncelli. Classification of Melodies by Composer with Hidden Markov Models. In *Proceedings of the First International Conference on WEB Delivering of Music*, pages 88–95, Firenze, Italy, 2001.
8. Camilo Rueda and Frank D. Valencia. Situation: A Constraint-Based Visual System for Musical Compositions. In Carlos Agon, editor, *The OM's Composer Book*, IRCAM Centre Pompidou, France. To appear.
9. Taisuke Sato and Yoshitaka Kameya. PRISM: A symbolic-statistical modeling language. In *Proceedings of the 15th International Joint Conference on Artificial Intelligence*, pages 1330–1335, Nagoya, Japan, 1997.
10. Taisuke Sato and Yoshitaka Kameya. Parameter learning of logic programs for symbolic-statistical modeling. *Journal of Artificial Intelligence Research (JAIR)*, 15:391–454, 2001.
11. Jon Sneyers. MIDI files of automatically generated music. Available at *http://www.cs.kuleuven.be/~jon/automatic_composition/*.
12. Charlotte Truchet, Gérard Assayag, and Philippe Codognet. Visual and Adaptive Constraint Programming in Music. In *International Computer Music Conference (ICMC01)*, La Havana, Cuba, September 2001.

Using Dominators for Solving Constrained Path Problems

Luis Quesada, Peter Van Roy, Yves Deville, and Raphaël Collet

Université catholique de Louvain,
Place Sainte Barbe, 2, B-1348 Louvain-la-Neuve, Belgium
{luque, pvr, yde, raph}@info.ucl.ac.be

Abstract. Constrained path problems have to do with finding paths in graphs subject to constraints. We present a constraint programming approach for solving the Ordered disjoint-paths problem (ODP), i.e., the Disjoint-paths problem where the pairs are associated with ordering constraints. In our approach, we reduce ODP to the Ordered simple path with mandatory nodes problem (OSPMN), i.e., the problem of finding a simple path containing a set of mandatory nodes in a given order. The reduction of the problem is motivated by the fact that we have an appropriate way of dealing with OSPMN based on *DomReachability*, a propagator that implements a generalized reachability constraint on a directed graph based on the concept of graph variables.

The *DomReachability* constraint has three arguments: (1) a flow graph, i.e., a directed graph with a source node; (2) the dominance relation graph on nodes and edges of the flow graph; and (3) the transitive closure of the flow graph.

Our experimental evaluation of *DomReachability* shows that it provides strong pruning, obtaining solutions with very little search. Furthermore, we show that *DomReachability* is also useful for defining a good labeling strategy. These experimental results give evidence that *DomReachability* is a useful primitive for solving constrained path problems over directed graphs.

1 Introduction

Constrained path problems have to do with finding paths in graphs subject to constraints. One way of constraining the graph is by enforcing reachability between nodes. For instance, it may be required that a node reaches a particular set of nodes by respecting some restrictions like visiting a particular set of nodes or edges in a given order. We find instances of this problem in Vehicle routing problems [PGPR96, CL97, FLM99] and Bioinformatics [DDD04].

An approach to solve this problem is by using concurrent constraint programming (CCP) [Sch00, Mül01]. In CCP, we solve the problem by interleaving two processes: propagation and labeling. Propagation consists in filtering the domains of a set of finite domain variables, according to the semantics of the constraints that have to be satisfied. Labeling consists in defining the way the search tree is created, i.e., which constraint is used for branching.

In this paper, we present a propagator called *DomReachability*, that implements a generalized reachability constraint on a directed graph. The *DomReachability* constraint

P. Van Hentenryck (Ed.): PADL 2006, LNCS 3819, pp. 73–87, 2006.

has three arguments: (1) a flow graph, i.e., a directed graph with a source node; (2) the dominance relation graph on nodes and edges of the flow graph; and (3) the transitive closure of the flow graph. The dominance relation graph represents a dominance relation that identifies nodes common to all paths from a source to a destination. By extending the dominator graph we can also identify edges common to all paths from a source to a destination.

Due to the fact that the arguments of *DomReachability* are graph variables that can be partially instantiated, the problem modelled with *DomReachability* can be understood as finding a flow graph that respects the partial instantiations of the flow graph, the dominance relation graph and the transitive closure. For instance, we may be interested in finding a subgraph of a given graph where a node j is reached from a node s and j is dominated by a set of nodes ns with respect to s.

Applicability. The *DomReachability* propagator is suitable for solving the Simple path with mandatory nodes problem [Sel02, CB04]. This problem consists in finding a simple path in a directed graph containing a set of mandatory nodes. A simple path is a path where each node is visited only once. Certainly, this problem can be trivially solved if the graph has no cycle, since in that case there is only one order in which we can visit the mandatory nodes [Sel02]. However, the presence of cycles makes the problem NP-complete, since we can easily reduce the Hamiltonian path problem [GJ79, CLR90] to this problem.

Note that we can not trivially reduce Simple path with mandatory nodes to Hamiltonian path. One could think that optional nodes (nodes that are not mandatory) can be eliminated in favor of new edges as a preprocessing step, which finds a path between each pair of mandatory nodes. However, the paths that are precomputed may share nodes. This may lead to violations of the requirement that a node should be visited at most once.

Figure 1 illustrates this situation. Mandatory nodes are drawn with solid lines. In the second graph we have eliminated the optional nodes by connecting each pair of mandatory nodes depending on whether there is a path between them. We observe that the second graph has a simple path going from node 1 to node 4 (visiting all the mandatory nodes) while the first one does not. Therefore the simple path in the second graph is not a valid solution to the original problem since it requires node 3 to be visited twice. Note that the Simple path problem with only one mandatory node, which is equivalent to the 2-Disjoint paths problem [SP78], is still NP-complete.

In general, we can say that the set of optional nodes that can be used when going from a mandatory node a to a mandatory node b depends on the path that has been traversed before reaching a. This is because the optional nodes used in the path going from the source to a can not be used in the path going from a to b.

From our experimental measurements, we observe that the suitability of *DomReachability* for dealing with Simple path with mandatory nodes relies on the following aspects:

- The strong pruning that *DomReachability* performs. Due to the computation of dominators , *DomReachability* is able to discover non-viable successors early on.

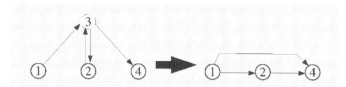

Fig. 1. Relaxing Simple path with mandatory nodes by eliminating the optional nodes

– The information that *DomReachability* provides for implementing smart labeling strategies. *DomReachability* associates each node with the set of nodes that it reaches. This information can be used to guide the search in a smart way. The strategy we used in our experiments tends to minimize the use of optional nodes.

An additional feature of *DomReachability* is its suitability for dealing with a problem that we call the Ordered simple path with mandatory nodes problem (OSPMN) where ordering constraints among mandatory nodes are imposed, which is a common issue in routing problems. Taking into account that a node i reaches a node j if there is a path going from node i to node j, one way of forcing a node i to be visited before a node j is by imposing that i reaches j and j does not reach i. The latter is equivalent to imposing that i is an ancestor of j in the extended dominator tree of the path. Our experiments show that *DomReachability* takes the most advantage of this information to avoid branches in the search tree with no solution.

Related work. The cycle constraint of CHIP [BC94, Bou99] $cycle(N, [S_1, \ldots, S_n])$ models the problem of finding N distinct circuits in a directed graph in such a way that each node is visited exactly once. Certainly, Hamiltonian Path can be implemented using this constraint. In fact, [Bou99] shows how this constraint can be used to deal with the Euler knight problem (which is an application of Hamiltonian Path). Optional nodes can be modelled by putting each optional node in a separate elementary cycle. However, this constraint is not implemented in terms of dominators.

Sellmann [Sel02] suggests some algorithms for discovering mandatory nodes and non-viable edges in directed acyclic graphs. These algorithms are extended by [CB04] in order to address directed graphs in general with the notion of strongly connected components and condensed graphs. Nevertheless, graphs similar to our third benchmark [SPMc] represent tough scenarios for this approach since almost all the nodes are in the same strongly connected component.

CP(Graph) introduces a new computation domain focussed on graphs including a new type of variable, graph domain variables, as well as constraints over these variables and their propagators [DDD04, DDD05]. CP(Graph) also introduces node variables and edge variables, and is integrated with the finite domain and finite set computation domain. Consistency techniques have been developed, graph constraints have been built over the kernel constraints and global constraints have been proposed. One of those global constraints is $Path(p, s, d, maxlength)$. This constraint is satisfied if p is a simple path from s to d of length at most $maxlength$. Certainly, Simple path with mandatory nodes can be implemented in terms of *Path*. However, the filtering algorithm of *Path* does not compute dominators, which makes *Path* also sensible to cases like SPMN_52a.

Dominators are commonly used in compilers for dataflow analysis [AU77]. Dominance constraints also appear in natural language processing, for building semantic trees from partial information. However, we are not aware of approaches using dominators for implementing filtering algorithms. Even though the information it provides is extremely useful, and can be computed efficiently.

Structure of the paper. The paper is organized as follows. In Section 2, we introduce *DomReachability* by presenting its semantics and pruning rules. In Section 3, we show how we can model Simple path with mandatory nodes in terms of *DomReachability*. Section 4 gives experimental evidence of the performance of *DomReachability* for this type of problem. In Section 5 we show a reduction of the Ordered disjoint-paths problem (ODP) to OSPMN, which can be solved by our approach.

2   The *DomReachability* Propagator

2.1   Extended Dominator Graph

Given a flow graph fg and its corresponding source s, a node i is a dominator of node j if all paths from s to j in fg contain i [LT79, SGL97]:

$$i \in Dominators(fg, j) \leftrightarrow i \neq j \land \forall p \in Paths(fg, s, j) : i \in Nodes(p) \quad (1)$$

where

$$p \in Paths(fg, i, j) \leftrightarrow \begin{cases} p \text{ is a subgraph of } fg \\ Nodes(p) = \{k_1, \ldots, k_n\} \land k_1 = i \land k_n = j \\ Edges(p) = \{\langle k_t, k_{t+1} \rangle \mid 1 \leq t < n\} \end{cases} \quad (2)$$

Note that the nodes unreachable from s are dominated by all the other nodes. However, the nodes reachable from s always have an *immediate* dominator, which can be defined as

$$i = ImDominator(fg, j) \leftrightarrow$$
$$\begin{cases} i \in Dominators(fg, j) \\ \neg \exists k \in Nodes(fg) : i \in Dominators(fg, k) \land k \in Dominators(fg, j) \end{cases}$$
$$(3)$$

This property allows to represent the whole dominance relation as a tree, where the parent of a node is its immediate dominator. The dominator tree can be used as an efficient representation of the relation, as there exists incremental algorithms for updating the tree [SGL97]. This paper only presents a non-incremental algorithm to compute the whole relation (see Figure 5).

Let us now consider the extended graph of fg, $Ext(fg)$, which is obtained by replacing the edges by new nodes, and connecting the new nodes accordingly. This graph can be formally defined as follows:

$$\langle N', E', s' \rangle = Ext(\langle N, E, s \rangle) \leftrightarrow \begin{cases} s' = s \\ N' = N \cup E \\ e = \langle i, j \rangle \in E \leftrightarrow \langle i, e \rangle \in E' \land \langle e, j \rangle \in E' \end{cases}$$
$$(4)$$

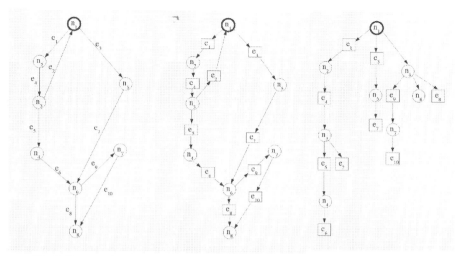

Fig. 2. Flow graph   **Fig. 3.** Extended flow graph   **Fig. 4.** Extended dominator tree

The extended dominator graph of fg is the dominator graph of its extended graph. Figures 2, 3 and 4 show an example of a flow graph, its extended graph, and its extended dominator tree, respectively. The extended dominator tree has two types of nodes: nodes corresponding to nodes in the original graph (*node dominators*), and nodes corresponding to edges in the original graph (*edge dominators*). The latter nodes are drawn in squares.

The extended dominator tree provides useful information. For instance, consider two node dominators i and j. If $\langle i, j \rangle \in Edges(DomTree(Ext(fg))) \setminus Edges(fg)$, there are at least two node-disjoint paths from i to j in the flow graph (as it is the case between nodes 1 and 6 in Figure 4). Note also that, if i is an ancestor of j in the extended dominator tree, and the path from i to j does not contain any edge dominator, there are at least two edge-disjoint paths from i to j in the flow graph.

2.2   The *DomReachability* Constraint

The *DomReachability* constraint is a constraint on three graphs:

$$DomReachability(fg, edg, tc) \tag{5}$$

where

- fg is a flow graph, i.e., a directed graph with a source node, whose set of nodes is a subset of N;
- edg is the extended dominator graph of fg; and
- tc is the transitive closure of fg, i.e,

$$\langle i, j \rangle \in Edges(tc) \leftrightarrow \langle i, j \rangle \in Edges(TransClos(fg))$$
$$\langle i, j \rangle \in Edges(TransClos(g)) \leftrightarrow \exists p : p \in Paths(g, i, j) \tag{6}$$

The above definition of *DomReachability* implies the following properties which are important for the pruning that *DomReachability* performs. These properties define relations between the graphs fg, edg and tc. These relations can then be used for pruning, as we show in the next section.

1. If $\langle i, j \rangle$ is an edge of fg, then i reaches j.

$$\forall \langle i, j \rangle \in Edges(fg) : \langle i, j \rangle \in Edges(tc) \tag{7}$$

2. If i reaches j, then i reaches all the nodes that j reaches.

$$\forall i, j, k \in N : \langle i, j \rangle \in Edges(tc) \wedge \langle j, k \rangle \in Edges(tc) \rightarrow \langle i, k \rangle \in Edges(tc) \tag{8}$$

3. If j is reachable from $s = Source(fg)$ and i dominates j in fg, then i is reachable from s and j is reachable from i:

$$\forall i, j \in N : \langle s, j \rangle \in Edges(tc) \wedge \langle i, j \rangle \in Edges(edg) \rightarrow \langle s, i \rangle \in Edges(tc) \wedge \langle i, j \rangle \in Edges(tc) \tag{9}$$

2.3   Pruning Rules

We implement the constraint (5) by the propagator that we note

$$DomReachability(\langle FG, s \rangle, EDG, TC). \tag{10}$$

FG, EDG and TC are graph variables, i.e., variables whose domain is a set of graphs [DDD05]. A graph variable G is represented by a pair of graphs $Min(G) \# Max(G)$. The graph g that G approximates must be a supergraph of $Min(G)$ and a subgraph of $Max(G)$, therefore $Min(G)$ and $Max(G)$ are called the lower and upper bounds of G, respectively. So, $i \in Nodes(G)$ holds if $i \in Nodes(Min(G))$, and $i \notin Nodes(G)$ holds if $i \notin Nodes(Max(G))$ (the same applies for edges). Notice that the source s of the flow graph FG is a known value.

The definition of the *DomReachability* constraint and its derived properties give place to a set of propagation rules. We show here the ones that motivate the implementation of incremental algorithms for keeping the dominance relation and the transitive closure of the flow graph. The others are given in [QVD05b]. A propagation rule is defined as $\frac{C}{A}$ where C is a condition and A is an action. When C is true, the pruning defined by A can be performed.

From property (7) we derive

$$\frac{\langle i, j \rangle \in Edges(Min(FG))}{Edges(Min(TC)) := Edges(Min(TC)) \cup \{\langle i, j \rangle\}} \tag{11}$$

From property (8) we derive

$$\frac{\langle i, j \rangle \in Edges(Min(TC)) \wedge \langle j, k \rangle \in Edges(Min(TC))}{Edges(Min(TC)) := Edges(Min(TC)) \cup \{\langle i, k \rangle\}} \tag{12}$$

From property (9) we derive, for $i \in Nodes(Min(FG))$,

$$\frac{\langle s, j \rangle \in Edges(Min(TC)) \wedge \langle i, j \rangle \in Edges(Min(EDG))}{Edges(Min(TC)) := Edges(Min(TC)) \cup \{\langle s, i \rangle, \langle i, j \rangle\}} \tag{13}$$

From definition (6) we derive

$$\frac{\langle i, j \rangle \notin Edges(TransClos(Max(FG)))}{Edges(Max(TC)) := Edges(Max(TC)) \setminus \{\langle i, j \rangle\}} \tag{14}$$

From definition (1) we derive

$$\frac{\langle i, j \rangle \in Edges(DomGraph(Ext(Max(FG))))}{Edges(Min(EDG)) := Edges(Min(EGD)) \cup \{\langle i, j \rangle\}} \tag{15}$$

where $DomGraph$ is a function that returns the dominator graph of a flow graph, i.e., $\langle i, j \rangle \in Edges(DomGraph(fg)) \leftrightarrow i \in Dominators(fg, j)$.

2.4   Implementation of *DomReachability*

DomReachability has been implemented using a message passing approach [VH04] on top of the multi-paradigm programming language Oz [Moz04]. In [QVD05a], we discuss the implementation of *DomReachability* in detail. In this section we simply refer to the update of the upper bound of TC and the lower bound of EDG. Both values should be updated when an edge is removed from $Max(FG)$. However, as explained in [QVD05a], we do not compute these values each time an edge is removed since this certainly leads to a considerably amount of unnecessary computation. This is due to the fact that these two values evolve monotonically. What we actually do is to consider all the removals at once and make one computation per set of edges removed.

```
GetDominators(fg)
    nodes₀ := DFS(fg, Source(fg))
    for i ∈ Nodes(fg) do
        doms(i) := if i ∈ nodes₀ then ∅ else Nodes(fg) \ {i} end
    end
    for i ∈ nodes₀ do
        nodes₁ := DFS(RemoveNode(fg, i), Source(fg))
        for j ∈ nodes₀ \ (nodes₁ ∪ {i}) do
            doms(j) := doms(j) ∪ {i}
        end
    end
    return doms
end
```

Fig. 5. Computation of Dominators

Currently, our way of updating TC's upper bound is simply by running DFS on each node of TC's upper bound. So the complexity of this update is $O(N * (N + E))$. Regarding EDG's lower bound, the set of dominators is computed by using the algorithm in Figure 5 (which is actually equivalent to Aho and Ullman's algorithm for computing dominators [AU77]). $doms(i)$ is the set of dominators of node i in fg. Let us assume that DFS returns the reachable nodes. $doms(i)$ is initialized with $\emptyset$ or $Nodes(fg) \setminus \{i\}$ depending on whether i is reached from $Source(fg)$ (since any node dominates an non-reached node). The basic idea of this algorithm is that, if $Source(fg)$ does not reach j after removing i then i dominates j. So, each node is removed in order to detect the nodes that it dominates. Therefore the computation of dominators is $O(N * (N + E))$ too.

3 Solving *Simple Path with Mandatory Nodes* with *DomReachability*

In this section we elaborate on the important role that *DomReachability* can play in solving Simple path with mandatory nodes. This problem consists in finding a simple path in a directed graph containing a set of mandatory nodes. A simple path is a path where each node is visited once, i.e., given a directed graph g, a source node src, a destination node dst, and a set of mandatory nodes $mandnodes$, we want to find a path in g from src to dst, going through $mandnodes$ and visiting each node only once.

The contribution of *DomReachability* consists in discovering nodes/edges that are part of the path early on. This information is obtained by computing dominators in each labeling step. Let us consider the following two cases[1]:

- Consider the graph variable on the left of Figure 6. Assume that node 1 reaches node 9. This information is enough to infer that node 5 belongs to the graph, node 1 reaches node 5, and node 5 reaches node 9.
- Consider the graph variable on the left of Figure 7. Assume that node 1 reaches node 5. This information is enough to infer that edges $\langle 1, 2 \rangle, \langle 2, 3 \rangle, \langle 3, 4 \rangle$ and $\langle 4, 5 \rangle$ are in the graph, which implies that node 1 reaches nodes 1,2,3,4,5, node 2 at least reaches nodes 2,3,4,5, node 3 at least reaches nodes 3,4,5 and node 4 at least reaches nodes 4,5.

Note that the Hamiltonian path problem (finding a simple path between two nodes containing all the nodes of the graph [GJ79, CLR90]) can be reduced to Simple path with mandatory nodes by defining the set of mandatory nodes as $Nodes(g) \setminus \{src, dst\}$.

The above definition of Simple path with mandatory nodes can be formally defined as follows.

$$SPMN(g, src, dst, mandnodes, p) \leftrightarrow \begin{cases} p \in Paths(g, src, dst) \\ NoCycle(p) \\ mandnodes \subset Nodes(p) \end{cases} \quad (16)$$

---

[1] In Figures 6 and 7, nodes and edges that belong to the lower bound of the graph variable are in solid line. For instance, the graph variable on the left side of Figure 6 is a graph variable whose lower bound is the graph $\langle \{1, 5\}, \emptyset \rangle$, and whose upper bound is the graph $\langle \{1, 2, 3, 4, 5, 6, 7, 8, 9\}, \{\langle 1, 2 \rangle, \langle 1, 3 \rangle, \langle 1, 4 \rangle, \langle 2, 5 \rangle, \langle 3, 5 \rangle, \langle 4, 5 \rangle, \langle 5, 6 \rangle, \langle 5, 7 \rangle, \langle 5, 8 \rangle, \langle 6, 9 \rangle, \langle 7, 9 \rangle, \langle 8, 9 \rangle \} \rangle$.

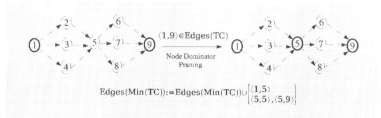

Fig. 6. Discovering node dominators

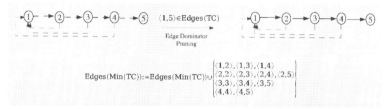

Fig. 7. Discovering edge dominator

$SPMN$ stands for "Simple path with mandatory nodes". $NoCycle(p)$ states that p is a simple path, i.e., a path where no node is visited twice. This definition of Simple path with mandatory nodes implies the following property.

$$DomReachability(p, edg, tc) \land \langle Source(p), dst \rangle \in Edges(tc) \land$$
$$mandnodes \subset \{i \mid \langle Source(p), i \rangle \in Edges(tc)\} \qquad (17)$$

This is because the destination is reached by the source and the path contains the mandatory nodes. This derived property and the fact that we can implement $SPMN$ in terms of the *AllDiff* constraint [Rég94] and the *NoCycle* constraint [CL97] suggest the two approaches for Simple path with mandatory nodes summarized in Table 1 (which are compared in the next section). In the first approach, we basically consider *AllDiff* and *NoCycle*. In the second approach we additionally consider *DomReachability*.

Table 1. Two approaches for solving Simple path with mandatory nodes

Approach 1	Approach 2
$SPMN(g, src, dst, mandnodes, p)$	$SPMN(g, src, dst, mandnodes, p)$
	$DomReachability(p, edg, tc)$
	$\langle Source(p), dst \rangle \in Edges(tc)$
	$mandnodes \subset \{i \mid \langle Source(p), i \rangle \in Edges(tc)\}$

4   Experimental Results

In this section we present a set of experiments that show that *DomReachability* is suitable for Simple path with mandatory nodes. In our experiments *Approach 2* (in Table 1) outperforms *Approach 1*. These experiments also show that Simple path with mandatory nodes tends to be harder when the number of optional nodes increases if they are

Table 2. Simple path with mandatory nodes instances

Name	Figure	Source	Destination	Mand. Nodes	Order
SPMN_22	[SPMa]	1	22	4 7 10 16 18 21	false
SPMN_22full	[SPMb]	1	22	all	false
SPMN_52a	[SPMc]	1	52	11 13 24 39 45	false
SPMN_52b	[SPMc]	1	52	4 5 7 13 16 19 22 24 29 33 36 39 44 45 49	false
SPMN_52full	[SPMd]	1	52	all	false
SPMN_52Order_a	[SPMc]	1	52	45 39 24 13 11	true
SPMN_52Order_b	[SPMc]	1	52	11 13 24 39 45	true

Table 3. Performance with respect to optional nodes

Opt. Nodes	Failures	Time
5	30	89
10	42	129
15	158	514
20	210	693
25	330	1152
32	101	399
37	100	402
42	731	3518
47	598	3046

Table 4. Simple path with mandatory nodes tests

Problem		SPMN		SPMN+R		SPMN+R+ND		SPMN+R+ND+ED	
Instance	Figure	Failures	Time	Failures	Time	Failures	Time	Failures	Time
SPMN_22	[SPMa]	+130000	+1800	91	6.81	40	6.55	13	4.45
SPMN_22full	[SPMb]	213	1.44	19	0.95	0	0.42	0	1.22
SPMN_52b	-	-	-	+900	+1800	+700	+1800	100	402
SPMN_52full	[SPMd]	3012	143	774	765	3	8.51	3	45.03
SPMN_52Order_a	[SPMc]	+12000	+1800	51	46.33	45	81	16	57.07
SPMN_52Order_b	-	+12000	+1800	+1500	+1800	81	157	41	117

uniformly distributed in the graph. We have also observed that the labeling strategy that we implemented with *DomReachability* tends to minimize the use of optional nodes (which is a common need when the resources are limited).

In Table 2, we define the instances on which we made the tests of Table 4[2]. The node id of the destination is also the size of the graph. The column Order is true for the instances whose mandatory nodes are visited in the order given. Notice that SPMN_52Order_b has no solution. The time measurements are given in seconds. The number of failures means the number of failed alternatives tried before getting the solution.

We have made four types of tests in our experiments: using *SPMN* without *DomReachability* (column "SPMN"), using *SPMN* and *DomReachability* but without considering the dominance graph (column "SPMN+R"), using *SPMN* and *DomReachability* with the dominance graph (column "SPMN+R+ND"), and using *SPMN* and *DomReachability* with the dominance graph of the extended flow graph (node+edge dominators (column "SPMN+R+ND+ED")).

As it can be observed in Table 4, we were not able to get a solution for SPMN_22 in less than 30 minutes without using *DomReachability*. However, even though the number of failures is still inferior, the use of *DomReachability* does not save too much time when dealing with mandatory nodes only. This is due to the fact that we are basing our

---

[2] In order to save space, the figures mentioned in the tables were dropped and made available through references [SPMa], [SPMb], [SPMc] and [SPMd].

implementation of *SPMN* on two things: the *AllDiff* constraint [Rég94] (that lets us efficiently remove branches when there is no possibility of associating different successors to the nodes) and the *NoCycle* constraint [CL97] (that avoids re-visiting nodes).

The reason why *SPMN* does not perform well with optional nodes is because we are no longer able to impose the global *AllDiff* constraint on the successors of the nodes since we do not know a priori which nodes are going to be used. In fact, one thing that we observed is that the problem tends to be harder to solve when the number of optional nodes increases. In Table 3, all the tests were performed using *DomReachability* on the graph of 52 nodes.

Even though, in SPMN_22, the benefit caused by the computation of edge dominators is not that significant, we were not able to obtain a solution for SPMN_52b in less than 30 minutes, while we obtained a solution in 402 seconds by computing edge dominators. So, the computation of edge dominators pays off in most of the cases, but node dominators should be computed in order to profit from edge dominators.

4.1 Labeling Strategy

DomReachability provides interesting information for implementing smart labeling strategies, due to the fact that it associates each node with the set of nodes that it reaches. This information can be used to guide the search in a smart way. For instance, we observed that, when choosing first the node i that reaches the most nodes and selecting as a successor of i first a node that i reaches, we obtain paths that minimize the use of optional nodes (as it can be observed in [SPMc]).

Nevertheless, in order to reduce the number of failures in finding the solution of [DPc] (which was solved in less than 100 failures), we favored the nodes that were closer to the mandatory nodes, i.e., if the successors of the chosen node are not mandatory the chosen successor is the one closest to the next mandatory node.

4.2 Imposing Order on Nodes

An additional feature of *DomReachability* is its suitability for imposing ordering constraints on nodes (which is a common issue in routing problems). In fact, it might be

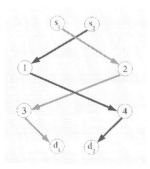

Fig. 8. Finding two disjoint paths

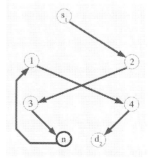

Fig. 9. Finding a simple path passing through n

the case that we have to visit the nodes of the graph in a particular (partial) order. We call this version the "Ordered simple path with mandatory nodes problem" *(OSPMN)*.

Our way of forcing a node i to be visited before a node j is by imposing that i reaches j and j does not reach i. The tests on the instances SPMN_52Order_a and SPMN_52Order_b show that *DomReachability* takes the most advantage of this information to avoid branches in the search tree with no solution. Notice that we are able to solve SPMN_52Order_a (which is an extension of SPMN_52a) in 57.07 seconds. We are also able to detect the inconsistency of SPMN_52Order_b in 117 seconds.

5   Reducing the Ordered Disjoint-Paths Problem to the Simple Path with Mandatory Nodes Problem

The k-Disjoint-paths problem consist in finding k pairwise disjoint paths between k pairs of nodes $\langle s_1, d_1 \rangle$, $\langle s_2, d_2 \rangle$, ..., $\langle s_k, d_k \rangle$. Both the node-disjoint version and the edge-disjoint version are NP-complete [SP78]. We will focus on the node-disjoint version.

Let us first look at the problem of reducing the 2-Disjoint-paths problem to SPMN. Suppose that we want to find two disjoint paths between the pairs $\langle s_1, d_1 \rangle$ and $\langle s_2, d_2 \rangle$ in g. Let g' and n be defined as follows.

$$
\begin{aligned}
&n \notin Nodes(g) \\
&g' = AddEdges(g_1, E_1 \cup E_2) \\
&g_1 = AddNode(g_2, n) \\
&g_2 = RemoveNodes(g, \{d_1, s_2\}) \\
&E_1 = IncEdges(g, d_1)[d_1/n] \\
&E_2 = OutEdges(g, s_2)[s_2/n]
\end{aligned}
\tag{18}
$$

Finding the two disjoint paths is equivalent to finding a simple path from s_1 to d_2 passing through n in g'. The correctness of this reduction relies on the fact that the concatenation of the two disjoint paths forms a simple path since each disjoint path is a simple path. Figure 9 shows the the reduction of the two disjoint paths problem of Figure 8. The path found in Figure 9 corresponds to the concatenation of the two disjoint paths of Figure 8.

Let us consider now an extended version of the 2 Node-disjoint path problem that we call *2 Ordered node-disjoint path (2ODP)*. In this version, each pair is associated with a set of mandatory nodes and an order relation on the mandatory nodes. That is, given the directed graph g and the tuples $\langle s_1, d_1, mn_1, order_1 \rangle$ and $\langle s_2, d_2, mn_2, order_2 \rangle$, the goal is to find two paths p_1 and p_2 such that p_1 is a path from s_1 to d_1 visiting mn_1 respecting $order_1$, p_2 is a path from s_2 to d_2 visiting mn_2 respecting $order_2$, and p_1 and p_2 are node-disjoint.

The 2ODP problem $\langle g, \langle \langle s_1, d_1, mn_1, order_1 \rangle, \langle s_2, d_2, mn_2, order_2 \rangle \rangle \rangle$ can be reduced to OSPMN $\langle g', s_1, d_2, mn', order' \rangle$ where g' is defined as in the previous reduction, $mn' = mn_1 \cup mn_2 \cup \{n\}$, n is defined as before, and

$$
order' = \begin{cases}
order_1 \cup \\
order_2 \cup \\
\{\langle n_1, n_2 \rangle \mid (n_1 \in mn_1 \wedge n_2 = n) \vee (n_1 = n \wedge n_2 \in mn_2)\}.
\end{cases}
\tag{19}
$$

ReduceODP($\langle g, \langle \langle s_1, d_1, mn_1, order_1 \rangle, \ldots, \langle s_k, d_k, mn_k, order_k \rangle \rangle \rangle$)
    $ospmn := \langle g, s_1, d_1, mn_1, order_1 \rangle$
    for $i \in \{2, 3, \ldots, k\}$ do
        $\langle g', s', d', mn', order' \rangle := ospmn$
        $ospmn := Reduce\_2\_ODP(\langle g', \langle \langle s', d', mn', order' \rangle, \langle s_i, d_i, mn_i, order_i \rangle \rangle \rangle)$
    end
    return $ospmn$
end

Fig. 10. Reducing ODP to OSPMN

The simple path traverses the nodes mn_1 in the order $order_1$, and the nodes mn_2 in the order $order_2$, the nodes mn_1 are visited before n and the nodes in mn_2 after n.

Let $Reduce\_2\_ODP$ be defined as

$$Reduce\_2\_ODP(ODPins) = OSPMNins$$
$$ODPins = \langle g, \langle \langle s_1, d_1, mn_1, order_1 \rangle, \langle s_2, d_2, mn_2, order_2 \rangle \rangle \rangle$$
$$OSPMNins = \langle g', s_1, d_2, mn', order' \rangle$$

$$\tag{20}$$

The function $ReduceODP$, which reduces any ordered disjoint path problem (ODP) to OSPMN, can be defined as shown in Figure 10. Certainly, we assume that the pairs $\langle s_1, d_1 \rangle, \langle s_2, d_2 \rangle, \ldots, \langle s_k, d_k \rangle$ are pairwise node-disjoint. However, this condition can be easily fulfilled by duplicating the nodes that are used by more than one pair.

Note that the conventional k node-disjoint paths problem can be trivially reduced to ODP. We simply need to map each pair $\langle s_i, d_i \rangle$ to $\langle s_i, d_i, \emptyset, \emptyset \rangle$. We used $ReduceODP$ to solve the case shown in [DPc]. In this case we were interested in finding 14 node-disjoint paths in a directed graph of 165 nodes.

6 Conclusion and Future Work

We presented *DomReachability*, a constrained graph propagator that can be used for solving constrained path problems. *DomReachability* is a propagator that reasons in terms of the three partially defined graphs that it has as arguments. Further definition of one of its graphs may cause the other two graphs to be further defined. After introducing the semantics and pruning rules of *DomReachability*, we showed how its use can speed up a standard approach for dealing with Simple path problem with mandatory nodes. Our experiments show that the gain is increased with the presence of optional nodes. The latter makes the problem harder, and standard approaches perform worse.

It is important to emphasize that both the computation of node dominators, and the computation of edge dominators play an essential role in the performance of *Dom-Reachability*. The reason is that each one is able to prune when the other can not. Notice that Figure 6 is a context where the computation of edge dominators cannot infer anything since there is no edge dominator. Similarly, Figure 7 represents a context where the computation of edge dominators discovers more information than the computation of node dominators.

As mentioned before, our current approach for maintaining the dominator graph and the transitive closure has complexity $O(N * (N + E))$. However, we are aware of $O(N + E)$ algorithms for updating these structures [SGL97, DI00]. In fact, there is a non-incremental algorithm for computing dominator trees that is more efficient than our current algorithm since it is $O(E\alpha(E, N))$, where $\alpha(E, N)$ is a functional inverse of Ackermann's function [LT79]. Certainly, our next step is to implement these algorithms since we believe that they will remarkably improve the performance of *DomReachability*.

Acknowledgements

We thank Eugene Ressler for pointing out that our former cut nodes [QVD05b] were actually dominators; Christian Schulte, Fred Spiessens and Grégoire Dooms for proofreading earlier versions of this paper; and Martin Oellrich for providing the instance solved in [DPc].

References

[AU77]   A. V. Aho and J. D. Ullman. *Principles of Compiler Design*. Addison-Wesley, 1977.

[BC94]   N. Beldiceanu and E. Contjean. Introducing global constraints in CHIP. *Mathematical and Computer Modelling*, 12:97–123, 1994.

[Bou99]   Eric Bourreau. *Traitement de contraintes sur les graphes en programmation par contraintes*. Doctoral dissertation, Université Paris, Paris, France, 1999.

[CB04]   Hadrien Cambazard and Eric Bourreau. Conception d'une contrainte globale de chemin. In *10e Journées nationales sur la résolution pratique de problèmes NP-complets (JNPC'04)*, pages 107–121, Angers, France, June 2004.

[CL97]   Yves Caseau and Francois Laburthe. Solving small TSPs with constraints. In *International Conference on Logic Programming*, pages 316–330, 1997.

[CLR90]   T. Cormen, C. Leiserson, and R. Rivest. *Introduction to Algorithms*. The MIT Press, 1990.

[DDD04]   G. Dooms, Y. Deville, and P. Dupont. Constrained path finding in biochemical networks. In *5èmes Journées Ouvertes Biologie Informatique Mathématiques*, 2004.

[DDD05]   G. Dooms, Y. Deville, and P. Dupont. CP(Graph):introducing a graph computation domain in constraint programming. In *CP2005 Proceedings*, 2005.

[DI00]   Camil Demetrescu and Giuseppe F. Italiano. Fully dynamic transitive closure: Breaking through the $O(n^2)$ barrier. In *IEEE Symposium on Foundations of Computer Science*, pages 381–389, 2000.

[DPc]   A disjoint-paths problem solved with *Reachability*. Available at *http://www.info.ucl.ac.be/˜luque/PADL06/DPcase.ps*.

[FLM99]   F. Focacci, A. Lodi, and M. Milano. Solving tsp with time windows with constraints. In *CLP'99 International Conference on Logic Programming Proceedings*, 1999.

[GJ79]   Michael Garey and David Johnson. *Computers and Intractability: A Guide to the The Theory of NP-Completeness*. W. H. Freeman and Company, 1979.

[LT79]   T. Lengauer and R. Tarjan. A fast algorithm for finding dominators in a flowgraph. *ACM Transactions on Programming Languages and Systems*, 1(1):121–141, July 1979.

[Moz04]   Mozart Consortium. The Mozart Programming System, version 1.3.0, 2004. Available at *http://www.mozart-oz.org/*.

[Mül01]   Tobias Müller. *Constraint Propagation in Mozart*. Doctoral dissertation, Universität des Saarlandes, Naturwissenschaftlich-Technische Fakultät I, Fachrichtung Informatik, Saarbrücken, Germany, 2001.

[PGPR96]   G. Pesant, M. Gendreau, J. Potvin, and J. Rousseau. An exact constraint logic programming algorithm for the travelling salesman with time windows, 1996.

[QVD05a]   Luis Quesada, Peter Van Roy, and Yves Deville. Reachability: a constrained path propagator implemented as a multi-agent system. In *CLEI2005 Proceedings*, 2005.

[QVD05b]   Luis Quesada, Peter Van Roy, and Yves Deville. The reachability propagator. Research Report INFO-2005-07, Université catholique de Louvain, Louvain-la-Neuve, Belgium, 2005.

[Rég94]   Jean Charles Régin. A filtering algorithm for constraints of difference in csps. In *In Proceedings of the Twelfth National Conference on Artificial Intelligence*, pages 362–367, 1994.

[Sch00]   Christian Schulte. *Programming Constraint Services*. Doctoral dissertation, Universität des Saarlandes, Naturwissenschaftlich-Technische Fakultät I, Fachrichtung Informatik, Saarbrücken, Germany, 2000.

[Sel02]   Meinolf Sellmann. *Reduction Techniques in Constraint Programming and Combinatorial Optimization*. Doctoral dissertation, University of Paderborn, Paderborn, Germany, 2002.

[SGL97]   Vugranam C. Sreedhar, Guang R. Gao, and Yong-Fong Lee. Incremental computation of dominator trees. *ACM Transactions on Programming Languages and Systems*, 19(2):239–252, March 1997.

[SP78]   Y. Shiloach and Y. Perl. Finding two disjoint paths between two pairs of vertices in a graph. *Journal of the ACM*, 1978.

[SPMa]   Spmn_22. Available at *http://www.info.ucl.ac.be/~luque/PADL06/test_22.ps*.

[SPMb]   Spmn_22full. Available at *http://www.info.ucl.ac.be/~luque/PADL06/test_22full.ps*.

[SPMc]   Spmn_52a. Available at *http://www.info.ucl.ac.be/~luque/PADL06/test_52.ps*.

[SPMd]   Spmn_52full. Available at *http://www.info.ucl.ac.be/~luque/PADL06/test_52full.ps*.

[VH04]   P. Van Roy and S. Haridi. *Concepts, Techniques, and Models of Computer Programming*. The MIT Press, 2004.

JQuery: A Generic Code Browser with a Declarative Configuration Language

Kris De Volder

University of British Columbia, Vancouver BC V6T 1Z4, Canada
kdvolder@cs.ubc.ca
http://www.cs.ubc.causers/~kdvolder/

Abstract. Modern IDEs have an open-ended plugin architecture to allow customizability. However, developing a plugin is costly in terms of effort and expertise required by the customizer. We present a two-pronged approach that allows for open-ended customizations while keeping the customization cost low. First, we explicitly limit the portion of the design space targeted by the configuration mechanism. This reduces customization cost by simplifying the configuration interface. Second, we use a declarative programming language as our configuration language. This facilitates open-ended specification of behavior without burdening the user with operational details.

Keywords: integrated development environment, program database, domain-specific language, logic programming.

1 Introduction

Customizability and extensibility are important design goals for modern IDEs. In a typical IDE we discern two levels of customizability. The first level is provided by GUI controls such as preference panes. These customizations are cheap[1]. Unfortunately their range is limited: one can chose between a finite set of predefined behaviors but one cannot define new behavior.

The second level of customizability is through a plugin architecture. For example, the Eclipse IDE plugin architecture allows one to implement IDE extensions in Java™ and dynamically link them with the IDE. Other modern IDEs offer similar mechanisms. Plugins add executable code to the IDE so new behavior can be defined. Unfortunately the cost of customization is comparable to developing a small GUI application.

We will refer to a customization mechanism's trade-offs, between open-endedness and customization cost, as its *customization-cost profile*. We argue that IDEs provide two extreme customization-cost profiles: one is open-ended and expensive, the other is cheap but limited. We claim that it is also possible and useful to design configuration mechanisms with cost profiles in between these two extremes.

---

[1] We are interested in the cost in terms effort and expertise required of a customizer. In this paper, words like "cost", "cheap" and "expensive" should be interpreted in this sense.

P. Van Hentenryck (Ed.): PADL 2006, LNCS 3819, pp. 88–102, 2006.

Fig. 1. Different Eclipse JDT Code Browsers

We present an approach that is flexible enough for open-ended customizations while remaining relatively cheap. There are two key ingredients. First, we explicitly limit ourselves to a portion of the design space referred to as the *targeted design space*. This reduces customization costs by allowing a simpler configuration interface. Second, we use a *declarative* programming language to facilitate open-ended specification of behavior without burdening the user with operational details.

We do not intend to provide direct evidence for our claims in their most general sense. Instead, we describe a concrete illustrative example, the JQuery tool, for one particular class of IDE extensions, code browsers. Applying these ideas to other types of IDE extensions is interesting for future research but is outside the scope of this paper.

2   The Targeted Design Space

In this section we examine the browsers provided by Eclipse JDT (Java Development Tools) environment, which is representative for the state of the art. This analysis serves two purposes. First, it serves as a basis to establish explicit bounds on the targeted design space. Second, it provides a concrete example of the two extreme customization-cost profiles.

Eclipse JDT offers multiple browsers to view and navigate source code. The core JDT browsers are shown in Figure 1. Each browser allows a developer to view and navigate their code in a different way: the *Package Explorer* (left) shows program structure in terms of modular containment relationships; the *Type Hierarchy* (middle) shows code structure in terms of inheritance relationships; and the *Call Hierarchy* (right) shows the structure of the static call graph.

Each of the browsers provides very similar functionality: a pane with a tree-viewer displaying icons and textual labels that represent program elements (packages, types etc.). The elements are organized hierarchically based on a particular relationship that exists between the elements. Double clicking an element reveals its source-code in a Java editor. Each view also has some buttons at the top, allowing some control over the contents and structure of the view. For example, the call hierarchy allows inverting the direction of the call edges; the package explorer allows hiding private and static elements; the type hierarchy allows showing/hiding an extra pane displaying the members of the selected type.

We see that Eclipse JDT browser configuration exhibits the two extreme customization-cost profiles: GUI buttons provide cheap but limited control over a browser's behavior but customization beyond this point is costly: in the best case the browser's source code can be used to develop a new plugin.

We end this section by establishing explicit bounds on JQuery's targeted design space. We decided to focus only on the core functionality observed in the various JDT browsers: a single browser pane containing a tree widget, but no support for additional control buttons or information panes. We also limited ourselves to browsers for a single Java program. In particular, it was not our goal to support browsing across multiple versions (e.g. CVS) or browsing of non-Java artifacts (e.g XML configuration files, build scripts etc.). These limitations delineate the targeted design space.

As a general principle, a customizer should not need to specify things that do not vary within the targeted design space. This principle served as a design guideline to simplify the configuration interface.

3   JQuery from a User's Perspective

JQuery is Java browser implemented as an Eclipse plugin. Unlike the standard Eclipse browsers, JQuery is generic: it can be configured to render many different types of views. We will argue that JQuery's customization-cost profile fits somewhere in between the two extremes offered by modern IDEs. This means that JQuery offers a more cost-effective creation of open-ended browser variations than a plugin architecture. However, it also means that customizing JQuery requires more expertise than clicking GUI buttons. Users may be reluctant to learn the configuration interface. Therefore in this section we present an example illustrating how JQuery 3.1.5 can already be used "out of the box".

The example is a fictional scenario in which a developer is exploring the JHotDraw [1] code base. JHotDraw is an application that lets users draw and manipulate a variety of figures such as rectangles, circles, etc. The developer wants to find out how figures are implemented and to find an example of a class that manipulates figures. Figure 2 shows a screenshot of JQuery at the end of her exploration. We explain the exploration step by step.

The starting point for exploration is typically a general purpose browser, such as a package explorer or a type hierarchy. To this end, JQuery provides a menu to select one of several "TopLevel" browsers. In this example the developer chooses to start with a JQuery view similar to an Eclipse package explorer. She then navigates down into the `org.jhotdraw.figures` package and discovers a number of classes that seem to correspond to different types of figures. Assuming there is a common base type for figures she decides to examine the supertypes of `ElbowHandle`. In JQuery, the browser's view can be extended to reveal relationships not yet shown. Right-clicking on a node brings up a contextual menu of

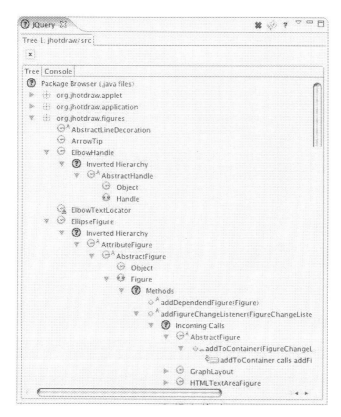

Fig. 2. Exploring Figures Implementation in JHotDraw

node-specific queries. The developer right-clicks on `ElbowHandle` and selects "Inheritance >> Inverted Hierarchy", which reveals the supertypes of `ElbowHandle` in an up-side-down inheritance hierarchy. Double clicking on a node brings the corresponding source code into view in the editor pane. Our developer inspects the source code of the supertypes of `ElbowHandle` and concludes that they are not what she is looking for. She then retraces her steps and tries browsing the supertypes of `EllipseFigure` instead. Among these she finds an interface called `Figure` which is what she was looking for. She decides to investigate what operations can be performed on Figures, expanding the view with the list of methods it defines. Finally, to find examples of classes that use `Figures` she decides to find all the places in the code that make calls to `addFigureChangeListener()`. This concludes the example.

This example adopted from our previous paper [11] shows how an exploration task may involve following several different types of relationships back and forth. It illustrates that JQuery supports this kind of "mixed-relationship browsing" by allowing the insertion of sub-browsers at any node in the tree. Our previous paper focused on the merits of this particular GUI design. The current paper focuses on the merits of its generic implementation and declarative configuration interface. We believe that it is one of the merits of the generic implementation to have enabled the conception of the "mixed-relation browser" GUI. Indeed, the predecessor of JQuery, QJBrowser [13], was also generic but it did not support mixed-relationship browsing. QJBrowser's generic browser model made adding that ability a straightforward next step.

4   Levels of Configurability

Although JQuery rests on top of a general purpose logic programming language called TyRuBa [8], it is not required for a JQuery user to be an expert TyRuBa programmer. It was illustrated in Section 3 how using JQuery "out of the box" requires no knowledge of logic programming. Furthermore, JQuery's configuration interface can be divided into two levels which we will refer to as the *basic* and the *advanced* configuration level. We draw the line between the levels based on how a user interacts with the configuration mechanism. A basic user only uses the JQuery GUI. An advanced user also edits configuration files in a separate text editor. Since configuration files are TyRuBa include files, advanced user's need to be familiar with programming in TyRuBa. Basic users are only exposed to TyRuBa via a dialog box in which they can edit a query. It suffices they have a basic understanding of TyRuBa expression syntax, but they do not need to know about inference rules or writing logic programs.

In the next two sections we will discuss both configuration levels in more detail. Each section begins with an explanation of the configuration interface and concludes with an argument placing its customization-cost profile at a different point between the two extremes.

5   Basic Configuration: "Instant" Browser Definitions

5.1   The Basic Configuration Interface

The key insight that sparked the JQuery design is that a code browser can be thought of as not much more than a tree-viewer widget for displaying and navigating query results. This is the main principle underlying JQuery browser definitions, consisting of two parts. The first part is a logic query executed over the *source model*, a database containing facts about the browsed program's structure. The purpose of the query is to select the elements to be displayed in the browser. We will refer to it as the *selection criterion*. The second part is an ordered list of (a subset of) the variables bound by the query. Its purpose is to define how to organize the query results into a tree. We will refer to it as the *organization criterion*.

A basic user can access and change the definition of any browser or subbrowser by double-clicking on its root node. Alternatively they can create a new browser by selecting "New TopLevel Query" from the menu. In each case they are presented with a dialog box like the one shown in Figure 3.

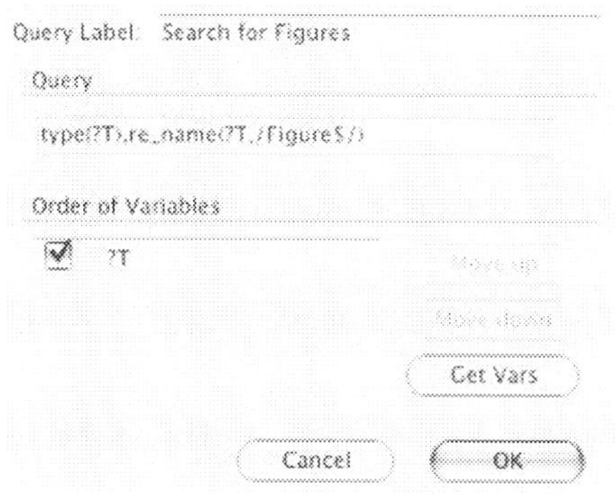

Fig. 3. Dialog box for editing browser definitions

We now look at some concrete examples that serve two purposes. First, they help clarify the meaning of selection and organization criteria. Second, they illustrate we can a create a broad variety of useful browsers.

The first example is shown in Figure 3. Its selection criterion finds all types (classes or interfaces) in the program whose name ends with "Figure". This is a useful query, exploiting a naming convention in JHotDraw to find classes that implement the `Figure` interface.

The query language used to express the selection criterion is the declarative logic programming language TyRuBa [8]. TyRuBa expression syntax is similar to Prolog's. One notable difference is that identifiers for denoting variables must start with a "?" character. This is convenient because it allows us to use names of Java methods, classes and variables as constants even when they start with a capital.

JQuery defines a number of TyRuBa predicates that provide access to the source model. In this example two such predicates are used: the `type` predicate is used to find all types declared in the program; the `re_name` predicate is used to restrict to types whose name matches the regular expression `/Figure$/`. These predicates are implemented by JQuery either by storing facts into the TyRuBa database or by means of logic inference rules. From a user's perspective this distinction is irrelevant. All that is required is that users are familiar with the semantics of the available predicates. The list of source model predicates is fairly extensive. A representative selection is shown in Table 1. For a more complete list we refer to the JQuery documentation [14]. These predicates provide access to a wealth of information about Java program structure: declaration context, inheritance hierarchy, location and targets of method calls, field accesses, where objects are created, location of compilation errors, method signatures, JavaDoc tags, etc.

The previous example's selection criterion only binds a single variable, making it ill-suited to illustrate the organization criterion. So let's extend the selection criterion as follows:

```
type(?T),re_name(?T,/Figure$/),method(?T,?M),returns(?M,?R)
```

Table 1. Selected predicates from JQuery's source model

Predicate	Description
package(?P)	?P is a package.
type(?T)	?T is a type defined in the program.
interface(?T)	?T is an interface defined in the program.
method(?M)	?M is a method defined in the program.
field(?F)	?F is a field defined in the program.
method(?T,?M)	?M is a method defined in type ?T.
returns(?M,?T)	Method ?M has return type ?T.
name(?E,?n)	Element (=package, type, method, field) ?E has name ?n.
re_name(?E,?regexp)	Element ?E has a name that matches ?regexp.
subtype(?Sub,?Sup)	?Sub is a direct supertype of ?Sup.
subtype+(?Sub,?Sup)	Transitive closure of subtype.
child(?E1,?E2)	?E2's declaration is directly nested inside ?E1.
reads(?reader,?field,?loc)	?field is read from ?reader at source location ?loc.

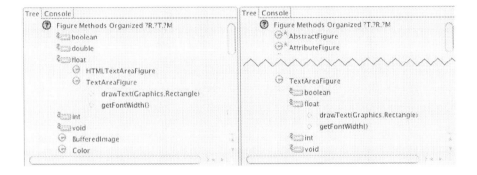

Fig. 4. Example: two different ways of organizing methods

This query additionally selects the methods (for each selected type) and the methods' respective return types. The results of this query can be organized in several ways. For example we can organize them primarily based on what type they are declared in by specifying a selection criterion ?T, ?R, ?M. Alternatively we can organize them primarily based on return type by specifying ?R, ?T, ?M. The resulting browsers are shown side by side in figure 4. To show the correspondence between both browsers, we have selected the same method (getFontWidth() from class TextAreaFigure returning a float) in each.

For our next example, we note that not all JHotDraw's figure classes follow the naming convention our first example relies on. This fact can be verified by formulating a selection criterion that finds violations of the naming convention:

```
name(?IFigure,Figure), subtype+(?IFigure,?Figure),
NOT( re_name(?Figure,/Figure$/) )
```

The resulting JQuery browser, displaying the values of all violating `?Figures`, could be very useful to refactor the offending classes and make them respect the naming convention. Note that it would be very difficult to accomplish this task with the standard Eclipse browsers and searching tools: even though Eclipse has a fairly extensive search facility, it is insufficient to formulate a precise enough query.

As a last example, assume that the developer who wishes to fix her code to adhere to the naming convention only has ownership of specific packages in the code base. The browser above is not as useful because it does not help her distinguish violating classes under her control from other classes. There are several ways in which she could get around this. If she knows how to characterize the packages under her control, for example based on a naming convention, then she could refine the query to remove classes not under her control. Alternatively, she could decide to organize the offending classes based on their package by changing the browser definition as follows:

```
selection:    name(?IFigure,Figure), subtype+(?IFigure,?Figure),
              NOT( re_name(?Figure,/Figure$/) ),
              package(?Figure,?P)
organization: ?P, ?Figure
```

The resulting browser lets the developer quickly see all packages that contain offending classes and navigate to those packages under her control.

These are only a few examples. Many other useful browser's can be defined by selecting and organizing Java code elements based on different combinations of properties and relationships such as their names, inheritance relations, field accesses, declaration context, method call targets, object creation, method signatures, JavaDoc tags, etc. The possibilities are endless.

We conclude this section by noting that sub-browser definitions, for which we gave no explicit example, work in exactly the same way except that their selection criterion may use a special `?this` variable to refer to the element at which the sub-browser is rooted.

5.2 The TyRuBa Language

We now discuss some specifics of the TyRuBa language. TyRuBa has a static type-and-mode system that was heavily inspired by Mercury's [10]. The TyRuBa inference engine follows a tabled evaluation [2] strategy. Both these features help making the query language more declarative than more conventional (i.e. Prolog-like) logic programming languages. The details of the TyRuBa language, its type and mode system and its tabled execution are beyond the scope of this paper. We refer the interested reader to [8] for more details. We will assume that the typical PADL reader has at least a passing familiarity with these more advanced logic programming language features and limit our discussion to how they may affect JQuery users and their required level of expertise.

Evidently, the type-and-mode system adds considerable complexity for users who need to understand it and provide additional type and mode declarations when defining predicates. However, these complications mostly affect advanced-level users, since basic users are not expected to declare or implement predicates. Most important for the basic user is how these features affect the formulation of logic expressions. The type and mode system actually helps rather than complicates this. First, the type-and-mode checker rejects some ill-formed queries with an error message. In a more Prolog-like language such queries might execute without returning any results, producing an empty browser. For example the following query which has its arguments ?loc and ?f accidentally switched will be rejected by the type checker:

```
field(?f),name(?f,"foobar"),reads(?m,?loc,?f)
```

Another advantage is that the mode system absolves the user from worrying about subexpression execution order. For example in the following query subexpressions can be executed in either order and this will yield the same result (the Figure interface in the JHotDraw code base):

```
type(?Figure), name(?Figure,Figure)
```

However, it is preferable to execute the name subexpression first because that will quickly retrieve all objects with name Figure (a small number) and then iteratively single out the ones that represent types. The other execution order will retrieve all types (a large number) and then iteratively test whether their name equals Figure. The TyRuBa mode system uses some simple heuristics based on the number of bound parameters and a predicate's declared modes to make an educated guess about the best execution order.

The second example is similar but more complex and illustrates that some execution orders are expressly prohibited by the mode system.

```
re_name(?drawMethod,/^draw/), interface(?IFigure),
name(?IFigure,Figure), subtype+(?IFigure,?Figure),
method(?Figure,?drawMethod)
```

In this query, the execution of the re_name subexpression must be postponed at least until the ?drawMethod variable is bound to an actual value. The TyRuBa mode system will pick an ordering that satisfies this constraint, as well as the preference to execute the name subexpression first.

Our experience suggests it is more intuitive for users unfamiliar with a logic programming language to write conjuncts in any order and think of them as semantically equivalent, than to consider the operational semantics of different execution orders.

5.3   Configuration-Cost Profile

We end this section with an analysis of the configuration-cost profile for the basic-level user. Recall that the customization-cost profile of a mechanism is a characterization of its cost versus flexibility trade-off. We therefore perform an analysis in terms of a) limitations of the mechanism b) cost of the mechanism. We will argue that both in terms of cost and limitations the basic-level configuration interface fits somewhere in the middle of the spectrum.

We can divide the user's cost into two kinds of effort: effort to learn the query language and effort to actually formulate a query. Both of these costs are clearly higher than respective costs to click on GUI buttons which requires little effort to learn or to use.

Both of these costs are at the same time considerably lower than similar costs associated with developing a plugin in Java. Specifically, learning to use a plugin architecture is very costly because the APIs and XML configuration files associated with a plugin architecture have a complexity that is orders of magnitude higher than that of the JQuery query language. As a point of comparison, we determined the minimal subset of Eclipse 3.1 public APIs that is required for the compilation of JQuery. This subset declares 241 public types and 2837 public methods. In contrast, the JQuery query language defines only 13 types and 53 predicates over those types. We believe the difference outweighs the advantage that plugin developers may gain from being able to program in the familiar Java language. A similar order-of-magnitude difference is apparent in the effort of formulating a query versus implementing a plugin. A typical query is a handful of lines of declarative code; the implementation of a plugin ranges in the thousands of lines. For example the implementation of JQuery itself consists of 11019 commented lines of Java code, not including the implementation of the query engine.

Of course, the reduction in complexity implies a loss of flexibility. The basic-level configuration interface does not provide full control over all aspects of a browser's behavior, or not even over some configurable aspects of the tool that are only accessible at the advanced level.

Some limitations that apply specifically to basic-level users are as follows. First, edits to a browser definition through the GUI only affect the current instance of the browser but not new instances created later. Second, the structure of JQuery's menus can not be changed by basic users because this requires editing the configuration files. Third, basic users cannot define browsers with recursive structure such as for example a type-hierarchy or call-hierarchy browser.

There are also limitations that are a result of the limits of the source model. Basically, if information about the program structure is not present in the source-model or derivable from it, than no amount of creativity can produce that information. These limitations affect basic and advanced users alike. A plugin implementor on the other hand has direct access to extensive APIs and if that is not sufficient they have the option of implementing their own program analyzer.

In conclusion, the above analysis puts JQuery's basic-level configuration cost profile clearly in the middle between GUI controls and plugins.

6   Advanced Configuration

In this section we discuss the level of configurability available to advanced users willing to learn the TyRuBa programming language and the structure of JQuery's configuration files. Compared to basic users advanced users gain additional abilities:

1. to effect permanent changes to an existing browser's definition.
2. to define new browsers and add them permanently to JQuery's menu hierarchy.
3. to define recursive browsers.
4. to extend the query language with new predicates.

6.1   The Advanced Configuration Interface

The principle behind the advanced configuration interface is that whenever JQuery needs to make a decision about what to display or do, and this is supposed to be configurable, JQuery launches a query, asking the TyRuBa engine what it should do. Thus, the configuration interface takes the form of a set of predicates that are declared by JQuery but implemented in configuration files. The configuration files are TyRuBa include files that get loaded dynamically by JQuery. These files provide logic facts and rules that determine a significant portion of JQuery's functionality. To save space we limit ourselves to discussing two illustrative examples.

The first example is the definition of the "Inverted Hierarchy" sub-browser shown in Figure 2 and its corresponding menu item in JQuery's GUI. The relevant predicate in the configuration interface is declared as follows:

```
// ------------------------------------------------------------------
// A menuItem is defined follows:
//
// menuItem(?this, label, queryStr, [varName0, varsName1, ...])
//        :- applicabilityExp.
// ------------------------------------------------------------------

menuItem :: Object, [String], String, [String]
MODES
    (BOUND,FREE,FREE,FREE) IS NONDET
END
```

We stress that the *declaration* of this predicate is *not* in the configuration files, but rather is provided by JQuery as part of its definition of the configuration interface. The role of the declaration is to establish a contract between the JQuery GUI which calls it, and the configuration files that provide the implementation. The "Inverted Hierarchy" menu item is defined by the following configuration rule:

```
menuItem(?this, ["Inheritance", "Inverted Hierarchy"],
        "inv_hierarchy(?this,?IH)", ["?IH"])
:- Type(?this).
```

When a user clicks on an element in the GUI, JQuery calls the `menuItem` predicate, binding the `?this` parameter to the element. The second parameter will be bound by the rule to a list of strings representing a path in the menu/sub-menu hierarchy. In this case it indicates the creation of a menu item "Inverted Hierarchy" in the "Inheritance" menu. This rule's condition appropriately restricts its

applicability to elements of type Type. The second and third parameters, also
bound by the rule, correspond to the selection and organization criterion for the
sub-browser created by invoking this menu. Their meaning is as described in
Section 5. However, for simplicity, we neglected to mention that when variables
are bound to list values, they are "unfolded" to construct consecutive levels of
the tree. This mechanism enables the definition of recursive browsers. In this
example, the inv_hierarchy auxiliary predicate, recursively constructs paths in
the inverted-hierarchy tree:

```
inv_hierarchy :: Type,[Type]
MODES   (B,F) IS NONDET    END

inv_hierarchy(?T, []) :- NOT(subtype(?,?T)).
inv_hierarchy(?Sub,[?Super|?R])
   :- subtype(?Super,?Sub), inv_hierarchy(?Super,?R).
```

Note: the ? variable in TyRuBa is similar to Prolog's _ variable.

As a second example, we show how this mechanism makes it possible to
dynamically construct menu structures dependent on properties of the element
clicked on:

```
menuItem(?this, ["Members","Methods..."], ?name],
        {child(??this,??M), method(??M),name(??M,?name)}, ["?M"], )
:- Type(?this), method(?this, ?M), name(?M, ?name).
```

The text within {} is a string template where variables inside the braces are
substituted by their values. Variable substitution can be prevented by escaping
them with an extra ?). Interesting in this example is how the variable ?name
bound by the rule's condition is used to construct the menu label as well as the
selection criterion.

6.2   Customization-Cost Profile

It should be clear by now that the advanced configuration level represents yet
another point in the configuration-cost profile spectrum which is situated somewhere in between that of the basic-level and the plugin architecture.

In comparison to the basic-level, this mechanism offers strictly more flexibility
than the basic level and at a strictly higher cost.

In comparison to plugins and in terms of flexibility, in spite offering a lot of
flexibility to specify new behavior in logic rules and queries, JQuery is bound
by the limitations of the targeted design space outlined in Section 2. Other limitations such as those caused by what is (not) reified by the source model also
still apply. In terms of cost, an advanced user must be fluent in the TyRuBa
programming language. This requires considerable effort in learning a non familiar and unconventional programming language. Assuming that the language
barrier can be overcome, the customization cost is an order of magnitude below that of implementing a plugin. As a point of comparison, the most complex
browser definition in JQuery's configuration files defines the "Method Hierarchy"

sub-browser showing how a given method is overridden repeatedly in different classes in its class hierarchy. It defines two auxiliary predicates (to construct a hierarchy of alternating methods and classes in two steps) and consists of a total of 24 lines of TyRuBa code. As another point of comparison, the two default configuration files "`topQuery.rub`" and "`menu.rub`" which define a total of 15 TopLevel browsers and 54 sub-browsers are 73 and 352 lines of TyRuBa code respectively (this includes blank lines and comments). Even when taken together there is still an order of magnitude difference from the typically thousands of lines of Java code required to implement a browser plugin.

7   Related Work

JQuery derives much of its flexibility and functionality from the expressive power of the underlying query engine. The idea of using structural queries — in a logic language or another sufficiently powerful query language — as a basis for constructing software development tools is not new. Some examples of other systems based on structural source code querying are SOUL [17], ASTLog [7], GraphLog [6], Coven [4] and Stellation [5]. SOUL is a logic query language integrated with the Smalltalk development environment. ASTLog is a logic query language for querying C++ abstract syntax trees. GraphLog is a logic based graphical query language in which both queries and query results are represented as Graphs. Coven and Stellation are software configuration management tools, equipped with an SQL-like query language for the retrieval of software units. In all these tools, software queries can be used by developers in the process of exploring code. However, they do not support the use of the query language in that same way that JQuery does as a means to configure browsers, sub-browsers and the menu hierarchy.

There are numerous tools (e.g. Rigi [12], SHriMP [16], Ciao [3], SVT [9] and GraphLog [6]) that provide different ways to visualize the structure of a software system. JQuery is related to these tools in that a code browser is one kind of visualization. SVT [9] is most closely related. It is a configurable software visualization framework that relies on Prolog as a configuration language. However, JQuery's differs in that its configuration language is more declarative and that its targeted design space is (deliberately) more limited. Consequently JQuery strikes a completely different balance between cost and flexibility of its configuration interface.

8   Discussion and Future Work

One area for future research is extending and broadening the targeted design space: to other types of IDE extensions and to be less Java specific.

A second area for future research is the generation of efficient implementations from declarative browser specifications. In this paper, we have talked about configuration cost entirely in terms of user effort. We have not considered runtime and memory efficiency of the browsers. Although efficiency was never the main concern for our work, it has become clear that it affects the practical usability of a tool like JQuery. Indeed, such concerns have been an ongoing issue and the TyRuBa query engine has had considerable work put into it in order to meet the demands of producing browsers from realistic code bases in an interactive environment. JQuery produced browsers, in its current implementation, cannot compete with hand-crafted plugins. However, we believe that the declarative nature of the specification should provide ample opportunities for automatic optimizations and compilation. This is a very interesting area for future research that could tap into a wealth of knowledge from databases and logic programming languages.

9   Conclusion

We discussed how modern IDEs offer two levels of configurability that have cost-profiles at the extreme ends of a spectrum. One mechanism is GUI-based and is very easy and cheap to use but offers limited flexibility. Another is very hard and expensive to use but allows complete control by linking in executable imperative-style code.

We argued that the space in the middle between those two extremes is also interesting and can be accessed by designing a configuration interface targeted for a particular domain on top of a declarative programming language. We illustrated this approach by presenting the JQuery tool, a highly configurable Java code browsing tool that employs a declarative logic programming language at the core of its configuration mechanism. We argued that JQuery achieves a very open-ended configuration model that is still orders of magnitude cheaper in terms of user effort than a typical plugin architecture.

Acknowledgments

This work was supported in part by IBM Canada, NSERC and the University of British Columbia. We thank the anonymous PADL reviewers for their constructive criticism. We thank Doug Janzen and Rajeswari Rajagopalan for their many contributions without which this paper would not have been possible.

References

1. JHotDraw. http://www.jhotdraw.org/, 2002.
2. Weidong Chen and David S. Warren. Tabled evaluation with delaying for general logic programs. *J. ACM*, 43(1):20–74, 1996.
3. Yih-Farn R. Chen, Glenn S. Fowler, Eleftherios Koutsofios, and Ryan S. Wallach. Ciao: A graphical navigator for software and document repositories. In *Proc. Int. Conf. Software Maintenance, ICSM*, pages 66–75. IEEE Computer Society, 1995.
4. Mark C. Chu-Carroll and Sara Sprenkle. Coven: brewing better collaboration through software configuration management. In *Proceedings of the eighth international symposium on Foundations of software engineering for twenty-first century applications*, pages 88–97. ACM, 2000.

5. Mark C. Chu-Carroll, James Wright, and David Shield. Aspect-oriented programming: Supporting aggregation in fine grained software configuration management. In *Proceedings of the tenth ACM SIGSOFT symposium on Foundations of software engineering*, pages 99–108. ACM, November 2002.

6. Mariano Consens, Alberto Mendelzon, and Arthur Ryman. Visualizing and querying software structures. In *ICSE '92: Proceedings of the 14th international conference on Software engineering*, pages 138–156, New York, NY, USA, 1992. ACM Press.

7. R.F. Crew. Astlog: A language for examining abstract syntax trees. In *Proceedings of the USENIX Conference on Domain-Specific Languages*, Santa Barbara, California, October 1997.

8. Kris De Volder. Tyruba website. http://tyruba.sourceforge.net.

9. Calum A. McK. Grant. *Software Visualization In Prolog.* PhD thesis, Queens College, Cambridge, December 1999.

10. F. Henderson, T. Conway, Z. Somogyi, and D. Jeffery. The mercury language reference manual, 1996.

11. Doug Janzen and Kris De Volder. Navigating and querying code without getting lost. In *AOSD '03: Proceedings of the 2nd international conference on Aspect-oriented software development*, pages 178–187, New York, NY, USA, 2003. ACM Press.

12. H. Muller, K. Wong, and S. Tilley. Understanding software systems using reverse engineering technology. In *The 62nd Congress of L'Association Canadienne Francaise pour l'Avancement des Sciences Proceedings (ACFAS)*, 1994.

13. Rajeswari Rajagopalan. Qjbrowser: A query-based approach to explore crosscutting concerns. Master's thesis, University of British Columbia, 2002.

14. Jim Riecken and Kris De Volder. Jquery website. http://jquery.cs.ubc.ca.

15. Martin P. Robillard and Gail C. Murphy. Concern Graphs: Finding and describing concerns using structural program dependencies. In *Proc. of International Conference on Software Engineering*, 2002.

16. M.-A. D. Storey, C. Best, and J. Michaud. Shrimp views: An interactive and customizable environment for software exploration. In *Proc. of International Workshop on Program Comprehension (IWPC '2001)*, 2001.

17. Roel Wuyts. Declarative reasoning about the structure of object-oriented systems. In *Proceeding of TOOLS USA '98 Conference*, pages 112–124. IEEE Computer Society Press, 1998.

A Hybrid BDD and SAT Finite Domain Constraint Solver

Peter Hawkins and Peter J. Stuckey

NICTA Victoria Laboratory,
Department of Computer Science and Software Engineering,
The University of Melbourne, Vic. 3010, Australia
{hawkinsp, pjs}@cs.mu.oz.au

Abstract. Finite-domain constraint solvers based on Binary Decision Diagrams (BDDs) are a powerful technique for solving constraint problems over finite set and integer variables represented as Boolean formulæ. Boolean Satisfiability (SAT) solvers are another form of constraint solver that operate on constraints on Boolean variables expressed in clausal form. Modern SAT solvers have highly optimized propagation mechanisms and also incorporate efficient conflict-clause learning algorithms and effective search heuristics based on variable activity, but these techniques have not been widely used in finite-domain solvers. In this paper we show how to construct a hybrid BDD and SAT solver which inherits the advantages of both solvers simultaneously. The hybrid solver makes use of an efficient algorithm for capturing the inferences of a finite-domain constraint solver in clausal form, allowing us to automatically and transparently construct a SAT model of a finite-domain constraint problem. Finally, we present experimental results demonstrating that the hybrid solver can outperform both SAT and finite-domain solvers by a substantial margin.

1 Introduction

Finite-domain constraint satisfaction problems (CSPs) are an important class of problems with a wide variety of practical applications. There are many competing approaches for solving such problems, including propagation-based constraint solvers and Boolean Satisfiability (SAT) solvers.

We have previously shown how to represent many finite-domain constraint problems using Binary Decision Diagrams (BDDs) by modeling problems in terms of Boolean variables and representing both variable domains and constraints as formulæ over these variables [10]. The BDD representation of these formulæ allows us to "package" together groups of Boolean variables, where each group represents a set, multiset, or integer variable, and to make inferences on the sets of values that each group of variables can take *simultaneously*. This allows us to describe bounds, domain, and other types of propagation using BDD operations.

Another important class of finite-domain CSPs is the class of Boolean Satisfiability problems. While there is a variety of algorithms for solving SAT problems,

P. Van Hentenryck (Ed.): PADL 2006, LNCS 3819, pp. 103–117, 2006.
© Springer-Verlag Berlin Heidelberg 2006

some of the most successful complete SAT solvers are based on variants of the Davis-Putnam-Logemann-Loveland (DPLL) algorithm [6]. The basic algorithm has existed for over forty years, and a great deal of effort has gone into producing robust and efficient implementations. Three key elements of a modern SAT solver are a suitable branching heuristic, an efficient implementation of propagation, and the use of conflict-directed learning [22].

Most SAT solvers operate on problems expressed as a set of clauses, (although recently there has been some interest in non-clausal representations for SAT problems [20]). This uniform representation allows the use of highly efficient data structures for performing unit propagation, and the generation of conflict clauses in order to avoid repeating the same subsearch, as well to drive heuristics that lead the search to new parts of the search space.

Modern SAT solvers are very effective on some kinds of problems, and practical SAT solvers such as MiniSAT [8] have been successfully applied to a wide range of problems including electronic circuit fault detection and software verification. The main disadvantage of SAT solvers is that some kinds of constraints are hard to model efficiently using clauses—for example the set constraint $|S| = k$ requires $\binom{n}{k-1} + \binom{n}{k+1}$ clauses to express, and the resulting propagation is weak.

Although both BDD and SAT solvers are Boolean solvers, they represent different tradeoffs in the general propagation-search paradigm: BDDs are expensive to manipulate but produce powerful propagation and minimize search, while SAT propagation is quick and weak, leading to more search but hopefully requiring less time overall. One of the unique advantages of the SAT solver comes from the use of nogood learning, which allows substantial search space reductions for structured problems. To a certain extent the strengths of each solver are complementary, and in this paper we show how to create a hybrid solver that inherits from both.

In this paper, we present a novel approach to combining a BDD-based finite-domain constraint solver and a SAT solver into an efficient hybrid constraint solver. While dual modeling is not new, the key contribution of this paper is an efficient algorithm for capturing the inferences of a finite-domain solver in clausal form. Not only does this allow us to use the conflict-directed learning and backjumping algorithms of a SAT solver in a finite-domain constraint solver, we can also use this algorithm to lazily construct a SAT model from a finite-domain constraint problem represented in BDD form, giving us some of the speed advantages of a SAT solver without the need for an explicit clausal model of a problem.

The contributions of this paper are:

- We show how we can construct a hybrid constraint solver by pairing finite-domain variables with a dual Boolean representation.
- We show how we can efficiently convert the inferences performed by a BDD based solver into clausal form. These inferences can be used to lazily construct a SAT model of a problem from a finite-domain model, and allow us to apply conflict-directed learning techniques to the inferences of a finite-domain solver.
- We demonstrate experimentally that combining BDD and SAT solvers can substantially improve performance on some set benchmarks.

2   Propagation-Based Constraint Solving, BDDs and SAT

In this section we introduce definitions and notation for the rest of the paper. Most of these definitions are standard (see e.g. [15]).

We consider a typed set of variables $\mathcal{V} = \mathcal{V}_I \cup \mathcal{V}_S$ made up of *integer* variables $\mathcal{V}_I$, for which we use lower case letters such as x and y, and *sets of integers* variables $\mathcal{V}_S$, for which we use upper case letters such as S and T.

A *domain* D is a complete mapping from a fixed (countable) set of variables $\mathcal{V}$ to finite sets of integers (for the integer variables in $\mathcal{V}_I$) and to finite sets of finite sets of integers (for the set variables in $\mathcal{V}_S$). A domain D_1 is said to be *stronger* than a domain D_2, written $D_1 \sqsubseteq D_2$, if $D_1(v) \subseteq D_2(v)$ for all $v \in \mathcal{V}$.

We frequently use *set range* notation: $[L .. U]$ denotes the set of sets of integers $\{A \mid L \subseteq A \subseteq U\}$ when L and U are sets of integers. A set is said to be *convex* if it can be expressed as a range. The *convex closure* of a set S is the smallest range that includes S, and is written $conv(S)$. For example $conv(\{\{1,3\}, \{1,4,5\}, \{1,4,6\}\}) = [\{1\} .. \{1,3,4,5,6\}]$. We lift the concepts of convex and convex closure to domains in the natural way.

A *valuation* θ is a mapping of integer and set variables to correspondingly typed values, written $\{x_1 \mapsto d_1, \ldots, x_n \mapsto d_n, S_1 \mapsto A_1, \ldots, S_m \mapsto A_m\}$. We extend the valuation θ to map expressions or constraints involving the variables in the natural way. Let *vars* be the function that returns the set of variables appearing in an expression, constraint or valuation. In an abuse of notation, we define a valuation θ to be an element of a domain D, written $\theta \in D$, if $\theta(v_i) \in D(v_i)$ for all $v_i \in vars(\theta)$.

A constraint is a restriction placed on the allowable values for a set of variables. We shall be interested in constraints over integer and set variables. We define the *solutions* of a constraint c to be the set of valuations θ that make that constraint true, i.e. $solns(c) = \{\theta \mid (vars(\theta) = vars(c)) \wedge (\models \theta(c))\}$

We associate a *propagator* with every constraint. A propagator f is a monotonically decreasing function from domains to domains, so $D_1 \sqsubseteq D_2$ implies that $f(D_1) \sqsubseteq f(D_2)$, and $f(D) \sqsubseteq D$. A propagator f is *correct* for a constraint c if and only if for all domains D: $\{\theta \mid \theta \in D\} \cap solns(c) = \{\theta \mid \theta \in f(D)\} \cap solns(c)$ This is a weak restriction since, for example, the identity propagator is correct for any constraints. We assume that all propagators are correct.

A *set bounds propagator* f for constraint c is a propagator that maps convex domains to convex domains. For set problems typically set bounds propagators are employed.

A *propagation solver* for a set of propagators F and a domain D repeatedly applies the propagators in F starting from the domain D until a fixpoint is reached.

2.1   Binary Decision Diagrams

A *Reduced Ordered Binary Decision Diagram* (ROBDD) is canonical representation of a propositional expression (up to reordering on the propositions), which permits an efficient implementation of many Boolean function operations, including conjunction ($\land$), disjunction ($\lor$), existential quantification ($\exists$). In an ROBDD each node is either 1 (true) or 0 (false) or of the form $n(v, t, e)$ where v is a Boolean variable, and t and e are ROBDDs. For more details the reader is referred to the work of Bryant [3]. The modeling of constraint problems using ROBDDs is discussed extensively in [10].

2.2 SAT and Unit Propagation

A *proposition* $p \in \mathcal{P}$ is a Boolean variable, where $\mathcal{P}$ denotes the universe of Boolean variables. A *literal* l is either a proposition p or its negation $\neg p$. The *complement* of a literal l, $\neg l$ is $\neg p$ if $l = p$ or p if $l = \neg p$. A *clause* C is a disjunction of literals. An *assignment* is a set of literals A such that $\forall p \in \mathcal{P}.\{p, \neg p\} \nsubseteq A$. An assignment A *satisfies* a clause C if one of the literals in C appears in A.

A SAT solver takes a conjunction (or set) of clauses and determines if there is an assignment that simultaneously satisfies all the clauses. Complete SAT solvers typically involve some form of the DPLL algorithm which combines search and propagation by recursively fixing the value of a proposition to either 1 (true) or 0 (false) and using unit propagation to determine the logical consequences of each decision made so far. The unit propagation algorithm finds all clauses $p_1 \lor p_2 \lor \ldots \lor p_k$ where at least $k - 1$ of the literals are known to be false, and asserts the remaining literal to be true (since it is the only possible way for the clause to be satisfied). If all k literals are known to be false, then we have discovered a conflict in the set of assignments made so far and we must backtrack. Unit propagation can be performed very efficiently by using watched literal techniques [16].

Modern SAT solvers make use of *nogood learning* in order to reduce the search space, and guide search away from unprofitable areas. Nogood learning relies on building an *implication graph* for values derived by unit propagation (although the graph is usually represented implicitly). The implication graph is a directed acyclic graph where the nodes $l@t$ are pairs of literal l and timestamp t indicating the time the literal became known.

Unit propagation on a clause $l_1 \lor \cdots \lor l_n$ from nodes $\neg l_1@t_1, \ldots, \neg l_{i-1}@t_{i-1}, \neg l_{i+1}@t_{i+1}, \ldots, \neg l_n@t_n, 1 \leq i \leq n$ adds a new node $l_i@t_i$ where t_i is the maximum timestamp $t_i = \max\{t_1, \ldots, t_{i-1}, t_{i+1}, \ldots, t_n\}$ as well as arcs $\neg l_j@t_j \rightarrow l_i@t_i, 1 \leq j \neq i \leq n$. If we discover a conflict from a clause $l_1 \lor \cdots \lor l_n$ using literals $\neg l_1@t_1, \ldots, \neg l_n@t_n$, we add a node $\perp@t$ where $t = max(t_1, \ldots t_n)$ and arcs $\neg l_i@t_i \rightarrow \perp@t, 1 \leq i \leq n$.

When we derive a contradiction then any cut across the graph that leaves the contradiction on one side (the conflict side), and all the decisions (nodes without incoming arcs) on the other side (the reason side) defines a *nogood*. Nogoods can be added to the solver's store of learnt clauses in order to assist with future decisions.

We have a choice of which cut of a conflict graph to take. The *decision cut* simply keeps all the decisions (nodes without parents) (which corresponds to the cut commonly chosen by Conflict-Directed Backjumping schemes in a CSP

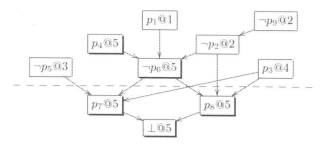

Fig. 1. An example implication graph, showing a possible set of implications on the set of clauses $(p_9 \vee \neg p_2) \wedge (\neg p_1 \vee p_2 \vee \neg p_4 \vee \neg p_6) \wedge (\neg p_3 \vee p_5 \vee p_6 \vee p_7) \wedge (p_2 \vee \neg p_3 \vee p_6 \vee p_8) \wedge (\neg p_7 \vee \neg p_8)$

context). A cut scheme that has been shown to be more effective experimentally in the SAT context, called 1-UIP [23], is to choose a cut that places only nodes with the same timestamp as the contradiction on the conflict side; of these, only nodes between the Unique Intersection Point (a node which dominates all nodes between the conflict and itself) closest to the conflict and the conflict itself are placed on the conflict side.

Example 1. Consider the implication graph shown in Figure 1. All the nodes with the same timestamp as the contradiction are shown with shadow. The 1-UIP cut is shown as the dashed line, since $\neg p_6$ is the closest node to the conflict which is included on all paths from the decision at time 5 to the conflict. The nogood generated is $p_2 \vee \neg p_3 \vee p_5 \vee p_6$. The decision cut generates $\neg p_1 \vee \neg p_3 \vee \neg p_4 \vee p_5 \vee p_9$.

3   A Hybrid SAT and Finite-Domain Constraint Solver

Since the powerful inference abilities of a finite-domain constraint solver and the efficient propagation and conflict-directed learning of a SAT solver are to some extent complementary, we would like to construct a hybrid solver that combines the advantages of both. Such a hybrid solver can be created through a process of dual modeling, where the same constraint problem is modeled in multiple cooperating solvers.

There are several important points we must consider when creating a dual model of a constraint problem:

- How should the problem variables and their domains be modeled in each solver?
- How should deductions be communicated between the two solvers during the search process?
- Which of the problem constraints be modeled in each solver, and how should they be modeled?
- How should the execution of the search procedure and the two solvers be scheduled?

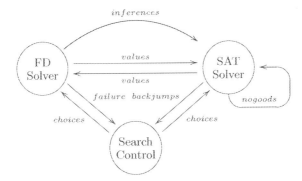

Fig. 2. Interactions between FD and SAT solvers and search

In the next three sections we outline our approach to these problems. An illustration of the interaction of the two solvers is shown in Figure 2.

3.1 Boolean Modeling of Constraint Variables and Domains

As a first step in constructing a hybrid model of a constraint problem, we need to establish how we will represent the constrained variables and their domains in each solver. Since finite-domain solvers are more expressive than Boolean models, it is reasonable to assume that we already have a finite-domain model for a problem, and we need only consider the how to represent finite-domain variables and domains in a propositional manner suitable for a SAT solver

Note that in the specific case of our hybrid solver the finite-domain solver is based on BDDs and also operates using a very similar Boolean model [10], but the discussion here is completely general and independent of the structure of the finite-domain solver.

Set variables are natural to model in terms of propositional logic. Suppose S is a set variable over a domain $[\emptyset \,..\, \{1, \ldots, n\}]$. We can model S as a set of propositions $P(S) = \{S_1, \ldots, S_n\}$, where $S_i \leftrightarrow i \in S$. Constraints then map to propositional formulæ over these variables. For example, the expression $S = A$ for some fixed set A in $[\emptyset \,..\, \{1, \ldots, n\}]$ is equivalent to the propositional formula $B(S = A) = \bigwedge_{i=1}^{n} S_i \leftrightarrow (i \in A)$.

Finite domain integer variables do not have such a natural propositional representation. Many encodings are possible — we outline here direct and log encodings (for more details, see, e.g. [21]).

In the *direct* or unary encoding, we model a finite domain integer variable x over a domain $\{0, \ldots, n\}$ by the propositions $P(x) = \{x_0, \ldots, x_n\}$ where x_i holds if and only if $x = i$. Since this representation would allow x to take on multiple values at once, we must also add constraints stipulating that x must take exactly one value: $(x_0 \vee \cdots \vee x_n) \wedge \bigwedge_{i=0}^{n-1} \bigwedge_{j=i+1}^{n} \neg x_i \vee \neg x_j$. The expression $x = i$ for a fixed value i is modeled by the propositional formula $B(x = i) = x_i \wedge \bigwedge_{j=0, j \neq i}^{n} \neg x_j$. Note that we can think of the direct encoding as encoding integers as singleton sets.

Another representation of finite domain integer variables is a *log* or binary encoding, which uses propositions $P(x) = \{x_0, x_1, \ldots, x_k\}$ that correspond to a binary representation $x = x_0 + 2x_1 + \cdots + 2^k x_k$, where $k = \lfloor \log_2 n \rfloor$. The expression $x = i$ for a fixed value i is modeled as the propositional formula $B(x = i) = \bigwedge_{j=0}^{k} (x_j \leftrightarrow i_j)$ where i_j, $0 \leq j \leq k$ is the jth bit of the binary encoding of the number i. The log encoding does not require any auxiliary constraints to ensure that each variable takes a single value. The log encoding is known to produce weaker unit propagation than the direct encoding [21] but produces smaller models in some cases and allows operations such as addition to be defined more compactly.

Since we can map set or integer values to propositional formulæ, we can easily map the domains of constrained variables as well. Given a variable v, we can define the propositional representation $B(D(v))$ of the domain $D(v)$ as $B(D(v)) = \bigvee_{d \in D(v)} B(v = d)$. Note that $B(D(v))$ is equivalent to a conjunction of propositions if v is a set variable and $D(v)$ is a convex set, or if v is an arbitrary integer variable in the direct encoding. However, it is important to note that with any of these encodings we can in theory represent arbitrary domains, not necessarily just those defined by conjunctions of propositions. However, SAT solvers are limited to domains represented as conjunctions of propositions, and hence we confine our attention to conjunctive domains in this paper.

Example 2. Consider the set variable S which ranges over $[\emptyset \mathbin{..} \{1, 2, 3\}]$, then $P(S) = \{S_1, S_2, S_3\}$. Then for the domain $D(S) = [\{1\} \mathbin{..} \{1, 2\}]$ we have $B(D(S)) = S_1 \wedge \neg S_3$. For the non convex domain $D'(S) = \{\{1\}, \{2, 3\}\}$ then $B(D'(S)) = (S_1 \wedge \neg S_2 \wedge \neg S_3) \vee (\neg S_1 \wedge S_2 \wedge S_3)$.

For an integer x ranging over $\{0, 1, 2, 3\}$ then the domain $D(x) = \{1, 2\}$ in the direct encoding is simply $B(D(x)) = \neg x_0 \wedge \neg x_3$, while in the log encoding it is $B(D(x)) = (x_0 \wedge \neg x_1) \vee (\neg x_0 \wedge x_1)$.

3.2   Channeling Constraints and Clause Generators

The most interesting part of constructing a dual solver is the channeling of information between the finite-domain and SAT solvers. The standard approach to channeling information between solvers is to create channeling constraints, which ensure that the domains of the corresponding variables in each solver are equal. While we could use such an approach when coupling a SAT solver and a finite-domain solver, simply communicating information about the values in a domain is insufficient to allow the SAT solver to build an inference graph and perform nogood computations. In order for the SAT solver to compute meaningful nogoods we also need to communicate the *reasons* for any deductions made by finite-domain constraint propagation.

Our basic strategy is for each proposition p inferred through finite-domain propagation we will derive an *inference clause*. An inference clause is a SAT clause that is a logical consequence of a finite-domain propagator, and that would have derived p through unit propagation from the variables that were fixed at the time that the finite-domain propagator deduced p. This new clause effectively encapsulates an inference of a finite-domain propagator in a form that the SAT solver can understand.

By adding inference clauses to the clause set of the SAT solver, we can perform nogood learning and conflict-directed backjumping on the inferences of the finite-domain solver. We can either add inference clauses explicitly to the SAT solver's store of learnt clauses, or extend the SAT solver so that inference clauses are used implicitly for performing nogood calculations. In the former case, we are effectively using finite-domain propagators as *generators* for SAT clauses, thus removing the need for a SAT model of the problem. As the search progresses and more inference clauses are added, effectively a SAT model of each finite domain constraint is constructed.

While it would be possible to augment any finite-domain solver to generate inference clauses by extending the propagator implementations on a case-by-case basis, since our FD solver is based on BDDs we can derive these clauses efficiently and automatically.

Let f be a propagator for a constraint c and D be a domain, and suppose $f(D) = D'$ where $D' \neq D$. Let $vars(c) = \{v_1, \ldots, v_n\}$. Clearly we have that $(c \wedge \bigwedge_{i=1}^{n} \bigvee_{x \in D(v_i)} v_i = x) \rightarrow \bigwedge_{i=1}^{n} \bigvee_{x \in D'(v_i)} v_i = x$. In the Boolean formalism this is equivalent to $(B(c) \wedge \bigwedge_{i=1}^{n} B(D(v_i))) \rightarrow \bigwedge_{i=1}^{n} B(D'(v_i))$, where $B(c)$ is a formula representing constraint c.

Now suppose $B(D)$ and $B(D')$ are conjunctions of propositions. This assumption holds if we restrict ourselves to use set bounds propagators [10]. We can treat these conjunctions as sets. Let $p \in B(D'(v_i)) \setminus B(D(v_i))$ be a *newly inferred proposition*. Then in any context where the constraint c holds, the clause $(\bigwedge_{i=1}^{n} B(D(v_i))) \rightarrow p$ or equivalently $(\bigvee_{i=1}^{n} \neg B(D(v_i))) \vee p$ also holds, and p would have been derived from this clause through unit propagation. We call this clause the *simple inference* of p, which we can add as a new (redundant) constraint.

Example 3. Consider the constraint $c \equiv |S| = x$ where S ranges over $[\emptyset \mathbin{..} \{1, \ldots, 5\}]$ and x ranges over $\{0, 1, 2, 3, 4, 5\}$. Let $D(S) = [\{1, 2\}, \{1, 2, 4\}]$ and $D(x) = \{3, 4, 5\}$. Then the strongest set bounds propagator f for c is such that $f(D) = D'$ where $D'(S) = [\{1, 2, 4\}, \{1, 2, 4\}]$, $D'(x) = \{3\}$.

In the Boolean representation $B(D(S)) = S_1 \wedge S_2 \wedge \neg S_3 \wedge \neg S_5$, $B(D(x)) = \neg x_0 \wedge \neg x_1 \wedge \neg x_2$, $B(D'(S)) = S_1 \wedge S_2 \wedge \neg S_3 \wedge S_4 \wedge \neg S_5$, and $B(D'(x)) = \neg x_0 \wedge \neg x_1 \wedge \neg x_2 \wedge x_3 \wedge \neg x_4 \wedge \neg x_5$. The newly inferred propositions are S_4, $\neg x_4$, $\neg x_5$, and x_3. Considering $\neg x_4$, we can see that the clause $(S_1 \wedge S_2 \wedge \neg S_3 \wedge \neg S_5 \wedge \neg x_0 \wedge \neg x_1 \wedge \neg x_2) \rightarrow \neg x_4$ or equivalently $\neg S_1 \vee \neg S_2 \vee S_3 \vee S_5 \vee x_0 \vee x_1 \vee x_2 \vee \neg x_4$ is valid and captures the deduction on x_4 made by the constraint propagation. Similarly we can produce one clause for each of the other propositions deduced by propagation.

The simple clauses generated above, while logically valid, are not minimal, and hence are unlikely to generate much useful propagation since they will only produce inferences when all but one of the Boolean variables in the clause are fixed. Since the decision variables of all of the variables involved in the constraint

```
mininf (p,c,P)
    let M := P
    let {p_1,...,p_m} := P
    for i := 1..m
        if ¬ sat(B(c) ∧ ¬p ∧ (M \ {p_i}))
            M := M \ {p_i}
    return M
```

Fig. 3. A generic algorithm for finding minimal reasons for inferences

are included in the clause, we are unlikely to revisit this particular combination of variable assignments again as the search progresses. In order to maximize the chance of generating useful inferences, we need to generate minimal reasons for each inference.

We define a *minimal inference* of p as follows. Let $P = \bigcup_{i=1}^{n} B(D(v_i)))$ be the set of candidate propositions for the minimal inference of p and let $M = \{m_1, \ldots, m_k\} \subseteq P$. We say M is a sufficient set of reasons for p if $(B(c) \wedge \bigwedge_{j=1}^{k} m_j) \rightarrow p$. We say M is a minimal set of reasons for p if M is a sufficient set of reasons for p and for any sufficient set $N \subseteq M$ we have $M = N$.

Example 4. For the propagation in Example 3 some minimal reasons define the inference clauses:

$$(S_1 \wedge S_2 \wedge \neg S_3 \wedge \neg S_5 \wedge \neg x_0 \wedge \neg x_1 \wedge \neg x_2) \rightarrow S_4$$
$$(\neg S_3 \wedge \neg S_5) \rightarrow \neg x_4$$
$$\neg S_3 \rightarrow \neg x_5$$
$$(S_1 \wedge S_2 \wedge \neg S_3 \wedge \neg S_5 \wedge \neg x_2) \rightarrow x_3$$

Note that other minimal reasons exist, e.g. $\neg S_5 \rightarrow \neg x_5$.

In general a minimal set of reasons is not unique. It is also possible that the same proposition would be inferred by multiple propagators, each propagator producing different minimal sets of reasons, and hence the reasons deduced for the value of a proposition depend on the order of execution of the propagators.

A generic algorithm for computing minimal reasons for inferences is shown in Figure 3. This algorithm needs $O(n)$ satisfiability checks where n is the number of candidate propositions. Such an algorithm would be prohibitive to use in general, although a divide-and-conquer version similar to the QUICKXPLAIN algorithm of [11] would perform better.

However, we can specialize this algorithm for use in a BDD context, leading to an efficient algorithm for inferring a minimal set of reasons for a deduction p. First we generate the BDD for $G = \bar{\exists}_{vars(P)} B(c) \wedge \neg p$, that is the constraint c with the information that p is false, restricted to the propositions P of interest in determining the minimal set M. We then recursively visit the BDD G determining whether each proposition in order is required for a contradiction. The resulting algorithm is shown in Figure 4.

```
BDDmininf(G,P,M)
    if G = 0 return M
    let G = n(v, Gᵥ, G₋ᵥ)
    let P = n(vₚ, Pᵥₚ, P₋ᵥₚ)
    if Pᵥₚ = 0 then l := ¬vₚ else l := vₚ
    if v = vₚ then
        if BDDsatconj(G₋ₗ,Pₗ) then return BDDmininf(Gₗ,Pₗ,M ∪ {l})
        else return BDDmininf(Gₗ ∨ G₋ₗ, Pₗ, M)
    else
        return BDDmininf(G,Pₗ,M)
```

Fig. 4. A BDD-based algorithm for finding minimal reasons for inferences

The algorithm works as follows. The initial call is $\mathsf{BDDmininf}(G,\ P,\ \emptyset)$. The first argument is the remaining BDD, the second the remaining set of possible reasons (represented as a conjunction BDD) and the last is the set of propositions in the minimal inference so far (which in practice is also represented by a BDD). The algorithm maintains the invariant that $G \wedge P$ is unsatisfiable.

If the BDD G is 0 ($false$) then no further reasons are required and we return the set M. The BDD cannot be 1 ($true$) since it must be unsatisfiable when conjoined with P. We find the literal l in P with the least variable v_P in the BDD variable ordering. If the variable v at the top of the BDD G is not the same then the literal l is irrelevant since it does not appear in G, and so we recurse, looking at the next least literal. Otherwise we check whether $G_{\neg l} \wedge P_l$ is satisfiable which corresponds to if the variable v takes the opposite value from l. If this is satisfiable then l is required to make a minimal inference, since removing it would lead to something satisfiable with the remainder P_l. Hence we add l to M and follow the l choice in the BDD G recursively. Otherwise l is not required, since the remainder of P is sufficient to ensure that both branches of G are unsatisfiable. We project out the variable v from G obtaining $G_v \vee G_{\neg v}$ (this requires building new BDD nodes) and recursively proceed.

Note that $\mathsf{BDDsatconj}(G, H)$ checks whether the conjunction H is a satisfying assignment for G, and simply requires following the path H in the BDD G. It does not require constructing new BDD nodes.

3.3   Constraint Modeling, Scheduling and Search

We have a great deal of flexibility in modeling the problem constraints in each solver. However, as discussed in Section 3.2, we do not need to construct a model of a constraint problem for the SAT solver — we can lazily construct it from the finite-domain model. However, it is also possible that in some cases better performance may be obtained by an explicit dual model, although this is not borne out by the experiments in Section 4. Due to space constraints we do not discuss explicit SAT models of constraint problems here.

We also have a great deal of flexibility in deciding how to schedule the propagation of the SAT and BDD solvers. In our solver, we choose to treat the SAT solver as a single "propagator" which is executed at a higher priority than any other propagator. This ensures that the cheap SAT inferences are performed before the relatively expensive finite-domain inferences. Various labeling heuristics can be used, and we present experimental results for a sequential labeling heuristic as well as the Variable-State-Independent-Decaying-Sum (VSIDS) SAT solver heuristic.

4   Experimental Results

We have implemented a hybrid BDD and SAT solver in the Mercury system [19]. The BDD solver makes use of the CUDD BDD package [18] while the SAT solver is an interface to MiniSAT [8], but exporting control of search to Mercury.

The "Social Golfers" problem (problem prob010 of CSPLib) is problem commonly used as a benchmark for set CSP solvers. The aim of this problem is to arrange $N = g \times s$ golfers into g groups of s players for each of w weeks, such that no two players play together more than once. We can model this problem as a set constraint problem using a $w \times g$ matrix of set variables v_{ij}, where $1 \leq i \leq w$ is the week index and $1 \leq j \leq g$ is the group index. See [10] for the model in detail, although in this paper we have added constraints that allocate the golfers in sequential order to the first week in order to remove symmetries.

All test cases were run on a cluster of 8 identical 2.4Ghz Pentium 4 machines with 1Gb RAM and 2Gb swap space. Each test case was repeated 3 times, and the lowest of the 3 results used. In the result tables: "*" denotes a test case without a solution, "—" denotes failure to complete a test case within 10 minutes, and "×" denotes an out of memory error.

From Table 1, we can see that the best of the hybrid solvers outperforms the BDD bounds and (split) domain solvers that were presented in [10] on almost all of the test cases.[1] Using simple clause learning (B+SB) is not useful, since the overhead of deriving and storing nogoods is not repaid through search space reduction. The most surprising column is perhaps B+M which shows the overhead of minimizing the clauses without reducing the search space. It appears that generating minimized nogoods requires less than double the time taken for the original propagation. Once we make use of the minimal clauses (B+MB) by recording nogoods and performing backjumping we often improve on the bounds solver, but interestingly adding all of the inferred clauses to the SAT solver (B+MA) can lead to substantial further reductions in the search space. The B+MA column corresponds to a hybrid where in some sense we lazily build a CNF model of the problem using only the "useful" clauses found by the BDD model.

Table 2 presents results obtained using a Variable-State-Independent-Decaying-Sum heuristic, which is commonly used by SAT solvers. This table also contains a comparison with the SAT solvers MiniSAT and zChaff, the pseudo-boolean SAT solver MiniSAT+, and a dual BDD and SAT model with all constraints but cardinality constraints duplicated as SAT clauses. It appears that as in the sequential case, the B+MA technique performs the best out of all of

---

[1] Note that the BDD bounds solver is substantially faster on these examples than solvers such as Eclipse or Mozart due to better modeling capabilities and a more efficient implementation language [10].

Table 1. Performance results for the Social Golfers problem, using a sequential, smallest-element-in-set labeling heuristic. "Domain" = BDD Domain solver of [10]. "Bounds" = BDD Bounds solver of [10]. "B+SB" = Bounds + simple clause learning + backjumping. "B+M" = Bounds + minimized clause learning, no backjumping. "B+MB" = Bounds + minimized clause learning + backjumping. "B+MA" = Bounds + adding minimized clauses to the SAT solver as learnt clauses.

Problem w-g-s	Domain time/s	Domain fails	Bounds time/s	Bounds fails	B+SB time/s	B+SB fails	B+M time/s	B+MB time/s	B+MB fails	B+MA time/s	B+MA fails
2-5-4	0.1	**0**	0.1	30	<0.1	28	0.1	0.1	23	0.1	11
2-6-4	**0.1**	**0**	0.4	2036	0.8	1212	1.2	0.5	499	**0.1**	45
2-7-4	0.3	**0**	1.2	4447	1.9	2087	3.7	0.8	534	**0.2**	90
2-8-5	1.3	**0**	—	—	—	—	—	—	—	**0.8**	472
3-5-4	0.2	**0**	**0.1**	30	**0.1**	28	**0.1**	**0.1**	23	**0.1**	11
3-6-4	1.3	**0**	1.3	2039	1.6	1215	2.5	1.0	502	**0.2**	48
3-7-4	8.0	**0**	3.6	4492	3.7	2131	7.7	1.8	551	**0.5**	99
4-5-4	0.5	**0**	**0.1**	30	0.2	28	0.2	0.2	23	0.2	11
4-6-5	98.0	**0**	19.6	12747	23.1	8600	33.5	9.9	2323	**0.7**	81
4-7-4	—	—	7.0	4498	6.3	2137	12.2	2.9	557	**0.8**	**105**
4-9-4	—	—	**1.5**	71	1.7	69	2.2	2.0	43	1.9	**32**
5-4-3 (*)	29.0	**5165**	87.6	63519	140.8	43402	190.9	52.3	10440	**12.0**	9568
5-5-4	2.9	**41**	5.4	2686	7.1	1661	12.6	9.4	1356	**2.3**	1167
5-7-4	—	—	11.9	4583	9.7	2195	19.7	4.6	608	**1.5**	**159**
5-8-3	7.3	**0**	**0.7**	14	**0.7**	13	0.9	0.9	13	0.9	12
6-4-3 (*)	22.4	2132	130.3	61647	183.8	42986	235.7	12.6	1774	**2.1**	**908**
6-5-3	1.4	**82**	3.0	1455	4.2	967	6.9	2.5	327	**0.9**	282
6-6-3	1.3	**0**	**0.3**	5	**0.3**	5	0.4	0.4	5	0.4	5
7-5-3	—	—	—	—	—	—	—	127.5	11945	**18.2**	**6154**
7-5-5 (*)	**<0.1**	**0**	0.9	131	1.0	131	1.2	1.0	99	0.8	100

the solvers. The SAT solvers are frequently disadvantaged in this comparison because the representation of the cardinality constraints frequently requires a very large number of clauses.

5   Related Work and Conclusion

At present we are unaware of any other BDD based propagation solvers than our own, so in that sense the work is completely novel. But at a feature level there are relationships with much previous work.

Modeling of finite domains as Booleans is well understood and a standard form of dual modeling (see e.g. [4]). There has been interest in encoding CSPs as SAT problems [21]. The novel part of our approach is representing the actions of a finite-domain propagator in terms of clausal inferences. Even though the propagation rules of [4] and membership rules of [1] used to model propagation are similar, they only define directional inferences for modeling the behavior of propagators, rather than directly modeling logical inferences.

Table 2. Performance results for the Social Golfers problem, using a VSIDS labeling heuristic. "B+MB" = Bounds + minimized clause learning + backjumping. "B+MA" = Bounds + adding minimized clauses to the SAT solver as learnt clauses. "Dual" = Bounds + minimized clause learning + backjumping + Dual SAT/BDD model. "MiniSAT" = MiniSAT SAT solver [8]. "zChaff" = zChaff SAT solver [16]. "MiniSAT+" = MiniSAT with Pseudo-boolean extensions [9].

Problem w-g-s	B+MB time /s	fails	B+MA time /s	fails	Dual time /s	fails	MiniSAT time /s	fails	zChaff time /s	fails	MiniSAT+ time /s
2-5-4	**0.1**	21	**0.1**	22	**0.1**	4	0.2	273	0.2	767	0.2
2-6-4	0.3	83	**0.1**	64	**0.1**	12	0.5	125	0.9	1850	0.3
2-7-4	0.7	161	**0.2**	119	**0.2**	10	1.4	282	2.7	2858	0.6
2-8-5	3.6	437	1.3	622	**0.8**	130	×	×	×	×	1.5
3-5-4	**0.1**	26	**0.1**	24	0.5	215	0.3	534	2.2	7018	0.6
3-6-4	0.5	102	**0.3**	58	1.5	374	0.9	488	2.0	2715	1.2
3-7-4	1.1	128	**0.6**	92	3.5	493	6.9	7517	3.3	2348	2.1
4-5-4	**0.2**	27	0.4	122	2.0	900	0.5	543	3.3	9580	1.2
4-6-5	2.1	186	**1.3**	304	9.7	2135	17.0	763	×	×	4.0
4-7-4	**1.0**	40	**1.0**	98	13.1	1546	53.8	47801	281.7	166710	4.7
4-9-4	**2.0**	35	**2.0**	59	41.3	2161	----	----	×	×	12.9
5-4-3 (*)	66.0	13126	5.6	5876	11.1	10750	**0.4**	4554	1.4	9044	1.2
5-5-4	9.4	667	1.9	581	2.4	785	**1.4**	3291	2.3	7230	2.6
5-7-4	2.2	96	**1.5**	104	29.3	3458	----	----	----	----	8.5
5-8-3	**1.3**	35	1.7	425	10.7	1212	----	----	46.6	110980	7.3
6-4-3 (*)	0.3	74	**0.2**	71	1.3	637	0.3	4307	0.8	5975	1.1
6-5-3	11.1	1062	4.3	2801	8.2	3669	**0.8**	7795	74.4	186858	2.2
6-6-3	**0.4**	16	1.0	275	5.6	1310	2.2	17869	2.6	11666	3.5
7-5-3	127.6	14237	18.0	7018	35.8	118876	66.1	197714	396.8	562386	**6.3**
7-5-5 (*)	86.1	2513	**2.0**	139	**1.4**	97	8.8	1858	16.9	6910	6.9

There is a substantial body of work on look back methods in constraint satisfaction (see e.g. Dechter [7], chapter 6), but there seems little evidence of success for look back methods that combine with propagation. The most successful combination appears to be Forward Checking with Conflict Directed Backjumping (FC-CBJ) [17]. But other work by Bessière and Regin [2] calls into question whether FC-CBJ should be considered competitive. They showed that maintaining arc consistency (MAC) with an appropriate search strategy is usually better than FC-CBJ, and that conflict directed backjumping did not appear to improve the empirical performance of MAC. We believe our results do not match this conclusion primarily because we are able to use the highly efficient data structures of a SAT solver for maintaining and propagating nogoods, as well as an efficient BDD-based algorithm for calculating dependencies, thus making conflict-directed backjumping a worthwhile investment.

The only propagation based solver we are aware of that incorporates nogoods is the PaLM system [12]. It has been used to investigate new search methods based principally on dynamic backtracking. Like most previous work on nogoods in CSPs it keeps explanations and derives nogoods based on the constraints and decisions made in the search, rather than a SAT solver which simply records the inferences. Effectively it always uses decision cuts, instead of the more powerful 1-UIP nogoods. The system has been used to show that nogoods can be used constructively inside a propagation based solver [13].

The closest work to our own is that of Katsirelos and Bacchus [14], which showed that one could use nogood technology derived from SAT for storing and managing nogoods in a CSP system using FC-CBJ. Unfortunately no results were presented that combined MAC with nogood recording, which appears to limit the performance of the resulting solver. Another difference is that they don't appear to record the FC inferences as clauses, acting rather like S+MB rather than S+MA. They also reported no success with using SAT-derived labeling heuristics, which does not match our experience. The closest work to our implication detection algorithm is that of Damiano and Kukula [5]. In this work, however, the BDDs are static and not used for finite-domain propagation.

The use of nogoods has lead to a substantial improvement in the ability of SAT solvers to solve practical problems. SAT solvers treat nogoods both more efficiently than traditional CBJ approaches, but also learn better nogoods from a conflict. Our work shows at least in the case of set bounds propagation there is an advantage to using nogoods, because we can quickly determine minimal inferences and make use of the clever SAT technology to both generate and efficiently propagate nogoods.

Although we have hybridized a BDD-based finite domain constraint solver, we could similarly hybridize a more conventional finite domain propagation constraint solver by hard coding the minimal inferences for each primitive constraint supported by the solver. The advantage of BDD-based approach is that it is completely generic, and requires no extra work to support the wide variety of constraints that can be modeled as BDDs and is surprisingly fast.

For future work, we intend to try combining nogood learning with domain propagation, although this is more difficult to achieve, and possibly of less value. We will also try adding a 0-1 Integer Linear Programming solver into the hybrid solver, in the hope of producing a solver with better optimization capabilities.

In conclusion, we have demonstrated that by combining finite-domain constraint propagation and SAT techniques we can produce a highly efficient hybrid solver, which outperforms either of the original solvers on benchmarks. The high performance of this solver is a result of an efficient algorithm for accurately capturing the inferences of a finite-domain constraint solver as SAT clauses.

References

[1] K. Apt and E. Monfroy. Constraint programming viewed as rule-based programming. *TPLP*, 1(6):713–750, 2001.
[2] C. Bessière and J.-C. Regin. MAC and combined heuristics: Two reasons to forsake FC (and CBJ?) on hard problems. In *Proceedings of CP96*, LNCS. Springer, 1996.

[3] R. E. Bryant. Symbolic Boolean manipulation with ordered binary-decision diagrams. *ACM Comput. Surv.*, 24(3):293–318, 1992. ISSN 0360-0300.

[4] C. Choi, J. Lee, and P. J. Stuckey. Propagation redundancy in redundant modelling. In F. Rossi, editor, *Proceedings of CP2003*, volume 2833 of *LNCS*, pages 229–243. Springer-Verlag, 2003.

[5] R. Damiano and J. Kukula. Checking satisfiability of a conjunction of BDDs. In *Proceedings of DAC '03*, pages 818–823, New York, NY, USA, 2003. ACM Press.

[6] M. Davis, G. Logemann, and D. Loveland. A machine program for theorem-proving. *Communications of the ACM*, 5:394–397, 1962.

[7] R. Dechter. *Constraint Processing.* Morgan Kaufmann, 2003.

[8] N. Eén and N. Sörensson. An extensible SAT-solver. In E. Giunchiglia and A. Tacchella, editors, *Proceedings of SAT 2003*, volume 2919 of *LNCS*, pages 502–518, May 2003.

[9] N. Eén and N. Sörensson. Minisat+. http://www.cs.chalmers.se/Cs/Research/FormalMethods/MiniSat/MiniSat+.html, 2005.

[10] P. Hawkins, V. Lagoon, and P. J. Stuckey. Solving set constraint satisfaction problems using ROBDDs. *Journal of Artificial Intelligence Research*, 24:109–156, July 2005.

[11] U. Junker. QUICKXPLAIN: Conflict detection for arbitrary constraint propagation algorithms. In *IJCAI'01 Workshop on Modelling and Solving problems with constraints (CONS-1)*, 2001.

[12] N. Jussien and V. Barichard. The PaLM system: explanation-based constraint programming. In *Proceedings of TRICS: Techniques foR Implementing Constraint programming Systems, a post-conference workshop of CP 2000*, pages 118–133, 2000.

[13] N. Jussien, R. Debruyne, and P. Boizumault. Maintaining arc-consistency within dynamic backtracking. In *Proceedings of CP2000*, volume 1894 of *LNCS*, pages 249–261, Singapore, Sept. 2000. Springer-Verlag.

[14] G. Katsirelos and F. Bacchus. Unrestricted nogood recording in CSP search. In *Proceedings of CP2003*, volume 2833 of *LNCS*, pages 873–877. Springer, 2003.

[15] K. Marriott and P. J. Stuckey. *Programming with Constraints: an Introduction.* The MIT Press, 1998.

[16] M. Moskewicz, C. Madigan, Y. Zhao, L. Zhang, and S. Malik. Chaff: Engineering an efficient SAT solver. In *39th Design Automation Conference (DAC 2001)*, June 2001.

[17] P. Prosser. Hybrid algorithms for the constraint satisfaction search. *Computational Intelligence*, 9(3):268–299, 1993.

[18] F. Somenzi. CUDD: Colorado University Decision Diagram package. [Online, accessed 31 May 2004], Feb. 2004. http://vlsi.colorado.edu/~fabio/CUDD/.

[19] Z. Somogyi, F. Henderson, and T. Conway. The execution algorithm of Mercury, an efficient purely declarative logic programming language. *Journal of Logic Programming*, 29(1–3):17–64, 1996.

[20] C. Thiffault, F. Bacchu, and T. Walsh. Solving non-clausal formulas with DPLL search. In *Proceedings of CP2004*, volume 3258 of *LNCS*, pages 663–678. Springer, 2004.

[21] T. Walsh. SAT vs CSP. In *Proceedings of CP2000*, volume 1894 of *LNCS*, pages 441–456. Springer, 2000.

[22] L. Zhang and S. Malik. The quest for efficient Boolean satisfiability solvers. In *Proceedings of CAV2002*, volume 2404 of *LNCS*, pages 17–36, July 2002.

[23] L. Zhang, C. Madigan, M. Moskewicz, and S. Malik. Efficient conflict driven learning in a Boolean satisfiability solver. In *Proceedings of International Conference on Computer Design (ICCAD)*, pages 279–285, 2001.

Adding Constraint Solving to Mercury

Ralph Becket[1], Maria Garcia de la Banda[2], Kim Marriott[2],
Zoltan Somogyi[1,3], Peter J. Stuckey[1,3], and Mark Wallace[2]

[1] Department of Computer Science and Software Engineering,
The University of Melbourne, Australia
[2] School of Computer Science and Software Engineering,
Monash University, Australia
[3] NICTA Victoria Laboratory, Australia

Abstract. The logic programming language Mercury is designed to support programming in the large. Programmer declarations in conjunction with powerful compile-time analysis and optimization allow Mercury programs to be very efficient. The original design of Mercury did not support constraint logic programming (CLP). This paper describes the extensions we added to Mercury to support CLP. Unlike similarly motivated extensions to Prolog systems, our objectives included preserving the purity of Mercury programs as much as possible, as well as avoiding any impact on the efficiency of non-CLP predicates and functions.

1 Introduction

Constraint logic programming (CLP) [9] is considered the archetypal form of constraint programming thanks to three properties inherited from logic programming: its declarativeness, which allows users to state problems simply and correctly, its relational nature, which suits the definition and usage of constraints, and its built-in backtracking, which simplifies the specification of search. However, declarativeness also complicates the implementation of efficient constraint solvers, since this often requires the use of programming techniques (such as destructive update or control of the goal execution order) that lack a straightforward declarative reading.

As a result, constraint solvers are often implemented in other (non-declarative) languages, thus achieving efficiency of constraint solving but incurring an interface overhead between the modelling language and the constraint solver. Not only must the solver interface allow constraints to be passed to the solver, but it must also support memory management and backtracking. Typically such functionality is not directly provided by external solvers, making the interface complex and unnecessarily inefficient. Furthermore, the common need to access internal solver information means that the representation of the constraint store and its efficient but non-declarative manipulation spreads throughout the CLP interface. Since virtually no CLP languages make a distinction between declarative and non-declarative code (effectively making all code non-declarative) CLP is,

P. Van Hentenryck (Ed.): PADL 2006, LNCS 3819, pp. 118–133, 2006.

in practice, less efficient and arguably no cleaner than constraint programming embedded within a procedural paradigm.

In contrast to CLP, Mercury [12] has explored a different direction for the logic programming paradigm: that of a purely declarative general purpose language designed to support well-engineered, efficient, large programs. This is achieved by including an effective module system, strong, expressive, and statically checked type, mode, and determinism systems, clear separation between declarative and non-declarative code, and extensive compiler optimizations.

The above characteristics make Mercury an excellent candidate for achieving our objective: to design and implement a CLP platform that retains the advantages of CLP without compromising on programming style, efficiency, or scalability. This objective is similar to that driving the design of the HAL language [3], which compiled to Mercury, adopted its module, type, mode, and determinism systems, and extended them to support solvers. We chose instead to extend Mercury to become itself a CLP language. Our reasons for doing this were basically software engineering reasons: the HAL compiler duplicates much of the work done by the Mercury compiler and generates Mercury code. It is significantly simpler and more efficient to have all this work done under one roof.

Our extension of Mercury builds on some of the authors' positive and negative experiences building and using HAL. Indeed, while the main change required to support constraint solving in Mercury (an extension to the mode system to allow constrained variables, as described in section 3.1) was done to support HAL's generation of Mercury code, the design of several key issues in this paper, such as the handling of solver types and solver interfaces, is improved significantly compared with HAL. We believe these changes extend Mercury's support for constraint programming a significant step further, making it a clean declarative language for implementing efficient constraint solvers.

Our main contribution in this paper is a new design for solver types that provides a clean separation between the viewpoint of the solver user (the *external* view) which sees them as traditional solver variables, and the viewpoint of the solver implementor (the *internal* view) which sees them as data structures used to access the information required by the external view. Our extension supports this duality through the use of two different types with different instantiation states, linked together by a new solver type declaration. Several "solver interface cast" functions are automatically generated from this solver type declaration to allow easy conversion from one type and instantiation state to the others.

The two different types and instantiation states make it easier for solver implementors to provide a purely declarative interface to users, while still using imperative techniques. Thus, only solver implementors need to peek below the "purity" hood. This solution is not only semantically cleaner than that used in HAL, but also more powerful.

The rest of the paper is organized as follows. Section 2 introduces the necessary background. Section 3 describes the changes required to allow Mercury programs to use solvers written in other languages, while Section 4 describes the features we added to allow solvers to be written in Mercury itself, possibly as hybrid solvers written on top of other solvers. The last section provides comparisons to related work.

2 Background

While the syntax of Mercury is based on the syntax of Prolog, semantically the two languages are very different due to Mercury's purity; its type, mode, determinism and module systems; and its support for evaluable functions. Mercury has a strong Hindley-Milner type system very similar to Haskell's. Mercury programs are statically typed; the compiler knows the type of every argument of every predicate (from declarations or inference) and every local variable (from inference).

The initial version of the mode system classified each predicate argument as either input or output. If input, the argument passed by the caller must be a ground term; if output, the argument passed by the caller must be a distinct free variable, which the predicate or function will instantiate to a ground term. The extensions we describe later in this paper introduce other instantiation states and modes. It is possible for a predicate or function to have more than one mode; the usual example is append, which has two principal modes: append(in,in,out) and append(out,out,in). We call each mode of a predicate or function a *procedure*. Each procedure has a determinism, which puts limits on the number of its possible solutions. Procedures with determinism *det* succeed exactly once; *semidet* procedures succeed at most once; *multi* procedures succeed at least once; while *nondet* procedures may succeed any number of times.

2.1 Foreign Code and Purity

Mercury supports access to code written in other languages by allowing the implementation of a Mercury predicate or function to be given in one of the languages supported by the Mercury compiler. On Unix systems, that means C; when generating code for .NET, it means C# or managed C++. For example, the syntax for defining a function sin/1 in C is:

```
:- func sin(float) = float.
:- pragma foreign_proc("C", sin(X::in) = (Result::out), [promise_pure],
                       "Result = sin(X);").
```

The arguments of the foreign_proc pragma give the language of the code, the name of the predicate or function together with its arguments and their modes, a list of attributes, and the foreign code itself. The promise_pure attribute is part of the Mercury purity system, which classifies every predicate into one of the following three categories:

pure — the predicate is referentially transparent: the set of values it computes for its output arguments is completely determined by the values of the input arguments. Calls to such predicates may be optimized away or reordered freely.

impure — the predicate is not referentially transparent: the set of values it computes for its output arguments may depend on the current state of the computation in an arbitrary way. The execution of a call to an impure predicate may affect the behavior of future calls to impure and semipure predicates in an arbitrary manner. Calls to such predicates cannot be optimized away or reordered.

semipure — again, the predicate is not referentially transparent. However, the execution of a call to a semipure predicate cannot affect the behavior of future calls to impure and semipure predicates. Calls to such predicates can be optimized away or reordered *only* within the fenceposts formed by the surrounding impure calls.

Thus, predicates that write (and possibly read) state beyond their arguments are impure, while those that read but do not write are semipure:

```
:- semipure pred get_global(globaltype::out) is det.
:- pragma foreign_proc("C", get_global(X::out), [promise_semipure],
                          "X = some_global_variable;").
:- impure pred set_global(globaltype::in) is det.
:- pragma foreign_proc("C", set_global(X::in),   [],
                          "some_global_variable = X;").
```

Mercury allows programs to use impure code to implement a pure interface. Non-pure calls must be marked, and the user must promise that the predicate at the interface behaves as a pure predicate (i.e., its outputs depend only on its inputs). One example is the solutions predicate, which returns all solutions of a given goal as a sorted list. While this interface is purely declarative, the implementation of solutions uses a failure-driven loop patterned after Prolog's findall. After every success of the given goal, it saves the solution in a global variable and backtracks; when the goal has no more solutions, it picks up the list of recorded solutions from the global variable, sorts them and returns the result. This code is clearly impure, but the effect of this impurity is not visible outside solutions, because no other part of the system looks at that global variable. While predicates implemented in foreign languages are impure by default, Mercury predicates are pure unless they call semipure or impure predicates.

2.2   Type-Specific Representation and Equality

Since all types are known at compile time, term representation is specialized for each type. A given bit pattern may thus mean one term if it represents a value of type t1, and another for a value of type t2. The generic unify and compare predicates take an extra input describing the type of the arguments, which is used to invoke the specific unify or compare predicate for that type. These type-specific unify and compare predicates are usually created automatically by the compiler from the type definition, but programmers are allowed to define their own unify and/or compare predicates. For Mercury types defined in foreign languages, this is the only way unification and comparison *can* be defined. Additionally, this can also be useful for Mercury types on which semantic equality differs from structural equality, as it is the case when using unordered lists that may contain duplicates to represent sets. The type declaration:

```
:- type set_unordlist(T) ⟶ unord(list(T))
        where equality      is sort_elimdups_and_unify,
              comparison is sort_elimdups_and_compare.
```

specifies that for values of type set_unordlist(T), where T can be any type, unification should be defined by the sort_elimdups_and_unify predicate. User-defined equality imposes a proof obligation on the programmer, who must ensure that the equality predicate satisfies the usual properties of reflexivity, transitivity, commutativity and, most importantly, equivalence under replacement of equal objects. In other words, given A = B, it should be possible to substitute B for A in any call in the program without changing the call's results, with the exception of calls to semipure and impure predicates, which are known not to be referentially transparent [6].

3   Interfacing to External Solvers

The easiest way to add constraint solving capability to a Mercury program is to provide an interface to an existing solver such as CPLEX [2] written in a foreign language. The natural way to do this is to create a module that exports the operations of the external solver together with an abstract type representing the variables that participate in the constraints. This requires an extension of the mode system, an extension that is also needed for writing solvers entirely in Mercury, as we will discuss in section 4.

3.1   New Versus Old Variables

The standard version of the Mercury mode system requires the compiler to know exactly which goal binds each variable. This is inherently impossible to achieve in constraint programs since, given a sequence of constraints, the particular constraint that fixes the value of a variable is frequently data dependent. We therefore added an instantiation state called old which indicates the variable is known to a solver and thus may be constrained, but it is not known whether it is ground. For example, a finite domain variable might be known to be greater than 3 and smaller than 7 (thus, it is not free), but its exact value might not be known yet (thus, it is not semantically ground either).

All variables start life in instantiation state new. For ordinary variables life is simple: at some point known to the compiler they become ground. For variables that occur in constraints, things are a bit more complex. When they first become known to their constraint solver (at a point known to the compiler) they change from new to old. Their instantiation state stays old as more constraints are added to them, unless they participate in an operation that is *known* to fix their value, in which case they become ground. However, most constrained variables die old.

The predicate or function that first makes a variable known to a solver takes that variable from instantiation state new to old (referred to as argument mode no, after their initials). In most cases, this is a specialized initialization predicate that does nothing else. Usually, solver operations work only on variables that have already been initialized, so they take solver variables from instantiation state old to old, which we abbreviate as argument mode oo. In some solvers, adding a constraint can be more efficient if some of its variables are known not to have previous constraints on them. In such cases, the solver may export operations that both initialize a variable and put a constraint on it. For example, a function like addition (+) on a constrained float type cfloat may be declared as

```
:- pred   cfloat + cfloat = cfloat.
:- mode oo + oo = no is det.
```

The set of things user programs can do with old variables is restricted to passing them around, putting them into data structures, and calling the operations of their solver module. (This is enforced by the definition of their type being visible only in the solver module; they are not distinguished syntactically from other variables.) Since the concrete representation of old variables is usually just an index into the constraint store, unifying them with a term or with another variable using Mercury's usual structural equality is not meaningful. Solver programmers must avoid this unsoundness by defining type-specific equality predicates for the types of constrained variables.

3.2 *Tell* Versus *Ask* Goals

Solver operations can usually be divided into two classes, *tells* and *asks* (some operations are both). While tell operations add new constraints to the store, ask operations inspect the store, usually to decide whether a constraint is entailed by it or not. Thus, tell operations are usually semidet, since they might find the resulting store to be inconsistent. It is also possible for a tell operation to be det if it works with fresh (new) variables, as in the addition example above.

Tell operations can be (and usually are) pure. Even though their implementation includes side-effects (updates to the global constraint store), these are not visible to the solver user as long as the solver ensures the operations are order-independent, i.e., the consistency or inconsistency of the store does not depend on the order in which constraints are added. Consider the Herbrand constraint solver built into every Prolog system. A unification is a tell operation which adds a new Herbrand constraint to the store, and it is implemented via side-effects such as making one variable point to another. Nevertheless, from the user's point of view, the solver maintains referential transparency and is thus pure.

Unfortunately, tell constraints can cause problems when appearing in a negated context, i.e., in the body of a negation or in the condition of an if-then-else (if C then T else E is semantically equivalent to $(C \wedge T) \vee (\neg \exists C \wedge E)$). This is because tell constraints often have arguments of mode oo, and Mercury cannot decide whether these arguments become further constrained by the tell. If they are, this is unsound since the negated goal binds variables visible from the outside. This can, for example, destroy the commutativity of conjunction: if X and Y are initially unconstrained, then executing X $\geq$ Y, not(X $<$ Y) should succeed, whereas not(X < Y), X ≥ Y would fail (X < Y would succeed after constraining X and Y, so its negation would fail). Tell constraints occuring in negated contexts should be translated to ask constraints (see e.g. [4]). Our current solution is to implicitly make impure any goal occurring in a negated context that contains a nonlocal variable with inst old. In these cases, it is up to the programmer to decide whether such goals really are pure and add a purity promise if they are.

The result of executing an ask constraint depends upon the state of the constraint store, and thus upon when it is executed. Whereas tell goals can be reordered arbitrarily with respect to each other, ask goals should not be reordered with respect to tell goals. Furthermore, since some ask goals also change the constraint store, they should not be reordered with respect to other ask goals either. The simplest way to achieve this is to make them impure. This is also semantically desirable, since the undisciplined use of ask goals can break referential transparency. Consider the ask constraint fixed(X) which succeeds if solver variable X is fixed to a unique value. The goals fixed(X), X = 3 and X = 3, fixed(X) would have different behaviour.

4   Writing Constraint Solvers in Mercury

We want to allow programmers to write solvers directly in Mercury, either from scratch, or using other solvers. This requires significant additional changes to the language.

4.1   Solver Types

Solver users see constrained variables as black boxes whose implementation is hidden, and which spend most of their life in instantiation state old. Solver writers, on the other hand, must know the constraint variable's structure and must be able to manipulate it. For efficiency, this usually requires constraint variables to have a more concrete instantiation state such as ground. While the notion of abstract data types can be used to provide the user's view, we need a new mechanism, which we call *solver types*, to support the solver writer's view.

Solver types are for variables whose values may have constraints placed on them. Solver types are exported abstractly, i.e., their definition stays hidden and the only operations users can invoke on their values are those exported by the solver module. The following provides the module interface of the solver we will use as our running example:

```
:- solver type po_vertex.
:- pred init(po_vertex::no) is det.
:- pred eq(po_vertex::oo, po_vertex::oo) is semidet.
:- pred '<'(po_vertex::oo, po_vertex::oo) is semidet.
:- pred '≤'(po_vertex::oo, po_vertex::oo) is semidet.
:- impure pred order(list(po_vertex)::in, list(po_vertex)::out) is semidet.
```

The first line declares po_vertex to be an abstract solver type, while the other lines declare the operations available on it. The init predicate creates a fresh variable of the solver type; eq, <, and ≤ each tell the solver to impose the constraint they stand for; and order asks for a total order consistent with the partial order required by the constraints imposed so far, using the supplied order as a preference to break any ties.

The implementation section of the solver module defines some auxiliary types (vertex is a type synonym for integers, and constraint is a type with data constructors, lt for less-than constraints and le for less-than-or-equal-to constraints), and then gives the actual definition of the solver type as follows:

```
:- type vertex      == int.
:- type constraint  ---> lt(vertex, vertex) ; le(vertex, vertex).

:- solver type po_vertex where
      representation  is vertex,
      equality        is eq,
      initialisation  is init,
      constraint_store is
          [ mutable(counter, int, 0),
            mutable(constraints, set(constraint), empty_set) ].
```

The following subsections explain the various parts of this declaration.

4.2   The External and Internal Views of Solver Types

A solver type presents the "external" view of a constrained variable, which is the only view available to its users. Every solver type also has an underlying *representation* type, which presents the "internal" view visible only to the solver implementation. This representation type is specified by the representation is vertex part of the declaration.

In our example, a constrained variable of solver type po_vertex is represented by a variable of type vertex, which is just a synonym for integer. These two types are semantically quite different. Equating two values of type vertex simply requires testing whether two integers are the same, while equating two values of type po_vertex requires adding a new eq constraint to the store and testing its consistency. For instance, let V_1 and V_2 be two currently unconstrained variables of type po_vertex with internal representations 42 and 69, respectively. While V_1 = V_2 should succeed, constraining the two solver variables to behave identically with respect to all other solver operations, 42 = 69 should fail.

We can distinguish between these two kinds of equality thanks to Mercury's support for user-defined equality. The "equality is eq" part of the declaration indicates to Mercury that equality for values of solver type po_vertex is defined by the eq predicate, rather than by the default structural equality relation. (The Mercury compiler and runtime system together implement the unification $V_1 = V_2$ in the previous paragraph by calling eq(V_1, V_2).) Values of the internal type vertex, on the other hand, will use the standard equality definition for integers. This separation into two types allows solver writers to ensure the referential transparency of exported predicates and functions, something that must be done by any declarative language with true programmer defined equality. [1]

Separating the external, solver type from the internal, representation type also allows their treatment to differ in other respects, such as making just one of them an instance of a type class, or providing different implementations for the methods of a type class. For example, consider an overloaded predicate show for pretty-printing. Applying show to a vertex should simply print an integer (since a vertex *is* an integer), but showing a po_vertex could, for instance, list the constraints on the vertex.

4.3   Converting Between Internal and External Views

We need to provide ways of moving from the external type with its external instantiation state (old) to the internal type with its internal instantiation state (usually ground, but see section 4.6), and vice versa. The solver type declaration allows the Mercury compiler to automatically create the two casting functions required by the solver writer to do this. For our running example, these functions are:

```
:- impure func from_old_po_vertex(po_vertex::oo) = (vertex::out).
:- impure func to_old_po_vertex(vertex::in)      = (po_vertex::no).
```

where from_old_po_vertex takes an old po_vertex value and returns its internal ground vertex representation, while the dual function to_old_po_vertex takes a ground vertex value and returns the corresponding old po_vertex. Note that by default, internal representations are ground values. This can be overridden in the solver type declaration if, for example, the internal representation is defined in terms of another solver type.

The casting functions are impure because a semantically non-ground value of the external type may be (and typically is) represented by a ground value of the internal type. No declarative reading can be given to such a relationship. While the value of the external type may be further constrained, this does not affect the already ground value of the internal type. In the internal view, this is usually reflected only in the constraint store, which is not an argument to the casting functions.

Operationally, cast functions are just the identity function. Calls to these functions are guaranteed to be optimized away, and thus have no performance cost. They exist only to bridge the "semantic gap" between a solver type and its internal representation.

4.4   The Constraint Store

The value of a solver variable cannot be understood in isolation from the constraint store of its solver. The

---

[1] Languages like Haskell sidestep the same problem by treating the (possibly user-defined) equality relation == as having no relation to the equality = used for referential transparency. This is not possible in a relational language due to the pervasive, implicit use of equality.

```
constraint_store is
    [ mutable(counter, int, 0),
      mutable(constraints, set(constraint), empty_set) ].
```

part of the declaration indicates that the constraint store for the po_vertex type
is stored in two mutable global variables, one containing the id of the next vertex
to be allocated (each new vertex is given a different integer identifier), the other
containing the set of constraints in the store. In this case, the store may contain
only lt and le constraints (this example represents equality constraints as a pair of
le constraints). Initially no vertexes have been created and the set of constraints
is empty. More complex solvers would have more sophisticated data structures.

The Mercury compiler automatically creates two access predicates for each
mutable variable, which in this case will have the signatures

```
:- semipure pred get_counter(int::out) is det.
:- impure    pred set_counter(int::in) is det.
:- semipure pred get_constraints(set(constraint)::out) is det.
:- impure    pred set_constraints(set(constraint)::in) is det.
```

Exported solver predicates start by reading (parts of) the store from these global
variables and finish by updating them, if necessary. Updates to the global variables are trailed to ensure they are automatically undone on backtracking.

4.5   Solver Operations

The functionality of the solver derives from the functions and predicates that it
exports. In practice, this is where the bulk of the solver code lies. This code uses
predicates and functions created by the compiler from solver type declarations
to map the external types and instantiations to internal ones and vice versa,
and to lookup and modify information in the global solver state. For example,
the less-than-or-equal-to constraint listed in the solver type interface might be
defined as in figure 1.

If there is an existing path from X to Y in the constraint graph, then the
constraint $X \leq Y$ is already entailed and we return. (The path predicate looks for

```
A ≤ B :-
    promise_pure(
        impure X = from_old_po_vertex(A),
        impure Y = from_old_po_vertex(B),
        semipure get_constraints(Arcs_0),
        ( if    path(X, Y, Arcs_0, _)
          then true
          else  not path(Y, X, Arcs_0, strict),
                Arcs = set.insert(Arcs_0, le(X, Y)),
                impure set_constraints(Arcs)
        )
    ).
```

Fig. 1. The code of the predicate that adds a less-than constraint

acyclic paths in $Arcs_0$, and tracks whether the path traverses a strict constraint or not.) Otherwise, if there is an existing *strict* path from Y to X (implying Y < X), then we fail, since the constraint X ≤ Y is inconsistent with the current constraint graph. Otherwise we add le(X, Y) to the constraint graph and update the global constraint store.

4.6 Hybrid Solvers

It is also possible to define a new solver type in terms of other solver types. Figure 2 shows how a lexicographically ordered solver type could be defined in terms of the po_vertex solver (this example is purely illustrative: in practice a user of the po_vertex type would just use a pair of po_vertexes directly rather than hiding the representation behind another solver type). The solver type declaration contains an extra attribute, any is bound(lex_rep(old, old)), which specifies that the instantiation state of the representation type that corresponds to the inst old of the external type is not ground, but rather the function symbol lex_rep wrapped around two old values.

```
:- solver type lex where
      representation is lex_rep,
      any           is bound(lex_rep(old, old)),
      equality      is eq_lex,
      initialisation is init_lex.

:- type lex_rep ⟶ lex_rep(po_vertex, po_vertex).

:- pred init_lex(lex::no) is det.
init_lex(A) :-
      promise_pure(
          init(A₁), init(A₂), impure A = to_old_lex(lex_rep(A₁, A₂))
      ).

:- pred eq_lex(lex::oo, lex::oo) is semidet.
eq_lex(A, B) :-
      promise_pure(
          impure lex_rep(A₁, A₂) = from_old_lex(A),
          impure lex_rep(B₁, B₂) = from_old_lex(B),
          A₁ = B₁, A₂ = B₂
      ).

:- pred '≤'(lex::oo, lex::oo) is nondet.
A ≤ B :-
      promise_pure(
          impure lex_rep(A₁, A₂) = from_old_lex(A),
          impure lex_rep(B₁, B₂) = from_old_lex(B),
          ( A₁ < B₁ ; A₁ = B₁, A₂ ≤ B₂ )
      ).
```

Fig. 2. Defining a solver type in terms of another solver type

5   Related Work

Mercury's focus on purity while not neglecting efficiency (quite the contrary!) leaves very few directly competing logic programming languages. The closest relative is HAL [3], which itself used Mercury as an implementation language. The vast bulk of other logic programming systems supporting the implementation of constraint solvers can reasonably be described as Prolog extensions (e.g. [1, 5, 7, 11]). Oz [10] supports constraint programming, but any new constraint solvers have be written in a foreign language (C++).

5.1   Prolog-Based Systems

Key characteristics of Prolog-based systems are a dynamic type system, no mode checking, support for aliasing of all variables, and dependence on impure language features while lacking any mechanism for distinguishing pure code from impure code. The lack of a static type system means that program variables all have the same "universal type". Even in systems with optional type declarations, such as CIAO [7], the compiler cannot optimize the representation of a term to its type without breaking the assumptions of e.g. the debugger and the garbage collector. The compiler therefore cannot optimize the representation of solver types either. Because the absence of a mode system allows variables to become aliased before they become ground, every variable must be initialised before use. It also means that every time the system wants to look up the value of a variable, it needs to be prepared to follow a chain of aliasing pointers first. These characteristics make it very difficult to build fast Prolog systems (e.g. implementors must write program analyses if they wants to optimize away dereferencing). Prolog systems that have been extended to support constraint programming typically use *attributed variables* [8] to associate solvers with variables. This complicates the representation of variables even further, and makes unification more complex and expensive due to the need to check at many steps whether any attributed solver goals have to be invoked. However, the biggest drawback of building constraints on top of attributed variables is that code built that way has no clear, well-defined boundary between the pure external view and the internal impure view, which makes programs harder to maintain and to optimize.

The Mercury compiler, by contrast, knows the type of every variable, and each type has a separately optimized low-level representation. Thanks to the mode system, the Mercury compiler also knows at each point whether a given variable is new, old, or ground. Consequently, new variables may contain just junk data, and do not require any kind of initialization. Only *solver type* variables need to be initialized, at the point where their instantiation state changes from new to old (or to ground). Because new Mercury variables cannot be aliased (Mercury uses code reordering to ensure that at least one side of a unification is old or ground before the unification is carried out), variables do not need to be dereferenced. A particular solver *might* use aliasing as part of its implementation of equality, but that is an implementation decision made by the solver programmer and can have no effect on the performance of variables with other types, which have separate representations. For example, a Herbrand solver type for terms with Prolog-style unification could use a WAM-style [13] representation, where variables may be aliased and would therefore need dereferencing. On the other hand, a solver type interfacing to a SAT solver might unify variables by simply adding clauses equating the two variables to its constraint store. Similarly, because solver variables are handled exclusively by solver implementations, solvers can immediately inspect their variables' values. There is no need for a general attribute variable mechanism, and thus no overhead is incurred by non-solver types.

Mercury also gets additional speed from the Mercury compiler's ability to optimize away some computations and to reorder some others (e.g. to make failure happen earlier). The Mercury compiler is allowed to exercise this ability only on pure code; removing or reordering impure code could change the program's output. Mercury programmers often write clear, maintainable code, even if it is inefficient, if they know the compiler can eliminate the inefficiency. Our solver type design allows and indeed encourages solver writers to keep both solver interfaces and the codes of the solvers themselves as pure as possible, and requires them to cleanly separate out the impure code. This preserves maximum freedom for the compiler and allows programmers to maintain a declarative programming style. This has genuine advantages for both compiler implementors (optimizations are easier to implement) and constraint programmers (declarative code is more maintainable). These are real advantages not available with Prolog-based approaches.

5.2   HAL

Like Mercury, HAL also has external and internal views of solver types. But rather than making these genuinely distinct types, the external view is a specially handled renaming of the solver type representation. Outside the solver module, a HAL solver type is an abstract type whose values typically have instantiation state old and whose equality is defined by a programmer specified predicate in the solver module. Inside the solver module, the solver type is a concrete type, values of that type have a different instantiation state (usually ground), and the applicable equality semantics is structural equality rather than the equality predicate used for the external view.

The first problem with this approach is that referential transparency is much more complicated for solver types, since what equality means for such terms is different depending upon whether a unification occurs inside or outside the solver module. This means for example that code performing such unifications must not be subject to intermodule optimizations such as inlining. The second is that the solver type module cannot define predicates in terms of the external view. For example, in the Mercury po_vertex solver module the programmer can define equality of po_vertexes in terms of $\leq$ for po_vertexes:

$$eq(A, B) :- A \leq B, B \leq A.$$

In a HAL solver module, however, A and B would be viewed as integers (the representation view), hence the integer version of $\leq$ would be used instead of the po_vertex version, which has quite different properties! To see the third problem, consider a showable class the debugger may use to print values. We would like different things printed in the internal and the external views, but with the HAL approach, this is not possible, since there is only one type.

The Mercury approach avoids these problems by making the external and internal views distinct types and requiring the programmer to explicitly cast between them. We feel the modest amount of extra typing required is more than compensated for by the increased flexibility, clarity, and protection from errors.

6   Experimental Evaluation

The results presented here are solely presented to illustrate that the Mercury approach can be used to implement competitive solvers. The benchmark programs for each language are as similar as possible, although the solver type implementations are obviously different in each case. It is important to bear in mind that the performance of a given solver is determined much more by how it is implemented than in what language: the better algorithm will usually win! Using the exact same algorithm on all systems usually isn't feasible, and even when it is, a given algorithm may be a better fit for one system than for another. This is why despite our best efforts, the benchmarks here are far from being apples-to-apples comparisons. That said, it seems clear that Mercury is generally faster than HAL and Eclipse.

Table 1. Benchmark results

Problem	Size	Reps	Mercury	HAL	Eclipse
serialize	10,000	2,000	63.5	98.9 (1.56)	164.9 (2.60)
	7,500	3,000	68.4	96.5 (1.41)	180.1 (2.63)
	5,000	4,000	58.8	69.0 (1.17)	152.6 (2.60)
warplan		100	8.8	8.2 (0.93)	12.0 (1.36)
hanoi	10	20,000	15.2	17.3 (1.14)	31.7 (2.09)
	13	2,000	12.5	18.6 (1.48)	25.5 (2.04)
	16	200	10.8	18.5 (1.72)	31.9 (2.95)
qsort	10,000	200	45.9	55.4 (1.21)	221.5 (4.83)
	7,500	400	52.5	63.2 (1.21)	241.2 (4.59)
	5,000	800	48.7	58.4 (1.20)	204.9 (4.21)
laplace	10	6,000	28.1	32.2 (1.15)	72.7 (2.59)
	20	400	20.0	32.7 (1.64)	47.8 (2.39)
	30	50	15.9	33.3 (2.01)	37.7 (2.37)
matmul	10	2,000	12.2	37.4 (3.07)	60.9 (4.99)
	20	200	14.8	33.5 (2.26)	52.1 (3.52)
	30	40	14.3	38.3 (2.68)	42.6 (2.98)
mortgage		1,000	26.9	19.4 (0.72)	1140.0 (42.0)
fib	12	1,000	104.9	100.1 (0.95)	1667.3 (15.9)

These benchmarks were run on a PC with dual 933MHz Pentium III CPUs and 2 GBytes of RAM running Linux kernel version 2.4.3. All times are given in seconds and performance relative to Mercury is also given in parentheses for all other benchmark times. The compiler versions used were Mercury rotd-2005-08-21, the last development release of the HAL compiler (work on HAL ceased in 2004), and Eclipse 5.8. The CPLEX benchmarks were linked against CPLEX 7.0.

Table 1 gives the results. serialize, warplan, hanoi, and qsort are standard Prolog benchmarks to test performance on Herbrand constraints, i.e. Prolog-style unification. HAL's superior performance on warplan, the most challenging of this group of benchmarks, reflects the considerable effort expended by the HAL team on efficient Herbrand types.

laplace, matmul, fib, and mortgage test solver interfaces to CPLEX [2], an off-the-shelf linear constraint optimizer. laplace computes a matrix using Laplace's equation. matmul inverts a matrix of prime numbers by multiplying it with a matrix of variables and equating the result with the unit matrix. mortgage computes mortgage costs on a $120,000 dollar loan over 120 years at 1% interest and then runs the same computation backwards. fib takes a naive approach to computing Fibonacci numbers in the forward direction. In laplace and matmul, constraints are "batched" together and solved once at the end of the query. In mortgage and fib, constraints are incrementally checked for consistency because they control recursive loops. We believe HAL's superior performance on these two benchmarks is due simply to the fact we haven't had as much time to optimize this part of Mercury's interface to CPLEX.

7   Conclusions

We have extended Mercury with the instantiation old and solver types. When we began this work, we thought supporting solver types would be a straightforward and relatively uninteresting design problem. In the end it required several attempts and a great deal of careful thought to arrive at a clean design that could be implemented efficiently without sacrificing referential transparency.

So far, we have used these new Mercury features to implement a Herbrand solver, a propagation based finite domain solver, and a BDD-based set solver, as well as interfaces to CPLEX and SATZ (a SAT solver). We have found the solver type mechanisms to be easy to use, and in each case, the interface of the solver seen by its users is totally pure, with the exception of ask predicates.

We have evaluated the performance of some of the above solvers against comparable solvers in other languages. The results are very encouraging: in the benchmarks we have run, Mercury is the fastest system in almost all cases.

The system we have described is now available in releases-of-the-day from the Mercury web site. The full source code of our running example is also available from there, next to this paper on the papers page.

We would like to thank Fergus Henderson for many useful discussions, and NICTA and the Australian Research Council for their support.

References

1. B-Prolog. www.sci.brooklyn.cuny.edu/~zhou/bprolog.html.
2. ILOG CPLEX. www.cplex.com.
3. B. Demoen, M. Garcia de la Banda, W. Harvey, K. Marriott, and P.J. Stuckey. An overview of HAL. In *Proceedings of the Fourth International Conference on Principles and Practices of Constraint Programming*, pages 174–188, 1999.
4. G.J. Duck, M. García de la Banda, and P.J. Stuckey. Compiling ask constraints. In B. Demoen and V. Lifschitz, editors, *Proceedings of the 20th International Conference on Logic Programming*, LNCS, pages 105–119. Springer-Verlag, 2004.
5. ECLiPSe. http://www.icparc.ic.ac.uk/eclipse/.
6. F. Henderson, T. Conway, Z. Somogyi, D. Jeffery, P. Schachte, S. Taylor, and C. Speirs. The Mercury language reference manual. Available from http://www.cs.mu.oz.au/mercury/, 2000.
7. M. Hermenegildo, F. Bueno, D. Cabeza, M. Garcia de la Banda, P. López, and G. Puebla. The CIAO Multi-Dialect Compiler and System: An Experimentation Workbench for Future (C)LP Systems. In *Parallelism and Implementation of Logic and Constraint Logic Programming*. Nova Science, Commack, NY, USA, April 1999.
8. C. Holzbaur. Metastructures vs. attributed variables in the context of extensible unification. In *Proceedings of PLILP '92*, number 631 in LNCS, pages 260–268. Springer-Verlag, 1992.
9. J. Jaffar and J.-L. Lassez. Constraint logic programming. In *Proceedings of POPL '87*, pages 111–119, 1987.
10. Mozart. http://www.mozart-oz.org.
11. SICStus Prolog. http://www.sics.se/sicstus/.
12. Z. Somogyi, F. Henderson, and T. Conway. The execution algorithm of Mercury: an efficient purely declarative logic programming language. *Journal of Logic Programming*, 29:17–64, 1996.
13. D.H.D. Warren. An abstract Prolog instruction set. Technical Report 309, SRI International, Menlo Park, U.S.A., Oct. 1983.

Modeling Genome Evolution with a DSEL for Probabilistic Programming

Martin Erwig and Steve Kollmansberger

School of EECS,
Oregon State University
{erwig, kollmast}@eecs.oregonstate.edu

Abstract. Many scientific applications benefit from simulation. However, programming languages used in simulation, such as C++ or Matlab, approach problems from a deterministic procedural view, which seems to differ, in general, from many scientists' mental representation. We apply a domain-specific language for probabilistic programming to the biological field of gene modeling, showing how the mental-model gap may be bridged. Our system assisted biologists in developing a model for genome evolution by separating the concerns of model and simulation and providing implicit probabilistic non-determinism.

Keywords: Functional Programming, Probabilistic Programming, Haskell, Genome Evolution.

1   Introduction

A primary occupation of scientists is to devise models of observable processes. These models may be formal and mathematical, or informal ideas and sketches. In general, such models cannot be executed, simulated nor verified directly. Instead, scientists have had to translate their model first into a programming language. Traditionally, simulations for scientific models were written in the programming language of their day, such as Fortran or C. Later simulations were also written in mathematical packages such at MatLab. Recently, some researchers have developed domain-specific modeling tools for biological processes [9,11,15,4,3].

Many of these approaches, however, are merely speculation and have not been used in an actual research application. In addition, many of them are limited to only the particular given model, and so general computation cannot be mixed with the scientific specification. For example, the bio-ambients approach requires any model to be given in terms of a hierarchical chain of interacting objects [15]. On the other hand, some approaches are too general, forcing scientists to adapt their ideas to fit the general-purpose constructs given by the system. For example, the pathway logic system presents a general algebraic rewrite approach without specific support for constructs that may appear in biological systems [4].

We approach the problem driven by a specific application: In conjunction with the Center for Gene Research at Oregon State University, we have developed a model for the evolution of microRNAs [2,1], which has enabled scientists

P. Van Hentenryck (Ed.): PADL 2006, LNCS 3819, pp. 134–149, 2006.

to predict what types of genome sequences are most likely to exhibit active microRNAs. This result is important since microRNAs are an essential regulatory mechanism for controlling gene expressiveness. The model is realized with the help of a domain-specific embedded language (DSEL) for probabilistic programming [5]. This paper reports on our process as well as results applicable to modeling a wide variety of scientific domains.

We have chosen a DSEL approach because it yields a language that offers constructs general enough to represent any computation, but specific enough to be very closely related to the model. We found that the scientists did not know at the outset all the precise details of the model they wanted to represent. Therefore, choosing a DSEL approach allowed rapid prototyping and iteration as we developed the model from the ground up. We constructed the DSEL in Haskell because it offered a number of unique features that allowed "behind-the-scenes" operation (through monads), allowing the written code to closely resemble the biological concepts.

The remainder of this paper is structured as follows. We introduce our approach to probabilistic functional programming in Section 2. In Section 3 we will show how this approach can be applied to a simple biological problem, the Lotka-Volterra predator-prey model. In Section 4 we will discuss the motivation, problem, and prototyping of the genome model. The final model and its scientific accomplishments will be presented in Section 5. A discussion of related work is given in Section 6. Conclusions are presented in Section 7.

2   Probabilistic Functional Programming

We have constructed a probabilistic functional programming (PFP) library [5,13] based on a DSEL approach. The foundational structure of probabilistic computing is a list of values and their associated probabilities, called a *distribution*, which is encapsulated in the type:

```
Dist a
```

The users of the library do not directly construct such distributions—instead, we provide a variety of functions which construct and operate on them. For example, the functions `uniform` and `normal` construct a distribution from a list of values. These distributions are of course discrete, so they can be considered as approximations.

We can extract probabilities from the distribution using predicates on values in the distribution, called *events*. The function ?? takes such a predicate and determines the probability (represented by a float value) that it is true in a given distribution.

```
type Event a = a -> Bool

(??) :: Event a -> Dist a -> Probability
```

We can consider a simple example of rolling dice. A regular die has a numeric value from one to six, and may land on any of those values with equal probability.

```
type Die = Int

die :: Dist Die
die = uniform [1..6]
```

We can simulate rolling an arbitrary number of dice by the following function dice. The function joinWith combines all pairs of values from two distributions with a given function while multiplying their probabilities. In this case, we are accumulating individual die rolls in a list. The function certainly constructs a distribution that consists of one value with 100% probability.

```
dice :: Int -> Dist [Die]
dice 0 = certainly []
dice n = joinWith (:) die (dice (n-1))
```

Now what if we wanted to determine how likely it would be that out of a certain number of rolls, a certain number of them would come up six? Since we are producing a list, we can simply filter out all non-six values and count how long the remaining list is.

```
sixes :: (Int -> Bool) -> Int -> Probability
sixes p n = (p . length . filter (==6)) ?? dice n
```

If we wanted to determine the probability of rolling more than two sixes in a sequence of four die rolls, we could query:

```
> sixes (>2) 4
  1.6%
```

In many cases, distributions are not given directly. Instead, a series of steps are required for their construction, each one taking a value and producing a distribution. We call such a function a *transition*.

```
type Trans a = a -> Dist a
```

With transitions, distributions permit a sequenced form of computation known as a monad. In the probability monad, the function return indicates that a given value is certain. The bind operation >>= takes a distribution and a transition, threads the values in the first distribution through the transition and combines the resultant distributions. The observation that probability distributions form a monad is not new [6]. However, previous work was mainly concerned with extending languages by offering probabilistic expressions as primitives and defining suitable semantics [7,10,14,12].

Consider the case where we take a sum, roll a die and add its value to the sum. We may wish to repeat this process several times. We can employ a transition which takes the current sum `s` and adds each possible die roll `d` $\in$ `die` to the sum, which is expressed using the bind operation s follows.

```
die >>= (\d->return (s+d))
```

Using Haskell's `do` notation, this expression can be rewritten in a more readable way.

```
addDie :: Trans Int
addDie s = do d <- die
              return (s+d)
```

The statement `d <- die` can be thought of as universal quantification on the values in the distribution `die`.

In many cases, we want to repeat some transition multiple times. We create a constructor class `Iterate` for repeating various kinds of transitions, represented by the type constructor `c`.

```
class Iterate c where
    (*.)  :: Int -> (a -> c a) -> (a -> c a)
    while :: (a -> Bool) -> (a -> c a) -> (a -> c a)
```

In addition to iteration over distributions, we also iterate over randomized values. These are used to avoid monotonically increasing space usage (and thus, running out of memory) that can happen iterating with full distributions. For example, consider adding the value of `n` dice. At each step, the number of possible outcomes grows. All of these distributions will be combined and threaded again through the transition. In order to avoid space expansion, we provide random selection from distributions. In randomization, a distribution is created and one value selected at random based on the probabilities. A randomized transition is called an `RChange`, which takes a value and produces one randomized value. Random numbers are computed in the `IO` monad, for which we have created the synonym `R`.

```
type RChange a = a -> R a
```

Since an `RChange` produces only one value, we can thread the value through as many steps as we want and never worry about combinatorial explosion. Randomized values may be used in monads with the same syntax as distributions, but instead of being a universal quantification, it is a single selection: an existential quantification. We also provide the ability to construct randomized distributions by repeatedly sampling a particular randomized change. A randomized distribution (`RDist`) is some collection of values and probabilities that represents an approximation of the actual distribution. This is known as a Monte Carlo sampling. An randomized transition (`RTrans`) is a function that, given a value, produces such an approximation.

```
type RDist a  = R (Dist a)
type RTrans a = a -> RDist a
```

Continuing the dice example, we can establish iteration functions for rolling and summing the value of dice. The function `dieSum` rolls one hundred dice and adds them all together. The function `rDieSum` does the same, but uses randomization to only take ten walks through the space. The function `~*.` provides randomization of a transition and repeated walks to accumulate a randomized distribution.

```
dieSum = 100 *. addDie
rDieSum = (500,100) ~*. addDie
```

The randomized version offers considerable time and space savings. We can adjust the number of walks to spend more time gathering a better approximation, or to more quickly make a rough estimate. On the other hand, for a large number of steps, it is often impossible to run a full simulation.

The usual idea of iteration is to process a value repeatedly and return some final value. However, in some simulations we want to observe the evolution of a distribution over time. Since each step in an iteration produces an intermediate distribution, we can simply retain these distributions in a list rather than discard them. In general, a trace over any type of value can be represented as a list of that type. We call a trace of distributions a `Space`. This can be imagined as a three dimensional plane showing a slightly different distribution at each z value.

```
type Space a = [Dist a]
```

3   Probabilistic Modeling in Biology

The Lotka-Volterra predator-prey model [8] states that the population of predators and of prey can be described with mutually dependent equations. In particular, given the victims' growth factor (g), the predators' death factor (d), the search rate (s), and the energetic efficiency, (e), along with the current victim (v) and predator (p) population, a new population count can be determined with the equations $g * v - s * v * p$ (for victims) and $d * p + e * v * p$ (for predators). These new populations can then be rethreaded as input to create a simulation over time.

Consider the case when the growth and death rate are not a known constant, but exist within some probability distribution. We can define them, for example, using a normal curve.

```
growth = normal [1.01, 1.02 .. 1.10]
death  = normal [0.93, 0.94 .. 0.97]
(s,e)  = (0.01,0.01)
```

The data that we are simulating is the population of victims and predators. We can represent the population as a tuple of floats.

```
type Pop = (Float,Float)
```

Recall that we previously stated that distributions could be thought of as a monad. Monadic sequencing is very helpful in this case. We can create a transition which, given a Pop, produces a distribution of Pop based on the four distributions given above. The equations can be presented in the usual way, letting the monad do the heavy lifting of extracting values and combining probabilities.

In the transition dvp, all values are extracted by the monad from the distributions growth and death, and are then threaded through the equation, which is then recombined into a distribution of new values. In other words, this transition takes a current population and determines all possible new population values, and their probabilities.

```
dvp :: Trans Pop
dvp (v,p) = do g <- growth
               d <- death
               return (g*v - s*v*p `max` 0, d*p + e*v*p)
```

With an initial seed value, such as (v0,p0) = (15,15), we can now simulate the predator-prey model. However, if we tried this, we would quickly find that this is a case of strong combinatorial explosive, and we would be unable to simulate more than a handful of steps! The solution is to introduce randomization. This does not require any change to our transition, nor any modification of the equation. We simply use a function to perform 1000 randomized simulations (iteration of a randomized change) to produce a randomized distribution.

```
ppt n = ((1000,n) ~.. dvp) (v0,p0)
```

Of course, having the output come as a long list of values and probabilities is neither very interesting nor very useful. Therefore, we have developed a visualization module that presents information in a graph form.

We would like to visualize the generations (steps) on the X axis and the population count on the Y axis. In order to transform a distribution of population into a single value to plot we use the expected function which computes the expected value of a numeric distribution.

We can devise a function which operates on a randomized space to apply the expected function. First, the list of distributions must be extracted from the monad, then for each element in each distribution, either the first or the second element from the tuple (representing predator or prey) must be extracted, which is done by mapping a function f across all elements of each distribution. The expected function can be applied to each distribution in the space. The application of reverse is needed since traces are accumulated from the most recent value to the oldest value, but we want to plot the oldest value first.

```
getRE f rs = do rs' <- rs
                let rs'' = map (fmap f) rs'
                return (reverse (map expected rs''))
```

Finally, we can produce a chart with two lines: one for the predator and one for the prey. Note that the function plotRL takes a randomized list and turns it into a line on the graph. This list comes from calculating the expected value of each distribution in the randomized space.

```
fig1 = figP figure{title="Predator/Prey Simulation ",
                   xLabel="Time (generation)",
                   yLabel="Population"}
            [(plotRL v'){color=Green,label="Victim"},
             (plotRL p'){color=Red,label="Predator"}]
        where p = ppt 500
              v' = getRE fst p
              p' = getRE snd p
```

The plot created by this function is shown in Figure 1 on the left.

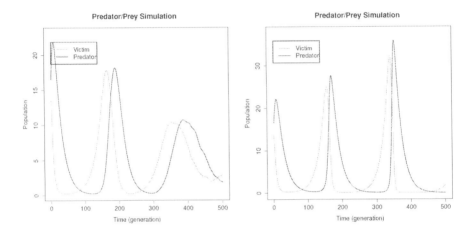

Fig. 1. Probabilistic (on the left) and deterministic (on the right) predator/prey simulation over 500 generations

Compared with the corresponding deterministic model with growth = 1.055 and death = 1.95 (shown in Figure 1 on the right), the probabilistic model demonstrates a quantitatively different behavior in how the peaks develop, suggesting that using probabilities in modeling has more effect than simply attempting to average the values and retain a deterministic approach. This conclusion is verified by Renshaw [16], who notes that stochastic predator-prey models almost always experience extinction after several generations.

4   Model Prototyping

In this section, we report on the gradual development of the genome model through iterations over several prototypes, followed by evaluations and discussions with biologists.

The most significant challenge we faced when developing this model was simply that the problem was not well defined; that is, the biologists did not know exactly what the model needed to represent. Thus, we have employed a method for rapid prototyping so that the model could evolve easily over time, which was essential to the project's success—the feedback and results from each step helped inform the biologists as to which direction would be most profitable to take. We conclude from our experience that any domain-specific language aimed at biologists, or scientists in general, should support rapid prototyping.

Biologists have determined that over generational time genomes experience evolutionary development. Part of this development includes parts of the genome being duplicated, and occasionally an inverted duplication. The duplications and inverted duplications can interact in some instances through microRNAs. MicroRNAs are transcribed from inverted duplications and can attach to duplicated genes to inhibit their expressiveness. In other words, when a duplication and inverted duplication are interacting, the genetic function of that duplication is suppressed. An important biological question is under what circumstances these microRNAs can develop.

To this end we had to model a genome that accumulates changes over time. The genome consists of multiple genes, which are either capable of interaction with inverted duplications or not, depending on the number of changes accumulated. The biologists felt that modeling various duplications of a single gene was sufficient. Therefore, the only information we need about each duplication (gene) is the number of changes it has accumulated. Our goal was to simulate how long any gene of the genome would remain in the state of interaction given a variety of initial conditions, such as varying rate of changes for different parts of the genome and different numbers of genes.

We started by constructing the genome as a list of duplications (also simply called genes) and inverted duplications. Duplications were simply represented as integers since the number of accumulated changes was the only information that mattered for this application. Inverted duplications had three significant parts that could accumulate changes, so we represented them with a three-tuple of integers. These three parts arise from the fact that an inverted duplication is strand of RNA folded onto itself. This can be viewed as two strands (sense and anti-sense) and a loop.

We then allowed a change to occur either in one of the parts of the inverted duplication or in one of the duplications. After discussing the model further, the biologists decided the inverted duplication needed only two components: a sense and an anti-sense. The loop was found to be non-significant. Since we were using high-level operations to express the model, the change was trivial.

Next, the biologists decided that merely having one inverted duplication was sufficient. Each duplication would then be compared against the inverted duplication to determine interaction. At this point, interaction was still a fuzzy concept, so we tried to clarify it into mathematical terms.

The biologists told us that, in the beginning, all the genes could interact with an inverted duplication. They called this state "full" interaction. Over evolutionary time, changes accumulate. If, for any duplication, the number of changes in that duplication plus the number of changes in the anti-sense of the inverted duplication were five or more, that duplication stopped interacting with the inverted duplication. In other words, the genetic function of that duplication could no longer be suppressed by a microRNA. If some duplications were interacting, the state was "partial". If none were interacting, the state was "none". In addition, if enough changes accumulated in the inverted duplication alone (a total of five between the sense and the anti-sense), then the inverted duplication was considered lost, and all interaction stopped. This behavior is directly implemented with the function `interaction`.

```
interaction :: Genome -> Interaction
interaction ((s,a),gs) | s+a>5 = Loss
                       | True  = if l==0 then None else
                                 if l==g then Full else Partial
                     where l=length ((filter (\n->a+n<=4)) gs)
                           g=length gs
```

It soon became apparent that this abstraction was not sufficiently detailed. The biologists told us that each gene actually needed to be divided into units. This meant that each duplication was now a list of n integers, each a place where changes could accumulate. We represented the inverted duplication as a list of n pairs (sense and anti-sense).

The additional complexity made the ideas of interaction and loss more interesting, as we had to match units in the genes with the units in the inverted duplication. We had to check each unit in a duplication against the corresponding anti-sense unit in the inverted duplication. If any had a sum of less than five changes, the duplication was still considered to interact. This concept is shown in Figure 2.

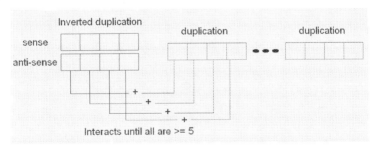

Fig. 2. The test of interaction

We made several additional changes before arriving at the final model, discussed in the next section, which the biologists found useful for generating predictions which they could test experimentally.

5   A Model of Genome Evolution

Our simulation finally ended up with a genome consisting of Dups and one inverted duplication IDup. In addition to a given number of Dups, we also had a given number of Units. Each gene was broken into that many units, and the sense and anti-sense of the inverted duplication also had that many units. We represented the inverted duplication with a list of Bins, where a Bin is simply a pair of units.

```
type Unit = Int
type Bin  = (Unit,Unit)

type Dup    = [Unit]
type IDup   = [Bin]
type Genome = (IDup,[Dup])
```

Initially, a change could randomly occur anywhere in any unit with equal probability. However, to model evolutionary pressure, we constructed several models which defined varying degrees of resilience for the gene parts. In particular, we used a "variable model" which allowed the genes to receive all the changes that fell on them, and a "family model" which allowed only one third of the changes to the duplications to accumulate. The names "variable" and "family" derive from the biologists' labels of different classes of genes, in particular, experiments which showed that some genes were essential to the functioning of an organism (thus were resistant to change) while others could change freely. The "family model" represents those genes which are resistant to change, while the "variable model" represents those which can freely change.

A model is a function which takes the number of genes in a genome and creates a probabilistic function which selects to accumulate a change in either the genes or the inverted duplication based on the number of genes.

```
type Model = Int -> Trans Genome
```

In the function mkModel to create a model, enumTT creates a distribution of transitions. Given the number of genes, x, and that there are 2 parts to the inverted duplication (sense and anti-sense), we make all units equally likely to experience a change. The function transAt performs a transition on a pair. The parameters 2 and 1 indicate which part of the pair should have the transition applied. Since genes are the second item in the pair, the gene transition performs the identity transition on the inverted duplication and a change on the genes, while for the inverted duplication we perform a correspondingly defined change and the identity transition on the genes. The definition for genes considers the probability given in gp, representing a family (gp = $\frac{1}{3}$) or variable (gp = 1) model, to determine whether to accept the change or ignore it.

At first glance, a simple uniform function would seem sufficient. However, since the genes and the idup contain an inequal number of accumulators, simply applying uniform would not give each accumulator an equal chance of being selected. Instead, we consider how many accumulators are present in each. The genome contains n genes, each with u units (accumulators). The inverted duplication contains u bins, each with two units. Thus, if x is the number of genes, then the total number of units is proportional to $2 + x$ (the two being from the inverted duplication) while the number of units in the genes is proportional to x. Thus, the probability of selecting a unit from the genes is $\frac{x}{2+x}$.

The functions chgGenes and chgIDup apply one change to either a list of duplications or a list of bins (an inverted duplication), respectively. The location of the change is a uniform distribution over all possible sites.

```
mkModel :: Float -> Model
mkModel gp v = enumTT [1-p,p] [genes,idup]
              where genes = transAt idT (chgGenes gp) 2
                    idup  = transAt chgIDup idT 1
                    x     = fromIntegral v
                    p     = x/(2+x)
```

A model that accepts all changes is defined by var and a model that accepts only one-third of changes to the genes is defined by fam.

```
var :: Model
var = mkModel 1

fam :: Model
fam = mkModel (1/3)
```

The state of interaction is defined as a function on the genome. The possibilities for interaction are Loss, None, Full and Partial.

```
data Interaction = Loss | None | Partial | Full
```

The state of Loss occurs when the pairs of the inverted duplication lined up sequentially had no pattern where the sum of changes between one sense and anti-sense was less than 11, the sum in the next less than 6, and the sum in the next less than 11. In other words, we rolled a 10-5-10 upper bound across the inverted duplication, and if no match was found, it was considered lost.

```
match x y z = x <= 10 && y <= 5 && z <= 10
```

The function defunct determines if an inverted duplication has been lost. This function takes three sequential pairs from an inverted duplication. Each pair (si,ai) consists of a sense si and anti-sense ai, which are represented as units accumulating changes. If the sum of the changes in the first pair and the third pair are less than or equal to 10, and the sum of the changes in the second (middle) pair is less than or equal to 5, then the inverted duplication is not defunct (not lost), so the function returns False. If the first three pairs do not, however, match the 10-5-10 pattern, then function shifts one pair down the sequence and looks again. If the function reaches the end of the sequence of pairs, and no sequence of three matching the pattern is found, the inverted duplication is considered lost. Implicitly, this means that all simulation models must have at least three units to be interesting.

```
defunct ((s1,a1):(s2,a2):(s3,a3):sx) |
    match (s1+a1) (s2+a2) (s3+a3) = False
defunct (_:sa2:sa3:sa) = defunct (sa2:sa3:sa)
defunct _ = True
```

If the inverted duplication is not lost, we proceed to inspect each gene to see if it interacts with the inverted duplication. Such interaction is determined by adding the changes in each unit in the gene to the anti-sense unit in the associated pair of the inverted duplication. If the sum is less than 5 for any unit, the gene is considered to interact with the inverted duplication.

```
interact :: IDup -> Dup -> Bool
interact i d = any (<=4) $ zipWith (+) (map snd i) (drop n d)
               where n = length d-length i
```

Gene interaction is tested for all genes, and the genome interaction state is determined by comparing the number of genes which interact with the total number of genes. If all genes interact, interaction is Full. If no genes interact, interaction is None. If some genes interact, interaction is Partial.

In this case, we define interaction as a function from a genome to an interaction state. The function interaction takes a Genome, which is a pair consisting of an inverted duplication i and a sequence of genes gs. The function defunct determines if the given inverted duplication is lost. If so, the interaction function always returns Loss. Otherwise, the number of genes g is determined by computing the length of the list gs, along with the number of genes currently interacting with the inverted duplication, which is determined by filtering the sequence of genes to retain only those that interact, and then counting them. These two values are then used to determine the interaction state as None, Partial or Full as described above.

```
interaction :: Genome -> Interaction
interaction (i,gs) | defunct i = Loss
                   | l==0      = None
                   | l==g      = Full
                   | otherwise = Partial
                      where l=length (filter (interact i) gs)
                            g=length gs
```

For each simulation run, we start with a genome that consists of an inverted duplication with no changes and a list of genes with no changes. We selected one of these genes to be the *founder gene* and set it aside. The remaining genes accumulated a given number of initial changes spread among them. The function g creates a `Genome` given an initial chance of changes c, the number of units per gene u and the number of genes n. This function first constructs the inverted duplication and genes with 0 changes. A list of $n-1$ of genes is constructed, which has the requested changes randomly applied. The function `chgGenes` here is the same as above; it applies one change per call to the given list of duplications. The parameter 1 indicates that it should not discard any changes. The founder gene, with no changes, is appended. This completes the creation of the genome. Once the genome is created, the model transition can be applied iteratively to produce a trace of the evolution.

```
g :: Float -> Int -> Int -> R Genome
g c u n = do gs' <- (m *. (random $ chgGenes 1)) gs
             return (zip f f,f:gs')
          where m  = round (fromIntegral n*c)
                f  = list u 0
                gs = list (n-1) f
```

Note the use of `random` to ensure that the change will produce a single randomized value rather than a distribution. This change is then iterated to select many randomized values, thus producing a randomized distribution, approximating the actual distribution.

We found that running a full simulation of the genome used tremendous amounts of memory and time, so we opted for randomized simulations, allowing the biologists to trade off between detail and time. In order to minimize memory usage, we performed the aggregation of traces at the outermost level. This avoids constructing a distribution during each simulation run, holding instead only a single randomized genome which is built into a randomized trace.

Changes were applied using the model until the interaction entered the state of `Loss`. Since these were randomized changes, we only accumulated an `RTrace`, which we then put together over many runs to produce an `RSpace`. We then analyzed each distribution to count how long the simulation stayed in partial interaction, as this was the configuration the biologists found interesting.

```
sumDiff :: [Dist Interaction] -> Float
sumDiff ds = sum (map (prob2Float . ((==Partial) ??)) ds)
```

We can then simply divide by the number of runs in the space to find the average time spent in interaction, which we can plot for varying models and number of genes. An example of the results is shown in Figure 3.

MicroRNAs are significant in determining the function of genes. However, it is not completely clear how about microRNAs have evolved—in particular, biologists note that microRNAs are not present with equal likelihood in all genes. Our model makes two concrete predictions about the presence of microRNAs: First, microRNAs are more likely to be found in "variable" genomes rather than "family" genomes, and second, as a probability per gene, microRNAs are more likely to be found in organisms with smaller genomes. Preliminary experimental results discussed in the forth-coming paper [1] supports both of these predictions.

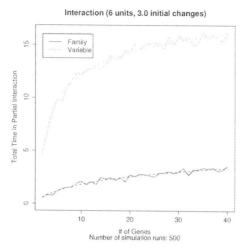

Fig. 3. Simulation results

6   Related Work

Work has been done on both probabilistic programming and modeling biological systems.

A theoretical, set-oriented treatment of probabilistic computations is given in [7]. The author points out that probabilistic computations can be considered in a monadic domain.

A monadic probability implementation is demonstrated by [14]. The authors show how probability distributions can be constructed using transitions similar to our own. The transitions can be combined monadically and operators are used to derive expected values and take samples. The authors also demonstrate a formal stochastic lambda calculus for representing probabilistic computations.

A randomized probabilistic language is demonstrated by Park, et al. [12]. Their method is based on sampling from probabilities, which can then be combined to form random results or probability distributions. Their method involves repeated sampling of the probability space, whereas our method can concretely represent this problem with deterministic probability distributions to find an exact probabilistic result.

An early attempt to model biological systems was done by McAdams and Shapiro [9]. The authors compared biological systems to electrical circuits noting that, like electrical circuits, biological systems operate in parallel and switches may describe activation or repression of either electricity or biological function.

Sato and Kameya [17] introduce a statistical logic learning language called PRISM based on Prolog. This language is designed for modeling uncertainty at a high level and can also infer parameters based on a set of given data.

A mathematical approach was taken by Nilsson and Fritzson with the Modelica system [11]. Modelica is an equation-oriented programming environment, which includes objects, allowing a direct modeling of biological components and the continuous mathematical models that direct their behavior. The authors also allow the introduction of thresholds, which allow discrete events to be modeled based on continuous value equations. A graphical environment exists, which allows straightforward access by mathematically trained scientists to develop Modelica models.

Regev et al. [15] introduce an abstraction method for representing biological components as units of computation. They call these components *ambients*. An ambient is an isolated computation environment which may contain, in a hierarchical fashion, other ambients. The authors also describe complex, multi-level models which include functions at the molecular, cellular, and anatomical level. These situations are modeled by having a set of ambients for each level of detail, and using the hierarchy to specify the range of influence. A language, BioSpi, is briefly described which includes the concept of ambients and is designed for systems biology simulations.

Eker et al. introduce a method they called "pathway logic" [4], which is an algebraic approach that allows analysis of the abstractions. For example, the authors point out that the equality of $(x+y)*(x-y)$ and $x^2 - y^2$ could be checked numerically for many possible values, but it can also be derived using a set of algebraic rewrite rules, which could form a proof. The authors define a specific set of rewrite rules involving proteins and cells and then show how analysis can provide several possible classes of results: explicit simulation, determining what constraints a given start state has on all future states (for example, if some property P is true, do we always reach a state that satisfies property Q?) and meta-analysis, which asks broadly which classes of starting states would satisfy some final criteria, thus allowing model disambiguation using actual data.

Pathway Modeling Language (PML) is introduced by Chang and Sridharan [3]. This language is based on the concept of binding sites—where two components have a compatible connector and so bind, allowing some private interactions and transformations, and then break apart with new connectors ready to bind to other components. They also provide for compartmentalization of reactions. This approach allows an event-oriented design where reactions happen as all preconditions are met and binding occurs. In this way, the order of reactions does not need to be explicitly specified.

7   Conclusions

High-level declarative languages, extended by suitable domain-specific abstractions, offer a great potential as executable modeling languages for scientists, because they support the incremental development of scientific models that can be instantly tested and easily revised and adapted.

We believe that typed functional languages are particularly well suited for this task since they allow the creation of type structures that closely reflect the modeled domains. This aspect gains in importance as scientific models evolve from being low-level and based on plain numbers toward incorporating higher-level (data) structures, such as sequences, tuples, and other data types, as evidenced by the presented application from genome evolution.

References

1. E. Allen, J. Carrington, M. Erwig, K. Kasschau, and S. Kollmansberger. Computational Modeling of microRNA Formation and Target Differentiation in Plants. 2005. In preparation.
2. J. C. Carrington and V. Ambros. Role of microRNAs in Plant and Animal Development. *Science*, 301:336–338, 2003.
3. Bor-Yuh Evan Chang and Manu Sridharan. PML: Toward a High-Level Formal Language for Biological Systems. In *Bio-CONCUR*, 2003.
4. Steven Eker, Merrill Knapp, Keith Laderoute, Patrick Lincoln, Jose Meseguer, and Kemal Sonmez. Pathway Logic: Symbolic Analysis of Biological Signaling. In *Pacific Symp. on Biocomputing*, pages 400–412, 2002.
5. M. Erwig and S. Kollmansberger. Probabilistic Functional Programming in Haskell. *Journal of Functional Programming*, 2005. To appear.
6. Giry, Michèle. A Categorical Approach to Probability Theory. In Banaschewski, Bernhard, editor, *Categorical Aspects of Topology and Analysis*, pages 68–85, 1981. Lecture Notes in Mathematics 915.
7. Jones, Claire and Plotkin, Gordon D. A Probabilistic Powerdomain of Evaluations. In *4th IEEE Symp. on Logic in Computer Science*, pages 186–195, 1989.
8. A. J. Lotka. The Growth of Mixed Populations: Two Species Competing for a Common Food Supply. *Journal of Washington Academy of Sciences*, 22:461–469, 1932.
9. Harley H. McAdams and Lucy Shapiro. Circuit Simulation of Genetic Networks. *Science*, 269(5224):650–656, 1995.
10. Morgan, Carroll and McIver, Annabelle and Seidel, Karen. Probabilistic Predicate Transformers. *ACM Trans. on Programming Languages and Systems*, 18(3):325–353, 1996.
11. Emma Larsdotter Nilsson and Peter Fritzson. Using Modelica for Modeling of Discrete, Continuous and Hybrid Biological and Biochemical Systems. In *The 3rd Conf. on Modeling and Simulation in Biology, Medicine and Biomedical Engineering*, 2003.
12. Park, Sungwoo and Pfenning, Frank and Thrun, Sebastian. A Probabilistic Language based upon Sampling Functions. In *32nd Symp. on Principles of Programming Languages*, pages 171–182, 2005.
13. PFP. Probabilistic Functional Programming Library, 2005. http://eecs.oregonstate.edu/~erwig/pfp.
14. Ramsey, Norman and Pfeffer, Avi. Stochastic Lambda Calculus and Monads of Probability Distributions. In *29th Symp. on Principles of Programming Languages*, pages 154–165, 2002.
15. Aviv Regev, Ekaterina M. Panina, William Silverman, Luca Cardelli, and Ehud Shapiro. BioAmbients: An abstraction for biological compartments. *Theoretical Computer Science, Special Issue on Computational Methods in Systems Biology*, 325(1):141–167, September 2004.
16. Renshaw, Eric. *Modelling Biological Populations in Space and Time*. Cambridge University Press, 1993.
17. T. Sato and Y. Kameya. Parameter Learning of Logic Programs for Symbolic-Statistical Modeling. *Journal of Artificial Intelligence Research*, 15:391–454, 2001.

Tabling in Mercury: Design and Implementation

Zoltan Somogyi[1] and Konstantinos Sagonas[2]

[1] NICTA Victoria Laboratory,
Department of Computer Science and Software Engineering,
University of Melbourne, Australia
[2] Department of Information Technology, Uppsala University, Sweden
zs@csse.unimelb.edu.au, kostis@it.uu.se

Abstract. For any LP system, tabling can be quite handy in a variety of tasks, especially if it is efficiently implemented and fully integrated in the language. Implementing tabling in Mercury poses special challenges for several reasons. First, Mercury is both semantically and culturally quite different from Prolog. While decreeing that tabled predicates must not include cuts is acceptable in a Prolog system, it is not acceptable in Mercury, since if-then-elses and existential quantification have sound semantics for stratified programs and are used very frequently both by programmers and by the compiler. The Mercury implementation thus has no option but to handle interactions of tabling with Mercury's language features safely. Second, the Mercury implementation is vastly different from the WAM, and many of the differences (e.g. the absence of a trail) have significant impact on the implementation of tabling. In this paper, we describe how we adapted the copying approach to tabling to implement tabling in Mercury.

1 Introduction

By now, it is widely recognized that tabling adds power to logic programming. By avoiding repeated subcomputations, it often significantly improves the performance of applications, and by terminating more often it allows for a more natural and declarative style of programming. As a result, many Prolog systems (e.g., XSB, YAP, and B-Prolog) nowadays offer some form of tabling. Mercury is a language with an efficient implementation and comes with a module and a strong type system that ease the development of industrial-scale applications. Like Prolog systems with tabling, Mercury aims to encourage a more declarative style of programming than "plain" Prolog. This paper discusses implementation aspects of adding tabling to Mercury.

When deciding which tabling mechanism to adopt, an implementor is faced with several choices. Linear tabling strategies [11, 3] are relatively easy to implement (at least for Prolog), but they are also relatively ad hoc and often perform recomputation. Tabled resolution strategies such as OLDT [9] and SLG [1] are guaranteed to avoid recomputation, but their implementation is challenging because they require the introduction of a suspension/resumption mechanism into the basic execution engine.

In the framework of the WAM [10], currently there are two main techniques to implement suspension/resumption. The one employed both in XSB and in YAP [5], that of the SLG-WAM [6], implements suspension via *stack freezing* and resumption using an

P. Van Hentenryck (Ed.): PADL 2006, LNCS 3819, pp. 150–167, 2006.

extended trail mechanism called the *forward trail*. The SLG-WAM mechanism relies heavily on features specific to the WAM, and imposes a small but non-negligible overhead on *all* programs, not just the ones which use tabling. The other main mechanism, CAT [2], completely avoids this overhead; it leaves the WAM stacks unchanged and implements suspension/resumption by incrementally saving and restoring the WAM areas that proper tabling execution needs to preserve in order to avoid recomputation.

For Mercury, we chose to base tabling on SLG resolution. We decided to restrict the implementation to the subset of SLG that handles stratified programs. We chose CAT as implementation platform, because the alternatives conflict with basic assumptions of the Mercury implementation. For example, Mercury has no trail to freeze, let alone a forward one, and freezing the stack *à la* SLG-WAM breaks Mercury's invariant that calls to deterministic predicates leave the stack unchanged. CAT is simply the tabling mechanism requiring the fewest, most isolated changes to the Mercury implementation. This has the additional benefit that it allows us to set up the system to minimize the impact of tabling on the performance of program components that do not use tabling; given an appropriate static analysis, the overhead can be completely eliminated.

This paper documents the implementation of tabling in Mercury (we actually aim to compute a specific minimal model of stratified programs: the perfect model). We describe how we adapted the CAT (Copying Approach to Tabling) mechanism to a different implementation technology, one which is closer to the execution model of conventional languages than the WAM, and present the additional optimizations that can be performed when tabling is introduced in such an environment. Finally, we mention how we ensure the safety of tabling's interactions with Mercury's if-then-else and existential quantification, constructs that would require the use of cut in Prolog.

The next section reviews Mercury and its implementation. Section 3 introduces tabling in Mercury, followed by the paper's main section (Section 4) which describes the implementation of tabling in detail. A brief performance comparison with other Prolog systems with tabling implementations based on SLG resolution appears in Section 5.

2   A Brief Introduction to Mercury

Mercury is a pure logic programming language intended for the creation of large, fast, reliable programs. While the syntax of Mercury is based on the syntax of Prolog, semantically the two languages are very different due to Mercury's purity, its type, mode, determinism and module systems, and its support for evaluable functions. Mercury has a strong Hindley-Milner type system very similar to Haskell's. Mercury programs are statically typed; the compiler knows the type of every argument of every predicate (from declarations or inference) and every local variable (from inference).

The mode system classifies each argument of each predicate as either input or output; there are exceptions, but they are not relevant to this paper. If input, the argument passed by the caller must be a ground term. If output, the argument passed by the caller must be a distinct free variable, which the predicate or function will instantiate to a ground term. It is possible for a predicate or function to have more than one mode; the usual example is append, which has two principal modes: append(in,in,out) and append(out,out,in). We call each mode of a predicate or function a *procedure*. The Mercury compiler generates different code for different procedures, even if they represent different modes of the same predicate or function. Each procedure has a determinism, which puts limits on the number of its possible solutions. Procedures with determinism *det* succeed exactly once; *semidet* procedures succeed at most once; *multi* procedures succeed at least once; while *nondet* procedures may succeed any number of times. A complete description of the Mercury language can be found at http://www.cs.mu.oz.au/research/mercury/information/doc-latest/mercury_ref.

The Mercury implementation. The front end of the Mercury compiler performs type checking, mode checking and determinism analysis. Programs without any errors are then subject to program analyses and transformations (such as the one being presented in Section 4) before being passed on to a backend for code generation.

The Mercury compiler has several backends. So far, tabling is implemented only for the original backend which generates low level C code [7], because it is the only one that allows us to explicitly manipulate stacks (see Section 4.3). The abstract machine targeted by this low level backend has three main data areas: a heap and two stacks. The heap is managed by the Boehm-Demers-Weiser conservative garbage collector for C. Since this collector was not designed for logic programming systems, it does not support any mechanism to deallocate all the memory blocks allocated since a specific point in time. Thus Mercury, unlike Prolog, does not recover memory by backtracking and recovers all memory blocks via garbage collection.

The Mercury abstract machine has two stacks: the *det stack* and the *nondet stack*. In most programs, most procedures can succeed at most once. This means that one cannot backtrack into a call to such a procedure after the procedure has succeeded, and thus there is no need to keep around the arguments and local variables of the call after the initial success (or failure, for semidet procedures). Mercury therefore puts the stack frames of such procedures on the det stack, which is managed in strict LIFO fashion.

Procedures that can succeed more than once have their stack frames allocated on the nondet stack. These frames are removed only when procedures fail. Since the stack frames of such calls stick around when the call succeeds, the nondet stack is not a true LIFO stack. Given a clause p(...) :- q(...), r(...), s(...), where p, q and r are all nondet or multi, the stack will contain the frames of p, q and r in order just after the call to r. After r succeeds and control returns to p, the frames of the calls to q and r are still on the stack. The Mercury abstract machine thus has two registers to point to the nondet stack: maxfr always points to the top frame, while curfr points to the frame of the currently executing call. (If the currently executing call uses the det stack, then curfr points to the frame of its most recent ancestor that uses the nondet stack.)

There are two kinds of frames on the nondet stack: *ordinary* and *temporary*. An ordinary frame is allocated for a procedure that can succeed more than once, i.e. whose determinism is nondet or multi. Such a frame is equivalent to the combination of a choice point and an environment in a Prolog implementation based on the WAM [10]. Ordinary nondet stack frames have five fixed slots and a variable number of other slots. The other slots hold the values of the variables of the procedure, including its arguments; these are accessed via offsets from curfr. The five fixed slots are:

prevfr The previous frame slot points to the stack frame immediately below this one. (Both stacks grow higher.)

redoip The redo instruction pointer slot contains the address of the instruction to which control should be transferred when backtracking into (or within) this call.

redofr The redo frame pointer slot contains the address that should be assigned to curfr when backtracking jumps to the address in the redoip slot.

succip The success instruction pointer slot contains the address of the instruction to which control should be transferred when the call of this stack frame succeeds.

succfr The success frame pointer slot contains the address of the stack frame that should be assigned to curfr when the call owning this stack frame succeeds; this will be the stack frame of its caller.

The redoip and redofr slots together constitute the failure continuation, while the succip and succfr slots together constitute the success continuation. In the example above, both q's and r's stack frames have the address of p's stack frame in their succfr slots, while their succip slots point to the instructions in p after their respective calls.

The compiler converts multi-clause predicate definitions into disjunctions. When executing in the code of a disjunct, the redoip slot points to the first instruction of the next disjunct or, if this is the last disjunct, to the address of the failure handler whose code removes the top frame from the nondet stack, sets curfr from the value in the redofr slot of the frame that is now on top, and jumps to the address in its redoip slot. Disjunctions other than the outermost one are implemented using temporary nondet stack frames, which have only prevfr, redoip and redofr slots [8].

The stack slot assigned to a variable contains garbage before the variable is instantiated; afterward, it contains the value of the variable. Since the compiler knows the state of instantiation of every visible variable at every program point, the code it generates will never look at stack slots containing garbage. This means that backtracking does not have to reset variables to unbound, which in turn means that the Mercury implementation does not need a trail.

3 Tabling in Mercury

In tabling systems, some predicates are declared *tabled* and use tabled resolution for their evaluation; all other predicates are *non-tabled* and are evaluated using SLD. Mercury also follows this scheme, but it supports three different forms of tabled evaluation: memoization (caching), loop checking, and minimal model evaluation. We concentrate on the last form, which is the most interesting and subsumes the other two.

The idea of tabling is to remember the first invocation of each call (henceforth referred to as a *generator*) and its computed results in tables (in a *call table* and an *answer table* respectively), so that subsequent identical calls (referred to as the *consumers*) can use the remembered answers without repeating the computation. Mercury programmers who are interested in computing the answers of tabled predicate calls according to the *perfect model* semantics can use the 'minimal_model' pragma. An example is the usual path predicate on the right.

```
:- pred path(int::in, int::out) is nondet.
:- pragma minimal_model(path/2).

path(A, B) :- edge(A, B).
path(A, B) :- edge(A, C), path(C, B).
```

Predicates with minimal_model pragmas are required to satisfy two requirements not normally imposed on all Mercury predicates. The first requirement is that the set of values computed by the predicate for its output arguments is completely determined by the values of the input arguments. This means that the predicate must not do I/O; it must also be *pure*, i.e., free of observable side-effects such as updating the value of a global variable through the foreign function interface. The second is that each argument of a minimal model predicate must be either fully input (ground at call and at return) or fully output (free at call, ground at return). In other words, partially instantiated arguments and arguments of unknown instantiation are not allowed. How this restriction affects the implementation of tabling in Mercury is discussed in the following section.

When a call to a minimal model predicate is made, the program must check whether the call exists in the call table or not. In SLG terminology [1], this takes place using the NEW SUBGOAL operation. If the subgoal *s* is new, it is entered in the table and this call, as the subgoal's generator, will use PROGRAM CLAUSE RESOLUTION to derive answers. The generator will use the NEW ANSWER operation to record each answer it computes in a global data structure called the *answer table* of *s*. If, on the other hand, (a variant of) *s* already exists in the table, this call is a consumer and will resolve against answers from the subgoal's answer table. Answers are fed to the consumer one at a time through ANSWER RETURN operations.

Because in general it is not known *a priori* how many answers a tabled call will get in its table, and because there can be mutual dependencies between generators and consumers, the implementation requires: (a) a mechanism to retain (or reconstruct) and reactivate the execution environments of consumers until there are no more answers for them to consume, and (b) a mechanism for returning answers to consumers and determining when the evaluation of a (generator) subgoal is *complete*, i.e. when it has produced all its answers. As mentioned, we chose the CAT suspension/resumption mechanism as the basis for Mercury's tabling implementation. However, we had to adapt it to Mercury and extend it in order to handle existential quantification and negated contexts. For completion, we chose the *incremental completion* approach described in [6]. A subgoal can be determined to be complete if all program clause resolution has finished and all instances of this subgoal have resolved against all derived answers. However, as there might exist dependencies between subgoals, these have to be taken into account by maintaining and examining the subgoal dependency graph, finding a set of subgoals that depend only on each other, completing them together, and then repeating the process until there are no incomplete subgoals. We refer to these sets of subgoals as *scheduling components*. The generator of some subgoal (typically the oldest) in the component is called the component's *leader*.

4   The Implementation of Tabling in Mercury

4.1   The Tabling Transformation and Its Supporting Data Structures

Mercury allows programmers to use impure constructs to implement a pure interface, simply by making a promise to this effect. The tabling implementation exploits this capability. Given a pure predicate such as path/2, a compiler pass transforms its body by surrounding it with impure and semipure code as shown in Fig. 3 (impure code may write global variables; semipure code may only read them). Note that the compiler promises that the transformed code behaves as a pure goal, since the side-effects inside are not observable from the outside.

As mentioned, the arguments of tabled procedures must be either fully input or fully output. This considerably simplifies the implementation of call tables. SLG resolution considers two calls to represent the same subgoal if they are *variants*, i.e., identical up to variable renaming. In Mercury, this is the case if and only if the two calls have the same ground terms in their input argument positions, because the output arguments of a call are always distinct variables. Conceptually, the call table of a predicate with n input arguments is a tree with $n + 1$ levels. Level 0 contains only the root node. Each node on level 1 corresponds to a value of the first input argument that the predicate has been called with; in general, each node on level k corresponds to a combination of the values of the first k input arguments that the predicate has been called with. Thus each node on level n uniquely identifies a subgoal.

The transformed body of a minimal model predicate starts by looking up the call table to see whether this subgoal has been seen before or not. Given a predicate declared as in the code shown in Fig. 1, the minimal model tabling transformation inserts the code shown on the same figure at the start of its procedure body.

```
:- pred p(int::in, string::in, int::out, t1::in, t2::out) is nondet.
:- pragma minimal_model(p/5).

p(In1, In2, Out1, In3, Out2) :-
    ...
```

```
        pickup_call_table_root_for_p_5(CallTableRoot),
impure  lookup_insert_int(CallTableRoot, In1, CallNode1),
impure  lookup_insert_string(CallNode1, In2, CallNode2),
impure  lookup_insert_user(CallNode2, In3, CallNode3),
impure  subgoal_setup(CallNode3, Subgoal, Status)
```

Fig. 1. Type-directed program transformation for arguments of tabled calls

We store all the information we have about each subgoal in a *subgoal structure*. We reach the subgoal structure of a given subgoal through a pointer in the subgoal's level n node in the call table. The subgoal structure has the following eight fields (cf. Fig. 2), which we will discuss as we go along: 1) the subgoal's status (*new, active* or *complete*); 2) the chronological list of the subgoal's answers computed so far; 3) the root of the

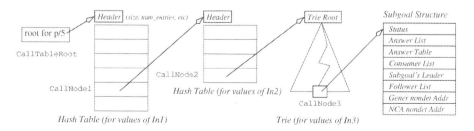

Fig. 2. Data structures created for the calls of predicate p/5

subgoal's answer table; 4) the list of the consumers of this subgoal; 5) the leader of the scheduling component this subgoal belongs to; 6) if this subgoal is the leader, the list of its followers; 7) the address of the generator's frame on the nondet stack; and 8) the address of the youngest nondet stack frame that is an ancestor of both this generator and all its consumers; we call this the nearest common ancestor (NCA).

In the code of Fig. 3, `CallTableRoot`, `CallNode1`, `CallNode2` and `CallNode3` are all pointers to nodes in the call tree at levels 0, 1, 2 and 3 respectively; see Fig. 2. `CallTableRoot` points to the global variable generated by the Mercury compiler to serve as the root of the call table for this procedure. This variable is initialized to NULL, indicating no child nodes yet. The first call to p/5 will cause `lookup_insert_int` to create a hash table in which every entry is NULL, and make the global variable point to it. The `lookup_insert_int` call will then hash In1, create a new slot in the indicated bucket (or in one of its overflow cells) and return the address of the new slot as `CallNode1`.

```
path(A, B) :-
  promise_pure (
    pickup_call_table_root_for_path_2(CallTableRoot),
    impure lookup_insert_int(CallTableRoot, A, CallNode1),
    impure subgoal_setup(CallNode1, Subgoal, Status),
    ( % switch on 'Status'
      Status = new,
      (
        impure mark_as_active(Subgoal),
        % original body of path/2 in the two lines below
        edge(A, C),
        ( C = B ; path(C, B) ),
        semipure get_answer_table(Subgoal, AnsTabRoot),
        impure lookup_insert_int(AnsTabRoot, B, AnsNode1),
        impure answer_is_not_duplicate(AnsNode1),
        impure new_answer_block(Subgoal, 1, AnsBlock),
        impure save_answer(AnsBlock, 0, B)
      ;
        impure completion(Subgoal),
        fail
      )
    ;
      Status = complete,
      semipure return_all_answers(Subgoal, AnsBlock),
      semipure restore_answer(AnsBlock, 0, B)
    ;
      Status = active,
      impure suspend(Subgoal, AnsBlock),
      semipure restore_answer(AnsBlock, 0, B)
    )
  ).
```

Fig. 3. Example of the tabling transformation on path/2

At later calls, the hash table will exist, and by then we may have seen the then current value of In1 as well; `lookup_insert_int` will perform a lookup if we have and an insertion if we have not. Either way, it will return the address of the slot selected by In1. The process then gets repeated with the other input arguments. (The predicates being called are different because Mercury uses different representations for different types. For example, integers are hashed directly but we hash the characters of a string, not its address.)

User-defined types. Values of these types consist of a function symbol applied to zero or more arguments. In a strongly typed language such as Mercury, the type of a variable directly determines the set of function symbols that variable can be bound to. The data structure we use to represent a function symbol from user-defined types is therefore a *trie*, a data structure which has extensively been used in tabled systems [4]. If the function symbol is a constant, we are done. If it has arguments, then `lookup_insert_user` processes them one by one the same way we process the arguments of predicates, using the slot selected by the function symbol to play the role of the root. In this way, the path in the call table from the root to a leaf node representing a given subgoal has exactly one trie node or hash table on it for each function symbol in the input arguments of the subgoal; their order is given by a preorder traversal of those function symbols.

Polymorphic types. This scheme works for monomorphic predicates because at each node of the tree, the type of the value at that node is fixed, and the type determines the mechanism we use to table values of that type (integer, string or float hash table for builtin types, a trie for user-defined types). For polymorphic predicates (whose signatures include type variables) the caller passes extra arguments identifying the actual types bound to those type variables. We first table these arguments, which are terms of a builtin type. Once we have followed the path from the root to the level of the last of these arguments, we have arrived at what is effectively the root of the table for a given monomorphic instance of the predicate's signature, and we proceed as described above.

4.2   The Tabling Primitives

The `subgoal_setup` primitive ensures the presence of the subgoal's subgoal structure. If this is a new subgoal, then `CallNode3` will point to a table node containing NULL. In that case, `subgoal_setup` will (a) allocate a new subgoal structure, initializing its fields to reflect the current situation, (b) update the table node pointed to by `CallNode3` to point to this new structure, and (c) return this same pointer as `Subgoal`. If this is not the first call to this procedure with these input arguments, then `CallNode3` will point to a table node that contains a pointer to the previously allocated subgoal structure, so `subgoal_setup` will just return this pointer.

`subgoal_setup` returns not just `Subgoal`, but also the subgoal's status. When first created, the status of the subgoal is set to *new*. It becomes *active* when a generator has started work on it and becomes *complete* once it is determined that the generator has produced all its answers.

What the transformed procedure body does next depends on the subgoal's initial status. If the status is *active* or *complete*, the call becomes one of the subgoal's consumers. If it is *new*, the call becomes the subgoal's generator and executes the original body of the predicate after changing the subgoal's status to *active*. When an answer is generated, we check whether this answer is new. We do this by using `get_answer_table` to retrieve the root of the answer table from the subgoal structure, and inserting the output arguments into this table one by one, as we inserted the input arguments into the call table. The node on the last level of the answer table thus uniquely identifies this answer.

`answer_is_not_duplicate` looks up this node. If the tip of the answer table selected by the output argument values is NULL, then this is the first time we have computed this answer for this subgoal, and the call succeeds. Otherwise it fails. (To make later calls fail, `answer_is_not_duplicate` sets the tip to non-NULL on success.) We thus get to call `new_answer_block` only if the answer we just computed is new.

`new_answer_block` adds a new item to the end of the subgoal's chronological list of answers, the new item being a fresh new memory block with room for the given number of output arguments. The call to `new_answer_block` is then followed by a call to `save_answer` for each output argument to fill in the slots of the answer block.

When the last call to `save_answer` returns, the transformed code of the tabled predicate succeeds. When backtracking returns control to the tabled predicate, it will drive the original predicate body to generate more and more answers. In programs with a finite perfect model, the answer generation will eventually stop, and execution will enter the second disjunct, which invokes the `completion` primitive. This will make the answers generated so far for this subgoal available to any consumers that are waiting for such answers. This may generate more answers for this subgoal if the original predicate body makes a call, directly or indirectly, to this same subgoal. The `completion` primitive will drive this process to a fixed point (see Sect. 4.5) and then mark the subgoal as *complete*. Having already returned all answers of this subgoal from the first disjunct, execution fails out of the body of the transformed predicate.

If the subgoal is initially *complete*, we call `return_all_answers`, which succeeds once for each answer in the subgoal's chronological list of answers. For each answer, calls to `restore_answer` pick up the output arguments put there by `save_answer`.

If the initial status of the subgoal is *active*, then this call is a consumer but the generator is not known to have all its answers. We therefore call the `suspend` primitive. `suspend` has the same interface as `return_all_answers`, but its implementation is much more complicated. We invoke the `suspend` primitive when we cannot continue computing along the current branch of the SLD tree. The main task of the suspension operation is therefore to record the state of the current branch of the SLD tree to allow its exploration later, and then simulate failure of that branch, allowing the usual process of backtracking to switch execution to the next branch. Sometime later, the `completion` primitive will restore the state of this branch of the SLD tree, feed the answers of the subgoal to it, and let the branch compute more answers if it can.

4.3   Suspension of Consumers

The `suspend` primitive starts by creating a *consumer structure* and adding it to the current subgoal's list of consumers. This structure has three fields: a pointer to this subgoal's subgoal structure (available in `suspend`'s `Subgoal` argument), an indication of which answers this consumer has consumed so far, and the saved state of the consumer.

Making a copy of all the data areas of the Mercury abstract machine (det stack, nondet stack, heap and registers) would clearly be sufficient to record the state of the SLD branch, but equally clearly it would also be overkill. To minimize overhead, we want to record only the parts of the state that contain needed information which can change between the suspension of this SLD branch and any of its subsequent resumptions. For consumer suspensions, the preserved saved state is as follows.

Registers. The special purpose abstract machine registers (`maxfr`, `curfr`, the det stack pointer `sp`, and the return address register `succip`) all need to be part of the saved state, but of all the general purpose machine registers used for parameter passing, the only one that contains live data and thus needs to be saved is the one containing `Subgoal`.

Heap. With Mercury's conservative collector, heap space is recovered only by garbage collection and never by backtracking. This means that a term on the heap will naturally hang around as long as a pointer to it exists, regardless of whether that pointer is in a current stack or in a saved copy. Moreover, in the absence of destructive updates, this data will stay unchanged. This in turn means that, unlike a WAM-based implementation of CAT, Mercury's implementation of minimal model tabling *does not need to save or restore any part of the heap.* This is a big win, since the heap is typically the largest area. The tradeoff is that we need to save more data from the stacks, because the mapping from variables to values (the current substitution) is stored entirely in stack slots.

Stacks. The way Mercury uses stack slots is a lot closer to the runtime systems of imperative languages than to the WAM. First of all, there are no links between variables because the mode system does not allow two free variables to be unified. Binding a variable to a value thus affects only the stack slot holding the variable. Another difference concerns the timing of parameter passing. If a predicate p makes the call q(A), and the definition of q has a clause with head q(B), then in Prolog, A would be unified with B at the time of the call, and any unification inside q that binds B would immediately update A in p's stack frame. In Mercury, by contrast, there is no information flow between caller and callee except at call and return. At call, the caller puts the input arguments into abstract machine registers and the callee picks them up; at return, the callee puts the output arguments into registers and the caller picks them up. Each invocation puts the values it picks up into a slot of its own stack frame when it next executes a call. The important point is that the only code that modifies a stack frame fr is the code of the procedure that created fr.

CAT saves the frames on the stacks between the stack frame of the generator (excluded) and the consumer (included), and uses the WAM trail to save and restore addresses and values of variables which have been bound since the creation of a consumer's generator. Mercury has no variables on its heap, but without a mechanism like the trail to guide the selective copying of stack slots which might change values, it must make sure that suspension saves information in *all* stack frames that could be modified between the suspension of a consumer and its resumption by its generator. The deepest frame on the nondet stack that this criterion requires us to save is the frame of the *nearest common ancestor* (NCA) of the consumer and the generator. We find the NCA by initializing two pointers to point to the consumer and generator stack frames, and repeatedly replacing whichever pointer is higher with the succfr link of the frame it points to, stopping when the two pointers are equal.

Two technical issues deserve to be mentioned. Note that we *must* save the stack frame of the NCA because the variable bindings in it may have changed between the suspension and the resumption. Also, it is possible for the nearest common ancestor of the generator and consumer to be a procedure that lives on the det stack. The expanded version of this paper [8] gives examples of these situations, motivates the implementation alternatives we chose to adopt, and argues for the correctness of saving (only) this information for consumers.

4.4   Maintenance of Subgoal Dependencies and Their Influence on Suspensions

We have described suspension as if consumers will be scheduled only by their nearest generator. This is indeed the common case, but as explained in Section 3 there are also situations in which subgoals are mutually dependent and cannot be completed on an individual basis. To handle such cases, Mercury maintains a stack-based approximation of dependencies between subgoals, in the form of scheduling components. For each scheduling component (a group subgoals that may depend on each other), its *leader* is the youngest generator G_L for which all consumers younger than G_L are consumers of generators that are not older than G_L. Of all scheduling components, the one of most interest is that on the top of the stack. This is because it is the one whose consumers will be scheduled first. We call its leader the *current leader*.

The maintenance of scheduling components is reasonably efficient. Information about the leader of each subgoal and the leader's *followers* is maintained in the subgoal structure (cf. Fig. 2). Besides creation of a new generator (in which case the generator becomes the new current leader with no followers), this information possibly changes whenever execution creates a consumer suspension. If the consumer's generator, G, is the current leader or is younger than the current leader, no change of leaders takes place. If G is older than the current leader, a *coup* happens, G becomes the current leader, and its scheduling component gets updated to contain as its followers the subgoals of all generators younger than G. In either case, the saved state for the consumer suspension will be till the NCA of the consumer and the current leader. This generalizes the scheme described in the previous section.

Because a coup can happen even after the state of a consumer has been saved, we also need a mechanism to extend the saved consumer states. The mechanism we have implemented consists of extending the saved state of all consumers upon change of leaders. When a coup happens, the saved state of all followers (consumers and generators) of the old leader is extended to the stack frame of the NCA of each follower and the new leader. Unlike CAT which tries to share the trail, heap, and local stack segments it copies [2], in Mercury we have not (yet) implemented sharing of the copied stack segments. It is our intention to implement and evaluate such a mechanism. However, note that the space problem is not as severe in Mercury as it is in CAT, because in Mercury there is no trail and no information from the heap is ever copied, which means that heap segments for consumers are naturally shared.

On failing back to a generator which is a leader, scheduling of answers to all its followers will take place, as described below. When the scheduling component gets completed, execution will continue with the immediately older scheduling component, whose leader will then become the current leader.

4.5   Resumption of Consumers and Completion

The main body of the `completion` primitive consists of three nested loops: over all subgoals in the current scheduling component S, over all consumers of these subgoals, and over all answers to be returned to those consumers. The code in the body of the nested loops arranges for the next unconsumed answer to be returned to a consumer of a subgoal in S. It does this by restoring the stack segments saved by the `suspend` primitive, putting the address of the relevant answer block into the abstract machine register assigned to the return value of `suspend`, restoring the other saved abstract machine registers, and branching to the return address stored in `suspend`'s stack frame. Each consumer resumption thus simulates a return from the call to `suspend`.

Since restoring the stack segments from saved states of consumers clobbers the state of the generator that does the restoring (the leader of S), the `completion` primitive first saves the leader's own state, which consists of saving the nondet stack down to the oldest NCA of the leader generator and any of the consumers it schedules, and saving the part of the det stack allocated since the creation of this nondet frame. To provide the information required for the second part of this operation, we extend every ordinary nondet stack frame with a sixth slot that contains the address of the top of the det stack at the time of the nondet stack frame's creation.

Resumption of a consumer essentially restores the saved branch of the SLD search tree, but restoring its saved stack segments *intact* is not a good idea. The reason is that leaving the `redoip` slots of the restored nondet stack frames unchanged resumes not just the saved branch of the SLD search tree, but also the departure points of all the branches going off to its right. Those branches have been explored immediately after the suspension of the consumer, because suspension involves simulating the failure of the consumer, thus initiating backtracking. When we resume a consumer to consume an answer, we do not want to explore the exact same alternatives again, since this could lead to an arbitrary slowdown. We therefore replace all the `redoips` in saved nondet stack segments to make them point to the failure handler in the runtime system. This effectively cuts off the right branches, making them fail immediately. Given the choice between doing this pruning once when the consumer is suspended or once for each time the consumer is resumed, we obviously choose the former.

This pruning means that when we restore the saved state of a consumer, only the success continuations are left intact, and thus the only saved stack frames the restored SLD branch can access are those of the consumer's ancestors. Any stack frames that are not the consumer's ancestors have effectively been saved and restored in vain.

When a resumed consumer has consumed all the currently available answers, it fails out of the restored segment of the nondet stack. We arrange to get control when this happens by setting the `redoip` of the very oldest frame of the restored segment to point to the code of the `completion` primitive. When `completion` is reentered in this way, it needs to know that the three-level nested loop has already started and how far it has gone. We therefore store the state of the nested loop in a global record. When this state indicates that we have returned all answers to all consumers of subgoals in S, we have reached a fixed point. At this time, we mark all subgoals in S as *complete* and we reclaim the memory occupied by the saved states of all their consumers and generators.

4.6   Existential Quantification

Mercury supports existential quantification. This construct is usually used to check whether a component of a data structure possesses a specific property as in the code:

```
:- pred list_contains_odd_number(list(int)::in) is semidet.
list_contains_odd_number(List) :- some [N] (member(N, List), odd(N)).
```

Typically the code inside the quantification may have more than one solution, but the code outside only wants to check whether a solution *exists* without caring about the number of solutions or their bindings. One can thus convert a multi or nondet goal into a det or semidet goal by existentially quantifying all its output variables. Mercury implements quantifications of that form using what we call a *commit* operation, which some Prologs call a *once* operation. The operation saves `maxfr` when it enters the goal and restores it afterward, throwing away all the stack frames that have been pushed onto the nondet stack in the meantime. The interaction with tabling arises from the fact that the discarded stack frames can include the stack frame of a generator. If this happens, the commit removes all possibility of the generator being backtracked into ever again, which in turn may prevent the generation of answers and completion of the corresponding subgoal. Without special care, all later calls of that subgoal will become consumers who will wait forever for the generator to schedule the return of their answers.

To handle such situations, we introduce of a new stack which we call the *cut stack*. This stack always has one entry for each currently active existentially quantified goal; new entries are pushed onto it when such a goal is entered and popped when that goal either succeeds or fails. Each entry contains a pointer to a list of generators. Whenever a generator is created, it is added to the list in the entry currently on top of the cut stack. When the goal inside the commit succeeds, the code that pops the cut stack entry checks its list of generators. For all generators whose status is not *complete*, we erase all trace of their existence and reset the call table node that points to the generator's subgoal structure back to a null pointer. This allows later calls to that subgoal to become new generators.

If the goal inside the commit fails, the failure may have been due to the simulated failure of a consumer inside that goal. When the state of the consumer is restored, it may well succeed, which means that any decision the program may have taken based on the initial failure of the goal may be incorrect. When the goal inside the commit fails, we therefore check whether any of the generators listed in the cut stack entry about to be popped off have a status other than *complete*. Any such generator must have consumers whose failure may not be final, so we throw an exception in preference to computing incorrect results. Note that this can happen only when the leader of the incomplete generator's scheduling component is outside the existential quantification.

4.7   Possibly Negated Contexts

The interaction of tabling with cuts and Prolog-style negation is notoriously tricky. Many implementation papers on tabling ignore the issue altogether, considering only the definite subset of Prolog. An implementation of tabling for Mercury cannot duck the issue. Mercury programs rely extensively on if-then-elses, and if-then-elses involve negation: "if C then T else E" is semantically equivalent to $(C \wedge T) \vee (\neg \exists C \wedge E)$. Of course, operationally the condition is executed only once. The condition C is a possibly negated context: it is negated only if it has no solutions. Mercury implements if-then-else using a *soft cut*: if the condition succeeds, it cuts away the possibility of backtracking to the else part only (the condition may succeed more than once).

If C fails, execution should continue at the else part of the if-then-else. This poses a problem for our implementation of tabling, because the failure of the condition does not necessarily imply that C has no solution: it may also be due to the suspension of a consumer called (directly or indirectly) somewhere inside C, as in the code below.

```
p(...) :- t_g(...), ( if ( ..., t_c(...), ... ) then ... else ... ), ...
```

If t_c suspends and is later resumed to consume an answer, the condition may evaluate to true. However, by then the damage will have been done, because we will have executed the code in the else part.

We have not yet implemented a mechanism that will let us compute the correct answer in such cases, because any such mechanism would need the ability to transfer the "generator-ship" of the relevant subgoal from the generator of t to its consumer, or something equivalent. However, we *have* implemented a mechanism that guarantees that incorrect answers will not be computed. This mechanism is the *possibly-negated-context stack*, or *pneg stack* for short. We push an entry onto this stack when entering a possibly negated context such as the condition of an if-then-else. The entry contains a pointer to a list of consumers, which is initially empty. When creating a consumer, we link the consumer into the list of the top entry on the pneg stack. When we enter the else part of the if-then-else, we search this list looking for consumers that are suspended. Since suspension simulates failure without necessarily implying the absence of further solutions, we throw an exception if the search finds such a consumer and abort execution. If not, we simply pop the entry of the pneg stack. We also perform the pop on entry to the then part of the if-then-else. Since in that case there is no risk of committing to the wrong branch of the if-then-else, we do so without looking at the popped entry.

There are two other Mercury constructs that could compute wrong answers if the failure of a goal does not imply the absence of solutions for it. The first is negation. We handle negation as a special case of if-then-else: $\neg G$ is equivalent to "if G then fail else true". The other is the generic all-solutions primitive builtin_aggregate, which serves as the basic building block for all of Mercury's all-solutions predicates. The implementation of builtin_aggregate uses a failure driven loop. To ward against builtin_aggregate(Closure,...) mistaking the failure of call(Closure) due to a suspension somewhere inside Closure as implying the absence of solutions to Closure, we treat the loop body as the condition of an if-then-else, i.e. we surround it with the code we normally insert at the start of the condition and the start of the else part (see [8] for the details).

Entries on both the cut stack and the pneg stack contain a field that points to the stack frame of the procedure invocation that created them, which is of course also responsible for removing them. When saving stack segments or extending saved stack segments, we save an entry on the cut stack or the pneg stack if the nondet stack frame they refer to is in the saved segment of the nondet stack.

5   Performance Evaluation

We ran several benchmarks to measure the performance of Mercury with tabling support, but space limitations allow presenting only some of them here.

Overhead of the grade with full tabling support. We compiled the Mercury compiler in two grades that differ in that one supports minimal model tabling, the form of tabling discussed in this paper, by including the cut and pneg stacks and the extra slot on nondet stack frames, and while the other, lacking these extras, supports only the other forms of tabling (memoization and loop checking). Enabling support for minimal model tabling without using it (the compiler has no minimal model predicates) increases the size of the compiler executable by about 5%. On the standard benchmark task for the Mercury compiler, compiling six of its own largest modules, moving to a minimal model grade with full tabling support slows the compiler down by about 25%. (For comparison, enabling debugging leads to a 455% increase in code size and a 135% increase in execution time.) First of all, it should be mentioned that paying this 25% cost in time

Table 1. Times (in secs) to execute various versions of transitive closure

benchmark	size	iter	chain				cycle			
			XSB	XXX	YAP	Mercury	XSB	XXX	YAP	Mercury
tc_lr +-	4K	200	0.62	0.51	0.28	0.58	0.63	0.52	0.28	0.59
tc_lr +-	8K	200	1.24	1.05	0.62	1.27	1.27	1.07	0.62	1.30
tc_lr +-	16K	200	2.57	2.15	1.51	2.47	2.62	2.12	1.48	2.61
tc_lr +-	32K	200	5.25	4.41	3.78	5.23	5.20	4.44	3.78	5.07
tc_lr --	2K	1	2.58	2.46	1.25	3.20	6.22	6.30	2.88	6.24
tc_rr --	2K	1	2.21	2.04	2.94	10.27	6.35	5.85	6.00	27.48

happens only if the user selects a grade with minimal model tabling support: programs that do not use minimal model tabling at all can use the default asm_fast.gc grade and thus not pay any cost whatsoever. Moreover, this 25% is probably an upper limit. (See also the results in Table 3 which overall show less than 19% overhead.) Virtually all of this cost in both space and time is incurred by the extra code we have to insert around possibly negated contexts; the extra code around commits and the larger size of nondet stack frames have no measurable overheads (see the data in [8]). If we had an analysis that could determine that tabled predicates are not involved (directly or indirectly) in a possibly negated context, this overhead could be totally avoided for that context. We are now working on such an analysis.

Comparison against other implementations of tabling. We compared the minimal model grade of Mercury (using rotd-06-10-2005, based on CAT) against XSB (2.7.1, based on the SLG-WAM), the XXX system (derived from XSB but based on CHAT) and YAP (version in CVS at 28 July 2005, based on SLG-WAM). XSB and XXX use *local scheduling* [6] in the default configuration while YAP uses *batched scheduling*. Mercury's scheduling strategy is similar but not identical to batched scheduling. All benchmarks were run on an IBM ThinkPad R40 laptop with a 2.0 GHz Pentium4 CPU and 512 Mb of memory running Linux. All times were obtained by running each benchmark eight times, discarding the lowest and highest values, and averaging the rest.

The first set of benchmarks consists of left- and right-recursive versions of transitive closure. In each case, the edge relation is a chain or a cycle. In a chain of size n, there are $n - 1$ edges of the form $k \rightarrow k + 1$ for $0 \leq k < n$; in a cycle of size n, there is also an edge $n \rightarrow 0$. We use two query forms: the query with the first argument input and the second output (+-) and the open query with both arguments output (--). The number of solutions is linear in the size of the data for the +- query and quadratic for --. The second set consists of versions of the same generation predicate with full indexing (i) or Prolog-style first-argument indexing only (p), with the same two kinds of queries. Each table entry shows how long it takes for a given system to run the specified query on the specified data *iter* times (iter=50 for the sg benchmarks). The tables are reset between iterations. In Tables 1 and 2, benchmarks use a failure driven loop or its equivalent to perform the iterations, while in Table 3 they use a tail-recursive driver predicate.

The rows for the +- query on left recursive transitive closure show all runtimes to be linear in the size of the data, as expected. Also, on left recursion, regardless of query, YAP is fastest, and XSB, XXX and Mercury are pretty similar. On right recursion, Mercury is slower than the other systems due to saving and restoring stack segments

Table 2. Times (in secs) to execute various versions of same generation

benchmark	XSB	XXX	YAP	Mercury
sg i +-	1.21	1.32	0.34	1.05
sg i --	3.53	3.89	1.07	2.43
sg p +-	83.56	58.17	34.58	32.14
sg p --	237.58	161.08	77.63	92.64

of consumers, and having to do so more times due to its different scheduling strategy (YAP doesn't do save/restore). It is unfortunate that not all systems implement the same scheduling strategy. However, local evaluation (i.e., postponing the return of answers to the generator until the subgoal is complete) is not compatible with the pruning that Mercury's execution model requires in existential quantifications, a construct not properly handled in Prolog systems with tabling. On the same generation (sg) benchmark, in which consumer suspensions are not created (variant subgoals are only encountered when the subgoals are completed), Mercury is clearly much faster than XSB and XXX, although it is still beaten by YAP in three cases out of four. Two reasons why Mercury's usual speed advantage doesn't materialize here are that (1) these benchmarks spend much of their time executing tabling's primitive operations, which are in handwritten C code in all four systems, and (2) the Prolog systems can recover the memory allocated by an iteration by resetting the heap pointer, whereas in Mercury this can be done only by garbage collection. (Although the benchmark programs are Datalog, the all-solutions predicate used by the benchmark harness allocates heap cells.)

Table 3 shows the performance of the same four systems on nine standard Prolog benchmarks that do not use tabling, taken from [7]. Mercury is clearly the fastest system by far, even when minimal model tabling is enabled but not used. It is beaten only on nrev and deriv, which spend *all* their time in predicates that are tail recursive in Prolog but not in Mercury.

It is very difficult to draw detailed conclusions from these small benchmarks, but we can safely say that we succeeded in our objective of concentrating the costs of tabling on the predicates that use tabling, reducing the performance of untabled predicates by at most 25%. We can confidently expect Mercury to be much faster than Prolog systems on programs in which relatively few consumer suspensions are encountered. The speed of Mercury relative to tabled Prolog systems on *real* tabled programs will depend on what fraction of time they spend in tabled predicates.

Table 3. Times (in secs) to execute some standard untabled Prolog benchmarks

benchmark iterations	cqueen 60K	crypt 30K	deriv 500K	nrev 300K	primes 150K	qsort 300K	queen 2K	query 100K	tak 1K	total
Mercury plain	1.92	5.44	5.61	7.99	6.43	6.37	4.77	0.70	0.52	39.8
Mercury tabled	3.26	7.17	4.96	7.08	8.80	7.41	5.83	0.89	1.80	47.2
YAP	9.16	9.14	4.08	4.53	20.89	15.35	12.40	6.44	12.50	94.5
XXX	15.27	10.86	8.08	6.94	31.66	21.72	22.09	17.46	17.30	151.4
XSB	23.64	17.23	11.58	16.71	thrashes	32.83	34.56	29.65	24.05	> 190.3

Our most promising avenues for further improvement of tabling in Mercury are clearly (1) improving the speed of saving and restoring suspensions and (2) implementing a scheduling strategy that reduces the number of suspensions and resumptions.

6   Concluding Remarks

Adapting the implementation of tabling to Mercury has been a challenge because the Mercury abstract machine is very different from the WAM. We have based our implementation on CAT because it is the only recomputation-free approach to tabling that does not make assumptions that are invalid in Mercury. However, even CAT required significant modifications to work properly with Mercury's stack organization, its mechanisms for managing variable bindings, and its type-specific data representations. We have described all these in this paper as well as describing two new mechanisms, the cut and the pneg stack, which allow for safe interaction of tabling with language constructs such as if-then-else and existential quantification. These constructs are either not available or not properly handled in other tabled LP systems.

In keeping with Mercury's orientation towards industrial-scale systems, our design objective was maximum performance on large programs containing some tabled predicates, not maximum performance on the tabled predicates themselves. The distinction matters, because it requires us to make choices that minimize the impact of tabling on non-tabled predicates even when these choices slow down tabled execution. We have been broadly successful in achieving this objective. Since support for tabling is optional, programs that do not use it are not affected at all. Even in programs that do use tabling, non-tabled predicates only pay the cost of one new mechanism: the one ensuring the safety of interactions between minimal model tabling and negation.

The results on microbenchmarks focusing on the performance of the basic tabled primitives themselves show tabling in Mercury to be quite competitive with that of other high-performance tabling systems. It is faster on some benchmarks, slower on some others, and quite similar on the rest, even though Mercury currently lacks some obvious tabling optimizations, such as sharing stack segment extensions among consumers. How the system behaves on real tabled applications, written in Mercury rather than Prolog, remains to be seen. Performing such a comparison across different languages is not a trivial task because many applications of tabling often rely on features (e.g., inspection of tables during runtime or dynamic modifications of the Prolog database) which are not available in Mercury. But one should not underestimate either the difficulty or the importance of adding proper tabling in a safe way to a truly declarative, high-performance LP system and the power that this brings to it.

References

1. W. Chen and D. S. Warren. Tabled evaluation with delaying for general logic programs. *J. ACM*, 43(1):20–74, Jan. 1996.
2. B. Demoen and K. Sagonas. CAT: the Copying Approach to Tabling. *J. of Functional and Logic Programming*, Nov. 1999.

3. H.-F. Guo and G. Gupta. A simple scheme for implementing tabled logic programming systems based on dynamic reordering of alternatives. In *Proceedings of ICLP'01*, pages 181–196, Nov/Dec. 2001.
4. I. V. Ramakrishnan, P. Rao, K. Sagonas, T. Swift, and D. S. Warren. Efficient access mechanisms for tabled logic programs. *J. of Logic Programming*, 38(1):31–54, Jan. 1999.
5. R. Rocha, F. Silva, and V. Santos Costa. On applying or-parallelism and tabling to logic programs. *Theory and Practice of Logic Programming*, 5(1 & 2):161–205, Jan. 2005.
6. K. Sagonas and T. Swift. An abstract machine for tabled execution of fixed-order stratified logic programs. *ACM Trans. on Prog. Lang. Syst.*, 20(3):586–634, May 1998.
7. Z. Somogyi, F. Henderson, and T. Conway. The execution algorithm of Mercury, an efficient purely declarative logic programming language. *J. of Logic Progr.*, 26(1–3):17–64, 1996.
8. Z. Somogyi and K. Sagonas. Minimal model tabling in Mercury. Available at http://www.mu.oz.au/research/mercury/information/papers.html, 2005.
9. H. Tamaki and T. Sato. OLD resolution with Tabulation. In *ICLP '86*, pages 84–98. 1986.
10. D. H. D. Warren. An abstract Prolog instruction set. Tech. Rep. 309, SRI International, 1983.
11. N.-F. Zhou, Y.-D. Shen, L.-Y. Yuan and J.-H. You. Implementation of a linear tabling mechanism. *J. of Functional and Logic Programming*, 2001(10), 2001.

Translating Description Logic Queries to Prolog

Zsolt Nagy, Gergely Lukácsy, and Péter Szeredi

Budapest University of Technology and Economics,
Department of Computer Science and Information Theory,
1117 Budapest, Magyar tudósok körútja 2., Hungary
{zsnagy, lukacsy, szeredi}@cs.bme.hu

Abstract. In this paper we present a novel approach for determining the instances of description logic concepts when huge amounts of underlying data are expected. In such cases, traditional description logic theorem proving techniques cannot be used due to performance problems. Our idea is to transform a concept description into a Prolog program which represents a query-plan. This transformation is done without any knowledge of the particular data. Data are accessed dynamically during the normal Prolog execution of the generated program. With this technique only those pieces of data are accessed which are indeed important for answering the query, i.e. we solve the original problem in a database friendly way. We evaluate the performance of our approach and compare it to several description logic reasoners.

Keywords: Description Logics, Reasoning, Instance retrieval, Query-plan, Prolog.

1 Introduction

The motivation for this work comes from our involvement in the development of a knowledge management tool-set for the integration of heterogeneous information sources, using methods and tools based on constraints and logic programming [4, 3].

The main idea of this approach is to collect and manage meta-information on the sources to be integrated. These pieces of information are stored in a model warehouse in the form of special models, constraints and mappings linking these models. We support models of different kinds. Some of them are based on the traditional object oriented paradigm, while others use *description logic* (DL) constructs as well. The model warehouse can be used to answer complex queries spanning over several data sources. The process of answering such queries is called *mediation*, during which we decompose complex integrated queries to simple queries answerable by individual information sources.

We thus have to query description logic concepts where the actual data – the so called ABox – is stored in databases. We found that it is practically impossible to use existing description logic inference systems for this task, as these are not capable of handling ABoxes stored externally. A further difficulty comes from the fact that the existing algorithms for querying description logic concepts need

P. Van Hentenryck (Ed.): PADL 2006, LNCS 3819, pp. 168–182, 2006.

to examine the whole ABox to answer a query. Because of this, we started to think about techniques which allow the separation of the inference algorithm from the data storage.

In our solution, the inference algorithm is divided into two phases. First we create a *query-plan* from a DL concept to be queried, without any knowledge of the actual data. Subsequently, this query-plan can be run on real data, to obtain the required results. We found that Prolog is suitable for executing such query plans, although in theory any language with sufficient expressive power could do the task. For example we could run a query plan in Oracle PL/SQL to reason on data stored in an Oracle database.

This paper is structured as follows: Section 2 gives a brief introduction to the description logic formalism and the critical issue of the *open world assumption*. Section 3 contains an overview of various approaches to handle open world assumption. In Section 4 we present a case study to introduce our ideas how to query description logic concepts in a database friendly way. Sections 5 and 6 give an outline of how DL concepts can be transformed to a query plan. In Section 7 we evaluate the performance of our approach and compare it to the other reasoning systems. Finally, Section 8 concludes this work with a summary and perspectives for future research.

2   Background

Description logics is a family of logic based languages used for knowledge representation. DL is used for describing the knowledge base of an application field (medical knowledge, configuration, nuclear engineering etc.). The terminological system of a description logic knowledge base consists of *concepts*, which represent sets of *objects*, and *roles* describing binary relations between pairs of objects. Objects are the instances occurring in the modelled application field, and thus are also called *instances* or *individuals*.

A description logic knowledge base consists of two parts: the *TBox* and the *ABox*. The TBox (terminology box) contains terminology axioms of form $C \sqsubseteq D$ (concept C is subsumed by D). The ABox (assertion box) stores knowledge about the individuals in the world: a concept assertion of form $C(i)$ denotes that i is an instance of C, while a role assertion $R(i,j)$ means that the objects i and j are related according to role R.

Concepts and roles may either be *atomic* (referred to by a concept name or a role name) or *composite*. A composite concept is built from atomic concepts using *constructors*. The expressiveness of a DL language depends on the constructors allowed for building composite concepts or roles.

In this paper we use the $\mathcal{ALC}$ description logic language. The $\mathcal{ALC}$ concepts are built from role names, concept names (atomic concepts), the top and bottom concepts ($\top$ and $\bot$) using the following constructors: intersection ($C \sqcap D$), union ($C \sqcup D$), negation ($\neg C$), value restriction ($\forall R.C$) and existential restriction ($\exists R.C$). Here C and D denote concepts and R is a role name. For an introduction to description logics we refer the reader to the first two chapters of [1].

The basic inference tasks concerning the TBox can be reduced to the problem of concept-satisfiability [1], where the goal is to determine if a given concept C is satisfiable with respect to a given TBox. Concept-satisfiability is usually decided using the tableau inference algorithm, which tries to build a model showing that C is satisfiable.

ABox-inference tasks require both a TBox and an ABox. In this paper we will deal with two ABox-reasoning problems: instance check and instance retrieval. In an *instance check* problem, a *query-concept* C and an individual i is given. The question is whether $C(i)$ is entailed by the TBox and the ABox. In an *instance retrieval* problem the task is to retrieve all the instances of a query-concept C, entailed by the TBox and the ABox. ABox-reasoning is usually also based on the tableau-algorithm. To infer that an individual i is an instance of a concept C, an indirect assumption $\neg C(i)$ is added to the ABox, and the tableau-algorithm is applied. If this reports inconsistency, i is proved to be an instance of C.

Simple instance-retrieval problems can be easily solved using an appropriate database query or Prolog goal. For example, the instances of the concept Novel $\sqcap \exists$hasTranslationTo.$\top$ (novels translated to some language) can be easily enumerated by an appropriate database query.

Open world assumption. Databases and Prolog use the the *closed world assumption* where any object not known to be an instance of C is treated as an instance of $\neg C$. No such assumption exists in DL inference tasks, which use the *open world assumption* (OWA). When reasoning under OWA, one is interested in obtaining statements which hold in all models of the knowledge base, i.e. those entailed by the knowledge base.

```
hasChild(Iocaste,Oedipus)        hasChild(Iocaste,Polyneikes)
hasChild(Oedipus,Polyneikes)     hasChild(Polyneikes,Thersandros)
Patricide(Oedipus)               ¬Patricide(Thersandros)
```

Fig. 1. The Iocaste ABox

A famous example of open world reasoning, presented in e.g. [1], is about the family of Oedipus and Iocaste. Let us consider the ABox shown in Figure 1. We will look for the answer to the following *instance retrieval* query: does a person exist in the ABox who has a patricide child, who in turn has a non-patricide child? Let us formalise this question using the $\mathcal{ALC}$ DL language:

$$\exists \texttt{hasChild}.(\texttt{Patricide} \sqcap \exists \texttt{hasChild}.\neg\texttt{Patricide}) \tag{1}$$

In the given ABox, Iocaste is an instance of this concept, in spite of the fact that one cannot *name* the child who has the desired property. Solving this problem requires *case analysis*: the child in question is either Polyneikes or Oedipus, depending on whether Polyneikes is a Patricide or not.

3   Possible Approaches

In the current stage of research, we address the instance check and instance retrieval problems under the following restrictions. Reasoning is over an empty TBox, and the ABox may only contain assertions of form $C(a)$, where C is an atomic or negated atomic concept[1], and $R(a, b)$, where R is a role name. The query-concept is built using the constructors of the $\mathcal{ALC}$ language.

Several techniques have emerged for dealing with case analysis in ABox-reasoning. An extreme case involves restrictions on the knowledge base to avoid the need for case analysis. For example, [7] suggests a solution called the *instance store*, where the ABox is stored externally, and is accessed in an efficient way. However, the ABox does not allow any axioms involving roles. Because of this restriction, most of the queries involving case analysis (like the Iocaste-query) are not expressible in the proposed framework.

The normal approach involves running a tableau-based DL reasoner able to answer ABox-inference questions, such as RACER. The main drawback of this approach is that current description logic inference engines require processing the whole ABox. Thus the instance retrieval tasks checks each instance name in the ABox whether it belongs to the query-concept, or not. Since our goal is to apply ABox-inference on a distributed knowledge base, where a large amount of instances is present at different locations, this is not acceptable.

Performance is also a main issue: when dealing with large amounts of instances, the traditional approach is slow and inefficient, even when TBox and ABox optimisation techniques are applied [6].

We suggest therefore using a database or a set of Prolog facts for storing the assertions of the ABox. In our solution, first the query is translated to an ABox-independent *query-plan*, which is an executable *Prolog-program*. This program generates all patterns that identify instances of the query-concept. In the second step, we execute the query-plan on the ABox to find the solution for the given instance check or instance retrieval problem.

For certain simple concepts there is a straightforward translation to Prolog. For example, the query-concept (1) can be represented by the following Prolog-clause:

$$\text{instance}(X) :- \text{hasChild}(X, Y), \text{patricide}(Y),$$
$$\text{hasChild}(Y, Z), \text{notPatricide}(Z). \tag{2}$$

In this clause, `notPatricide(Z)` invokes the predicate listing all individuals Z known to be non-patricide. However, this Prolog program does not return `Iocaste`, because it does not perform case analysis.

Obviously, using the `\+` operator (negation as failure) would not solve the problem: when `notPatricide(Z)` is replaced by `\+ patricide(Z)`, every instance not known to be patricide would be treated as non-patricide, which is incorrect.

---

[1] The restricted form of C is implied by the fact that we do not deal with TBox-reasoning in this paper.

An option is to extend the Prolog program above to perform case analysis using backtracking. Here, when testing whether an individual belongs to a concept, and there is no definite answer, we create a choice point: we first answer positively and then negatively. Subsequently – using some kind of meta programming – we make sure that both execution branches succeed, thus carrying out a case analysis. This approach, however, turns out to be unacceptably slow.

[8] suggests that the description logic knowledge base should be transformed into disjunctive datalog formulas, and reasoning should be performed using resolution. The motivation and goals of this work are similar to ours. While [8] allows much more general DL constructs (the $\mathcal{SHIQ}^-$ language, TBox), its implementation, KAON2 [9], is much slower then our approach, when run on simple problems, see Section 7.

[5] uses a direct transformation of $\mathcal{ALC}$ concepts into Horn-clauses, and poses some restrictions over the knowledge base, which disallow knowledge-base statements requiring disjunctive reasoning. In contrast, instead of a direct transformation, our approach involves extracting a query-plan from query-concepts using general resolution, and executing it in Prolog.

4   A Case Study

In Section 2 we have introduced an ABox describing the family of Iocaste and the query-concept (1). We will now modify (2), the direct translation of this query-concept, so that it performs case analysis. The resulting Prolog predicate instance(X) will enumerate all the instances of the concept (1) for an arbitrary ABox, represented by patricide/1, notPatricide/1 and hasChild/2 facts. First, we will focus on the instance check problem.

Our first task is to determine if an individual is an instance of the query-concept. Let us start by rewriting the Prolog clause (2) to its first order logic equivalent. In this form, notPatricide(Z) is replaced by $\neg Patricide(Z)$:

$$instance(X) \lor \neg hasChild(X,Y) \lor \neg Patricide(Y) \lor \neg hasChild(Y,Z) \lor Patricide(Z) \quad (3)$$

From the above clause and from the facts describing the ABox in Figure 1, we can easily prove that Iocaste is an instance of the query-concept, using general resolution. Such a proof is given in Figure 2. Here we denote the instances Iocaste, Oedipus, Polyneikes and Thersandros by individual names i, o, p and t, respectively. Clauses *(fact1)–(fact6)* represent the ABox, *(clause1)* is the above definition of *instance*, while *(clause2)* is the negation of *instance(i)*, the fact to be proved.

Since *instance* literals occur only in *(clause1)* and *(clause2)*, it is obvious that these clauses have to be resolved with each other, giving the resolvent *(resolv1)*. We then eliminate three literals of *(resolv1)* using *(fact1)*, *(fact5)* and *(fact3)* giving the result *(resolv4)*, which actually states the fact $Patricide(p)$. Then we resolve this fact with *(resolv1)* again, and subsequently eliminate the remaining literals, arriving at the empty clause *(resolv8)*.

In the proof in Figure 2, certain resolution steps used ABox facts, while others did not. It seems worthwhile rearranging the proof, so that all the steps indepen-

Clause name	Clauses used	Clause
(fact1)		$hasChild(i,o)$
(fact2)		$hasChild(i,p)$
(fact3)		$hasChild(o,p)$
(fact4)		$hasChild(p,t)$
(fact5)		$Patricide(o)$
(fact6)		$\neg Patricide(t)$
(clause1)		$instance(X) \vee$ $\neg hasChild(X,Y) \vee \neg Patricide(Y) \vee$ $\neg hasChild(Y,Z) \vee Patricide(Z)$
(clause2)		$\neg instance(i)$
(resolv1)	(clause1)(clause2)	$\neg hasChild(i,Y) \vee \neg Patricide(Y) \vee$ $\neg hasChild(Y,Z) \vee Patricide(Z)$
(resolv2)	(resolv1)(fact1)	$\neg Patricide(o) \vee$ $\neg hasChild(o,Z) \vee Patricide(Z)$
(resolv3)	(resolv2)(fact5)	$\neg hasChild(o,Z) \vee Patricide(Z)$
(resolv4)	(resolv3)(fact3)	$Patricide(p)$
(resolv5)	(resolv4)(resolv1)	$\neg hasChild(i,p) \vee$ $\neg hasChild(p,Z) \vee Patricide(Z)$
(resolv6)	(resolv5)(fact2)	$\neg hasChild(p,Z) \vee Patricide(Z)$
(resolv7)	(resolv6)(fact4)	$Patricide(t)$
(resolv8)	(resolv7)(fact6)	$\square$

Fig. 2. The proof of the Iocaste-problem using resolution

dent of the ABox are made at the beginning. This can obviously be carried out, as resolution is *commutative* and *associative*. In the case of our resolution proof, this means that the second use of *(resolv1)* should be moved up in the proof. Currently, this second use is against the fact *(resolv4)*: $Patricide(p)$. This literal is introduced in *(resolv1)*, so the rearrangement involves resolving *(resolv1)* against itself, unifying the positive and negative $Patricide$ literals. The result of this resolution step is the following:

$$\neg hasChild(i,P) \vee \neg hasChild(P,T) \vee Patricide(T) \vee$$
$$\neg hasChild(i,O) \vee \neg Patricide(O) \vee \neg hasChild(O,P) \qquad (resolv2')$$

In this clause we have renamed the variables in such a way that it is obvious how the six literals above can be eliminated by the clauses *(fact1)–(fact6)*.

We have thus shown that for our special query-concept and the corresponding ABox, the instance check problem can be solved using a two-phase resolution proof, where the first phase is independent of the ABox, and in the second phase, we always resolve against a fact describing an ABox-assertion.

Let us now consider the case of an arbitrary ABox. As in Figure 2, the only possible use of the $\neg instance(i)$ negative fact is to resolve it against the definition of the query-concept *(clause1)*, resulting in clause *(resolv1)*.

In the general case, an option is to finish the ABox-independent part of the proof at this point, and to try finding ABox-facts to eliminate all the literals of *(resolv1)*. Notice that *(resolv1)* is the same as the body of clause (3), with the $X = i$ substitution, so this alternative actually checks if i can be proven to be an instance of the query-concept directly, without case analysis.

The second option is to resolve *(resolv1)* against itself, as we have done in the previous example, producing *(resolv2′)*, which is the next pattern to be looked for in the ABox. Because our query-concept contains only a single pair of opposite literals, resolving it with itself can only be done in a single way.[2] Continuing the ABox-independent resolution options, we get the following clause when resolving *(resolv1)* against itself three times:

$$\neg hasChild(i, P_1) \lor \neg hasChild(P_1, T) \lor Patricide(T)$$
$$\neg hasChild(i, P_2) \lor \neg hasChild(P_2, P_1) \qquad (resolv3')$$
$$\neg hasChild(i, O) \lor \neg hasChild(O, P_2) \lor \neg Patricide(O)$$

Clauses *(resolv1)*, *(resolv2′)*, *(resolv3′)* etc. can be viewed as *query-patterns* for searching the database-representation of the ABox. These can easily be visualised as graphs, whose vertices correspond to objects, and edges denote roles. Each vertex is labelled with a set of concepts it is expected to belong to, while the edges are labelled with role-names. The first three query-patterns for the Iocaste-problem are shown in Figure 3 (to save space, the label *hasChild* is omitted from the edges, and the concept *Patricide* is abbreviated by P).

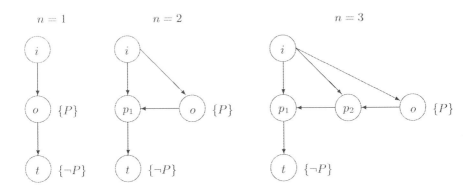

Fig. 3. The query-pattern using n instances of the clause *(resolv1)*

In this simple example the repetitive patterns can be captured by rewriting *(resolv1)* to the following Prolog clause:

```
patricide(Z) :- hasChild(i, Y), hasChild(Y, Z), patricide(Y).
```

This clause, together with (2), makes a Prolog program which correctly runs the instance(i) query, for an arbitrary ABox represented by the patricide and notPatricide facts. Note however, that now the clauses for the patricide/1

---

[2] If we had more occurrences of *Patricide* or $\neg Patricide$ literals or we had other opposite literals in the query-concept, we would have to explore more patterns.

predicate come in part from the ABox and in part from the query. To avoid this, we propose to introduce a new recursive predicate dPatricide/1 (deduced to be *Patricide*). This results in the Prolog program shown below. Since the program generates all possible patterns needed for answering the inference problem, this program will be considered the *query-plan* for the concept (1).

```
instance(i)            :- hasChild(i, Y), hasChild(Y, Z),
                          notPatricide(Z), dPatricide(Y).

dPatricide(Z)          :- patricide(Z).
dPatricide(Z)          :- hasChild(i, Y), hasChild(Y, Z),
                          dPatricide(Y).
```

This program is specialised to solve the instance check problem for a given individual i. In order to solve the more general instance retrieval problem, we replace every occurrence of the instance name i by a logic variable X. The second dPatricide clause however does not contain any reference to X (i.e. we do not know in dPatricide the instance all the query-paths start with), so X has to be passed to the predicate dPatricide increasing its arity to two, as shown below

```
instance(X)            :- hasChild(X, Y), hasChild(Y, Z),
                          notPatricide(Z), dPatricide(Y, X).

dPatricide(Z, _)       :- patricide(Z).
dPatricide(Z, X)       :- hasChild(X, Y), hasChild(Y, Z),
                          dPatricide(Y, X).
```

Executing the above query-plan on some ABoxes may lead to nontermination. This can occur when the ABox graph contains loops so that after one ore more iterations the dPatricide procedure calls itself with the same arguments as earlier. In order to avoid infinite loops, we need to modify the Prolog code, or use a Prolog system which supports tabling, e.g. XSB-Prolog [12].

Note that *(resolv1)* could be used to derive a Prolog clause dnotPatricide (deduced to be non-*Patricide*):

```
dnotPatricide(Z, _) :- notPatricide(Z).
dnotPatricide(Y, X) :- hasChild(X, Y), hasChild(Y, Z),
                       dnotPatricide(Z, X).
```

If such a clause is introduced, the notPatricide call in the body of instance is replaced by dnotPatricide. However, in this simple case of just two opposite literals being present in the query, one of the dPatricide and dnotPatricide predicates is sufficient, as any resolution proof can be transformed to a proof with the Prolog selection rule, which uses just one of these two predicates. Note that this does not hold in the general case.

5   Query-Plans for Tree-Concepts

In this section we outline the process of translating instance retrieval problems into executable query-plans, for the special case of so called *tree-concepts*. Such concepts are built using the intersection, existential restriction and atomic negation constructors only.

It is convenient to view tree-concepts as labelled graphs (actually trees) of the same kind as introduced in Figure 3. To transform a tree-concept $C = C_1 \sqcap \ldots \sqcap C_n$ ($n \geq 1$) into a graph rooted at vertex x, for each i, $1 \leq i \leq n$ do:

- if C_i is a possibly negated atomic concept, then add C_i to the label of x;
- otherwise $C_i = \exists R.D$. Create a new vertex y, add to the graph an edge from x to y with the label R, and recursively transform D into a graph rooted at y.

Note that the graph of a tree-concept is actually its simplest query pattern, i.e. the one not requiring case analysis. For example, the graph of concept (1) is the leftmost pattern in Figure 3.

We now show how to transform the graph of a tree-concept into a clause defining the given concept using first order logic. We assign distinct variables to the vertices of the tree-concept. The clause head is the positive literal $instance(X)$, where X is the variable assigned to the root of the tree. We then include body goals, i.e. negative literals of form $\neg R(U, V)$, for each edge $U \rightarrow V$ which has R as its label[3]. Finally, for each possibly negated atomic concept C in the label of vertex Y, we include the literal $\neg C(Y)$. For example, if we apply this procedure to the tree-concept (1), we get the clause (3).

It is obvious that the clause thus constructed captures the semantics of the tree-concept in question. Therefore – repeating the argumentation of our case study in Section 4 – this clause can be used to construct a proof that an instance i belongs to the concept C. Such a proof uses the following clauses: (a) $\neg instance(i)$, (b) the clause defining the concept C, and (c) the ABox facts. One has to start the ABox-independent part of the proof by first resolving (a) and (b), as only these contain $instance$ literals. Let us call the resolvent of these two clauses the *query-clause*. The only way to proceed is to resolve the query-clause against itself n times, $n = 0, 1, \ldots$ Each such resolution step obviously requires the presence of $\neg A(X)$ and $A(Y)$ literals in the query-clause. Such atomic concepts A, which occur both in negated and non-negated form in the query-concept, will be called *bipolar* concepts.

In the case study of the Iocaste-concept (1) we had a single bipolar atomic concept, $Patricide$, with just one positive and one negative literal. In the general case there are two new issues. First, because of multiple literals, we have to build two Prolog predicates for each bipolar concept A, one for "deducing" A and another for "deducing" $\neg A$ (cf. the dPatricide and dnotPatricide predicates of Section 4). The second problem is related to *factoring*: two identical literals in the resolvent have to be replaced by a single one. This problem can be solved using ancestor resolution [10], which can be easily implemented in Prolog by an additional argument in each predicate, which stores the list of ancestors, analogously to the techniques described in [11]. As an example let us consider the following concept:

---

[3] More precisely, U and V are the variables assigned to the end points of the edge.

$$\exists R.(A \sqcap \exists R.(\neg A \sqcap \exists R.(A \sqcap \exists R.\neg A)))) \tag{4}$$

The Prolog program corresponding to this query-concept is displayed below. To save space, only the first clause for dnotA is shown.

```
instance(X) :-      r(X,Y), r(Y,Z), r(Z,U), r(U,V),
                    dA(Y, X, [dA(Y)]), dnotA(Z, X, [dnotA(Z)]),
                    dA(U, X, [dA(U)]), dnotA(V, X, [dnotA(V)]).

dA(Z, _, _) :-      a(Z).                                            (c1)
dA(Z, _, Anc) :-    memberchk(dnotA(Z), Anc), !.                     (c2)
dA(Z, _, [_|Anc]) :- memberchk(dA(Z), Anc), !, fail.                (c3)
dA(Z, X, Anc) :-    r(X,Y), r(Y,Z), r(Z,U), r(U,V),
                    dA(Y, X, [dA(Y)|Anc]), dA(U, X, [dA(U)|Anc]),
                    dnotA(V, X, [dnotA(V)|Anc]).
dA(V, X, Anc) :-    r(X,Y), r(Y,Z), r(Z,U), r(U,V),
                    dA(Y, X, [dA(Y)|Anc]), dA(U, X, [dA(U)|Anc]),
                    dnotA(Z, X, [dnotA(Z)|Anc]).

dnotA(Z, _, _) :-   notA(Z).
(...)
```

In general, for each bipolar atomic concept A we create two Prolog predicates: dA/3 (deduced to be A) and dnotA/3 (deduced to be $\neg A$). The second argument, as in the case study, stores the root of the pattern, while the third contains the ancestor list. The first clause of these predicates is a simple renaming, as exemplified by (c1) above. The second clause, see (c2), caters for ancestor resolution, while the optional third clause, (c3), assures termination in the absence of tabling. The subsequent clauses are the contrapositives of the query-clause, which use one of the literals as the head, and the remaining ones as the body.

This translation scheme can be viewed as a much simplified special case of Stickel's Prolog Technology Theorem Prover (PTTP) approach [11]. If there are n occurrences of m distinct bipolar concepts, then $2m$ predicates with the total of $6m + n$ clauses are generated. Since the size of the clauses is is proportional to the size of the query-concept, we can say that the complexity of the tree-concept translation scheme is quadratic with the query-concept size.

6   Query-Plans for Arbitrary $\mathcal{ALC}$ Concepts

In this section we discuss how to create query patterns from arbitrary $\mathcal{ALC}$ concept expressions. This is done in two phases. First we transform the concept into a union of *tree-concepts*, in such a way that the deducible instances of the union are the same as those of the original concept. Next, we show how to transform a union of tree-concepts to Prolog code performing instance retrieval.

We start the first transformation with some simple steps:

1. *Negation normal form (NNF)*: transform the concept to NNF (negation appears only in front of atomic concepts, as described e.g. in [1]).

2. ∀- *and* ∃-*normalisation*: apply these two transformations wherever possible:

$$\forall R.(C \sqcap D) \rightsquigarrow \forall R.C \sqcap \forall R.D \quad \text{and} \quad \exists R.(C \sqcup D) \rightsquigarrow \exists R.C \sqcup \exists R.D$$

3. *Disjunctive normal form (DNF)*: transform all concepts C in subconcepts of form $\forall R.C$, and the query-concept itself to disjunctive normal form.

As a result of these transformations, the union-operator can only appear at the top level of the concept and inside ∀-concepts.

Let us consider an arbitrary concept of form $\forall R.C$, where $C \neq \top$. Notice that in $\mathcal{ALC}$ instance retrieval with respect to an empty TBox, no object can be inferred to be an instance of this concept.[4] Thus the set of inferable instances of such a $\forall R.C$ concept is empty.

However, if a ∀-concept appears in a composite expression, it may be incorrect to use this assumption. For instance, the concept $\forall R.C \sqcup \exists R.\neg C$ is obviously equivalent to $\top$. At the same time, if the assumption that the first union member generates no instance is used to reduce the instance retrieval problem to that of $\exists R.\neg C$, one clearly gets an incorrect result.

This anomaly is caused by the fact that instances of a concept can be inferred through case analysis. If we have a concept containing $\forall R.C$, as well as its negation, $\exists R.\neg C$ then one can argue that each individual should belong to either the first or the second subconcept. Any statement true under both of these assumptions is universally true.

For instance, in the case of the concept $F = (\forall R.C \sqcap D) \sqcup (\exists R.\neg C \sqcap E)$, we can use case analysis to show that $D \sqcap E \sqsubseteq F$, and so F and $F' = F \sqcup (D \sqcap E)$ are equivalent. Before dealing with ∀-concepts we will therefore apply the transformation $F \rightsquigarrow F'$.

In general, this transformation step is the following:

4. *Extension with subsumed concepts*: Let us view the concept union and intersection operators as taking sets of concepts as their argument. We still write these operators in infix notation, and by $F = C \sqcap D$ we mean that intersection F can be split into two sub-intersections C and D.

   Assume that the concept to be handled has a union subconcept of form $U = (C_1 \sqcap D_1) \sqcup \ldots \sqcup (C_n \sqcap D_n) \sqcup \ldots$, where

$$C_1 \sqcup \ldots \sqcup C_n \equiv \top \tag{5}$$

   In this case we replace U by $U \sqcup (D_1 \sqcap \ldots \sqcap D_n)$. We carry out this transformation in all possible ways. Finding the subconcepts satisfying (5) can be delegated to a TBox reasoner, such as RACER. We believe this will not be a bottleneck, as this is a "compile time" activity and the concepts to be retrieved are not expected to be very large.

This way we extend each union subconcept U to include all concept expressions which can be inferred to be subsumed by U. Now we turn to the elimination

---

[4] If the TBox was not empty and contained an axiom $A \sqsubseteq \forall R.C$, every instance of A would also be an (inferable) instance of $\forall R.C$.

of ∀-subconcepts. To support this transformation we introduce a special concept nil, which does not have any inferred instances. Note that any two occurrences of nil are different concepts, because their associated sets of instances may be different. It is also important to note that, from model theoretical viewpoint, $\mathtt{nil}^{\mathcal{I}}$ is not the empty set, so nil is different from ⊥.

The last transformation step is thus the following:

5. ∀-*elimination*: Substitute all occurrences of the concept $\forall R.C$ by nil. Apply the the following equalities to propagate nil values:

$$\begin{array}{lll} \mathtt{nil} \sqcap C = \mathtt{nil} & \mathtt{nil} \sqcup \bot = \mathtt{nil} & \exists R.\mathtt{nil} = \mathtt{nil} \\ \mathtt{nil} \sqcap \bot = \bot & \mathtt{nil} \sqcup C = C & \forall R.\mathtt{nil} = \mathtt{nil} \end{array}$$

Note that, after finishing the transformation, either the whole query-concept becomes nil, or no occurrences of nil remain within it.

After the five transformations have been carried out, we get a concept of form $C = C_1 \sqcup C_2 \sqcup \cdots \sqcup C_n$, where each C_i is a tree-concept. We now apply the technique described in Section 5 to each such tree-concept to produce Prolog clauses and then merge these to produce the program for the union concept. It is important to note that there is a single namespace: for each bipolar atomic concept A occurring in C there is a single dA and a single dnotA predicate in the program. If A occurs in, say both C_i and C_j, then both these union members contribute clauses to the dA and dnotA predicates. Obviously there is a single batch of initial clauses (cf. (c1)–(c3) in the Prolog code for concept (4)) for each such predicate.

As an example consider the following union of two tree-concepts, very similar to the Iocaste query-concept:

$$\exists R_1.(P \sqcap \exists R_1.\neg P) \sqcup \exists R_2.(P \sqcap \exists R_2.\neg P), \tag{6}$$

The Prolog code for this concept is shown below. Note that we have omitted the dnotP predicate, for reasons similar to those outlined at the end of the case study of Section 4.

```
instance(X) :- r1(X, Y), r1(Y, Z), notP(Z), dP(Y, X).
instance(X) :- r2(X, Y), r2(Y, Z), notP(Z), dP(Y, X).

dP(X, _) :- p(X).
dP(Z, X) :- r1(X, Y), r1(Y, Z), dP(Y, X).
dP(Z, X) :- r2(X, Y), r2(Y, Z), dP(Y, X).
```

The concept transformation steps described here can lead to exponential size increase in the worst case, because of the transformation to disjunctive normal form. Similarly, finding all the solutions of (5) may require exponential time. However we believe that this worst case behaviour is not typical. The complexity of the second phase, the generation of Prolog code from a union of tree-concepts, is quadratic (in the size of the concept), as outlined at the end of Section 5.

7   Evaluation

We have evaluated our solution by running the Prolog programs described in Section 4 using two Prolog systems. The corresponding instance retrieval problem was also run using other reasoners. We used RACER, which is, according to our knowledge, the fastest available tableau based ABox reasoner. We also evaluated the KAON2 [9] and the PTTP-based PROTEIN [2] systems. The tests were run under RACER 1.7.16, SICStus Prolog 3.12.0, XSB Prolog 2.7.1, KAON2 release 2005-10-17 and PROTEIN 2.33 on a Compaq Presario 2805 (1,4GHz Intel mobile CPU, 512MB RAM, Linux with 2.6.19 kernel). The results are shown in Figure 4. Each line of the table corresponds to a sample ABox. These ABoxes were generated randomly and contain at least one subgraph matching the Iocaste pattern of Figure 3.

The first column shows the size of the Iocaste pattern in the given ABox, which corresponds to the parameter n in Figure 3. The second and third columns show the number of the role and concept assertions present in the ABoxes. The fourth column contains the number of those irrelevant nodes which we added to the ABoxes as „noise". We did this in order to be able to measure how sensitive the inference engines are to this kind of ABox modification. By using irrelevant nodes we actually simulate real life situations, because in a database lookup it is rarely the case that the search pattern matches the whole content of the database.

pattern size (n)	role assertions	concept assertions	noise instances	RACER	SICStus	XSB	KAON2	PROTEIN
2	4	2	0	<0.001	<0.001	<0.001	0.049	0.030
10	20	2	0	<0.001	<0.001	<0.001	0.569	0.180
20	40	2	0	<0.001	<0.001	<0.001	-	99.110
100	200	2	0	0.500	0.002	0.002	-	-
500	1000	2	0	9.970	0.053	0.048	-	-
1000	2000	2	0	50.600	0.210	0.165	-	-
2	26	10	8	<0.001	<0.001	<0.001	0.049	0.050
2	48	11	16	0.050	<0.001	<0.001	0.047	0.060
2	233	64	76	0.100	<0.001	<0.001	0.051	0.130
2	555	140	196	0.340	<0.001	<0.001	0.048	0.210
2	4743	816	1196	11.930	<0.001	<0.001	0.052	5.290
2	32126	5373	7796	-	<0.001	<0.001	4.729	203.360

Fig. 4. Evaluation and comparison of our approach

The remaining five columns of Figure 4 show the times needed for enumerating all the instances of an Iocaste pattern in different software environments excluding loading and processing time. All values are given in seconds. For the test cases with very short runtime, we ran the programs multiple times. Timeout (when no result was returned in 10 minutes) is denoted by - (dash).

The total number of instances in each ABox is $n + 2 + noise$. The number of concept assertions is always less than the number of instances, as there are instances not belonging to any concepts, cf. Polyneikes in Figure 1.

The first six test cases are "clean" in that they contain nothing more but the Iocaste patterns themselves. In these there are only two concept assertions: one node belongs to the concept Patricide, and another to the concept ¬Patricide.

The results show that RACER scales quadratically when the pattern size is increased. KAON2 and PROTEIN fare much worse: they can only handle the simplest test cases. It can be seen that our program is several magnitudes faster than the others, including RACER: all of the tests were processed within a fraction of a second. Note, that our present solution is also quadratic in the number of individuals. This is however due to the fact that the Prolog code is not optimised. If we reorder the body of the dPatricide/2 clause as shown below[5], the runtime becomes linear (we do not show the corresponding runtimes):

```
dPatricide(Z, X)     :- hasChild(Y, Z), hasChild(X, Y),
                        dPatricide(Y, X).
```

In the second group of test cases we picked the smallest Iocaste pattern, then we added increasing amounts of irrelevant data to the ABoxes.

We conclude that for a large amount of irrelevant data RACER becomes unacceptably slow. In contrast, our solution is practically insensitive to the „noise", no matter how much we add. KAON2 and PROTEIN also seem to handle the irrelevant ABox information nicely, although in the big test cases they slow down.

8   Summary and Future Work

We have shown how to transform an arbitrary description logic concept formulated in the $\mathcal{ALC}$ language to a Prolog program performing the instance retrieval problem. We have handled case analysis, necessitated by the open world assumption, by systematically generating all patterns that are amenable to case analysis. At the same time we have shown that the Prolog program produced can be viewed as the ABox-independent part of a generic resolution proof. We have also evaluated our approach, showing that it can be faster than the traditional tableau-based approach by several magnitudes.

We view the current results as a first step. We plan to extend our algorithm to more elaborate DL languages (such as $\mathcal{SHIQ}$) and to allow TBox axioms as well. We will also work on the optimisation of the query plan, considering the use of target language specific elements (like cut, indexing, etc. in Prolog) to make the execution of the query plan more efficient.

Acknowledgements

The authors acknowledge the support of the Hungarian NKFP programme for the SINTAGMA project under grant no. 2/052/2004. We would also like to

---

[5] We also have to use indexing on multiple arguments in case of the hasChild/2 facts.

thank Tamás Benkő and the anonymous referees, for valuable comments on the drafts of this paper.

References

1. F. Baader, D. Calvanese, D. McGuinness, D. Nardi, and P. F. Patel-Schneider, editors. *The Description Logic Handbook: Theory, Implementation and Applications.* Cambridge University Press, 2003.
2. Peter Baumgartner and Ulrich Furbach. PROTEIN: A PROver with a theory extension INterface. In *Conference on Automated Deduction*, pages 769–773, 1994.
3. Tamás Benkő, Péter Krauth, and Péter Szeredi. A logic-based system for application integration. In *Proceedings of ICLP*, volume 2401 of *Lecture Notes in Computer Science*, pages 452–466. Springer, July 2002.
4. Tamás Benkő, Gergely Lukácsy, Attila Fokt, Péter Szeredi, Imre Kilián, and Péter Krauth. Information integration through reasoning on meta-data. In *Proceedings of the Workshop "AI Moves to IA", IJCAI'03, Acapulco, Mexico*, pages 65–77, 2003.
5. Benjamin N. Grosof, Ian Horrocks, Raphael Volz, and Stefan Decker. Description logic programs: combining logic programs with description logic. In *Proceedings of WWW '03*, pages 48–57, New York, NY, USA, 2003. ACM Press.
6. Volker Haarslev and Ralf Möller. Optimization techniques for retrieving resources described in OWL/RDF documents: First results. In *Proceedings of the Ninth International Conference KR2004, Whistler, Canada*. AAAI Press, 2004.
7. Ian Horrocks, Lei Li, Daniele Turi, and Sean Bechhofer. The Instance Store: DL reasoning with large numbers of individuals. In *Proceedings of DL2004, British Columbia, Canada*, 2004.
8. Ullrich Hustadt, Boris Motik, and Ulrike Sattler. Reasoning for Description Logics around SHIQ in a resolution framework. Technical report, FZI, Karlsruhe, 2004.
9. KAON2: Ontology management tool for the Semantic Web http://kaon2.semanticweb.org/.
10. R. Kowalski and D. Kuehner. Linear resolution with selection function. *Artificial Intelligence*, 2:227–260, 1971.
11. Mark E. Stickel. A Prolog technology theorem prover: a new exposition and implementation in Prolog. *Theoretical Computer Science*, 104(1):109–128, 1992.
12. David S. Warren. Programming in tabled Prolog (draft) http://www.cs.sunysb.edu/~warren/xsbbook/book.html.

Efficient Top-Down Set-Sharing Analysis Using Cliques

Jorge Navas[1], Francisco Bueno[2], and Manuel Hermenegildo[1,2]

[1] D. of C.S. and Electr. and Comp. Eng., U. of New Mexico, Albuquerque, NM, USA
[2] School of Computer Science, T.U. Madrid (UPM), Madrid, Spain
jorge@cs.unm.edu, herme@unm.edu
{bueno, herme}@fi.upm.es

Abstract. We study the problem of efficient, scalable set-sharing analysis of logic programs. We use the idea of representing sharing information as a pair of abstract substitutions, one of which is a worst-case sharing representation called a clique set, which was previously proposed for the case of inferring pair-sharing. We use the clique-set representation for (1) inferring actual set-sharing information, and (2) analysis within a top-down framework. In particular, we define the new abstract functions required by standard top-down analyses, both for sharing alone and also for the case of including freeness in addition to sharing. We use cliques both as an alternative representation and as widening, defining several widening operators. Our experimental evaluation supports the conclusion that, for inferring set-sharing, as it was the case for inferring pair-sharing, precision losses are limited, while useful efficiency gains are obtained. We also derive useful conclusions regarding the interactions between thresholds, precision, efficiency and cost of widening. At the limit, the clique-set representation allowed analyzing some programs that exceeded memory capacity using classical sharing representations.

1 Introduction

In static analysis of logic programs the tracking of variables shared among terms is essential. Arguably, the most accurate abstract domain defined for tracking sharing is the so called Sharing domain [JL92, MH92], which represents variable occurrences, i.e., the possible occurrences of run-time variables within the terms to which program variables will be bound. In this paper we study an alternative representation for this domain.

Example 1. Let $V = \{x, y, z\}$ be a set of variables of interest. A substitution such as $\{x/f(u_1, u_2, v_1, v_2, w), y/g(v_1, v_2, w), z/g(w, w)\}$ will be abstracted in Sharing as $\{x, xy, xyz\}$.[1] Sharing group x in the abstraction represents the occurrence of run-time variables u_1 and u_2 in the concrete substitution, xy represents v_1 and v_2, and xyz represents w. Note that the number of (occurrences of) run-time variables shared is abstracted away.

---

[1] To simplify notation, we denote a sharing group (a set of variables representing sharing) by the concatenation of its variables, e.g., xyz is $\{x, y, z\}$.

P. Van Hentenryck (Ed.): PADL 2006, LNCS 3819, pp. 183–198, 2006.

Sharing analysis has been used for inferring several interesting properties of programs; most notably (but not only), variable and goal independence. Several program variables are said to be independent if the terms they are bound to do not have (run-time) variables in common. Variable independence is the counterpart of sharing: program variables share when the terms they are bound to do have run-time variables in common. When we are talking of only two variables then we refer to pair-sharing, and when we track relations among more than two variables we refer to set-sharing. Sharing abstract domains are used to infer *possible* sharing, i.e., the possibility that shared variables exist, and thus, in the absence of such possibility, *definite* information about independence.

Example 2. Let $V = \{x, y, z\}$ be the variables of interest. A Sharing abstract substitution such as $\{x, y, z\}$ (which denotes the set of the singleton sets containing each variable) represents that all three variables are independent.

The Sharing domain has deserved a lot of attention in the literature in the past. It has been enhanced in several ways [Fil94, ZBH99]. It has also been extended with other kinds of information, the most relevant of which being freeness and linearity [JL92, CDFB96, HZB04], but also for example information about term structure [KS94, BCM94, MSJB95]. Its combination with other abstract domains has also been studied [CMB+93, Fec96]. In particular, in [ZBH99] an alternative representation for Sharing is proposed for the non-redundant domain of [BHZ02] and this representation is thoroughly studied for inferring pairsharing. A new component is added to abstract substitutions that represents sets of variables, the powerset of which would have been part of the original abstract substitution. Such sets are called *cliques*.

Example 3. Let V be as above. Consider the abstraction $\{x, xy, xyz, xz, y, yz, z\}$, i.e., the powerset of V (without the empty set). Such an abstraction conveys no information: there might be run-time variables shared by any pair of the three program variables, by the three of them, or not shared at all. However, abstractions such as this one are expensive to process during analysis: they penalize efficiency for no benefit at all. The clique that will convey the same information is simply the set V.

A clique is thus a compact representation for a piece of sharing which in fact does not convey any useful information. The precision and efficiency of using cliques for the case of inferring pair-sharing were reported in [ZBH99]. In [Zaf01] cliques were incorporated into the original Sharing domain, but precision and efficiency are again studied for the case of inferring pair-sharing. Here, we are interested in studying the substantially different case of inferring setsharing. Another important difference with previous work is that we develop the analysis for a top-down framework. This requires the definition of additional and non-trivial abstract functions in the domain. Such functions were not defined in [ZBH99, Zaf01], since bottom-up analyses were used there. We use the PLAI/CiaoPP framework [HBPLG99], which is an efficient implementation of a top-down analyzer using the fixpoint algorithms and optimizations described in [MH90, MH92, HPMS00].

The rest of the paper proceeds as follows. Notation and preliminaries are presented in Section 2, together with the representation based on cliques and the clique-domains for set-sharing and set-sharing with freeness. In Section 3 the required functions for top-down analysis are defined. In Section 4 we present an algorithm for detecting cliques, in Section 5 we introduce the use of the representation based on cliques as widening, and in Section 6 our experimental evaluation of the proposed analyses. Finally, Section 7 concludes.

2   Preliminaries

Let $\wp(S)$ denote the powerset of set S, and $\wp^0(S)$ denote the *proper powerset* of set S, i.e., $\wp^0(S) = \wp(S) \setminus \{\emptyset\}$. Let also $|S|$ denote the cardinality of a set S.

Let V be a set of variables of interest; e.g., the variables of a program. A *sharing group* is a set of variables of interest, which represents the possible sharing among them (i.e., that they might be bound to terms which have a common variable). Let $SG = \wp^0(V)$ be the set of all sharing groups. A *sharing set* is a set of sharing groups. The Sharing domain is $SH = \wp(SG)$, the set of all sharing sets.

Let F and P be sets of ranked (i.e., with a given arity) functors of interest; e.g., the function symbols and the predicate symbols of a program. We will use $Term$ to denote the set of terms constructed from V and $F \cup P$. Although somehow unorthodox, this will allow us to simply write $g \in Term$ whether g is a term or a predicate atom, since all our operations apply equally well to both classes of syntactic objects. We will denote $\hat{t}$ the set of variables of $t \in Term$. For two elements $s \in Term$ and $t \in Term$, $\hat{st} = \hat{s} \cup \hat{t}$.

For two elements $s_1 \in SH$, $s_2 \in SH$, let $s_1 \uplus s_2$ be their *binary union*, i.e., the result of applying union to each pair in their Cartesian product $s_1 \times s_2$. Let also s_1^* be the *star union* of s_1, i.e., its closure under union. Given terms s and t, and $sh \in SH$, we denote by sh_t the set of sets in sh which have non-empty intersection with $\hat{t}$, the set of variables of t. By extension, in sh_{st} we use $\hat{st}$ as the set of variables of t. Also, $\overline{sh_t}$ is the complement of sh_t, i.e., $sh \setminus sh_t$.

Analysis of a program proceeds by abstractly solving unification equations of the form $t_1 = t_2$, $t_1 \in Term$, $t_2 \in Term$. Let $solve(t_1 = t_2)$ denote the solved form of unification equation $t_1 = t_2$. The results of analysis are abstract substitutions which approximate the concrete substitutions that may occur during execution of the program. Let U be a denumerable set of variables (e.g., the variables that may occur during execution of a program). Concrete substitutions that occur during execution are mappings from V to the set of terms constructed from $U \cup V$ and F. Abstract substitutions are sharing sets.

2.1   Clique Domains

When a sharing set $sh \in SH$ includes the proper powerset of some set C of variables, the representation can be made more compact by using C to represent the same sharing that its powerset represents in the sharing set sh [ZBH99]. A *clique* is, thus, a set of variables of interest, much the same as a sharing group, but a clique C represents all the sharing groups in $\wp^0(C)$. For a clique C, we will use $\downarrow C = \wp^0(C)$. Note that $\downarrow C$ denotes all the sharing that is implicitly represented in a clique C. A *clique set* is a set of cliques. Let $CL = SH$ denote the set of all clique sets. For a clique set $cl \in CL$ we define $\Downarrow cl = \cup \{\downarrow C \mid C \in cl\}$. Note that $\Downarrow cl$ denotes all the sharing that is implicitly represented in a clique set cl. For a pair (cl, sh) of a clique set cl and a sharing set sh, the sharing that the pair represents is $\Downarrow cl \cup sh$.

The Clique-Sharing domain is $SH^W = \{(cl, sh) \mid cl \in CL, sh \in SH\}$, i.e., the set of pairs of a clique set and a sharing set [ZBH99]. An abstract unification operation $amgu^W$ is defined in [Zaf01] which uses a function $\overline{rel} : \wp(V) \times CL \longrightarrow CL$ (complement of rel), defined as:

$$\overline{rel}(S, cl) = \{\ C \setminus S \mid C \in cl\ \} \setminus \{\emptyset\}$$

which approximates the sharing not related to variables in S. We have used an equivalent definition of $amgu^W$ to the one in [Zaf01] (see [BNH05]).

Freeness can be introduced to the Clique-Sharing domain in the usual way [MH91], by including a component which tracks the variables which are known to be free. The Clique-Shfr domain is thus $SHF^W = SH^W \times V$. A method to define an abstract unification function for SH^W with freeness and linearity is outlined in [Zaf01]. We have used an abstract unification operation $amgu^{sf}$ for SH^W with freeness which is a simplification of the corresponding operation which results from the application of such method.

3   Abstract Functions Required by Top-Down Analysis

In top-down frameworks, the analysis of a clause $Head$:$-Body$ proceeds as follows. There is a goal $Goal$ for the predicate of $Head$, which is called in a context represented by abstract substitution $Call$ on a set of variables (distinct from $\hat{Head} \cup \hat{Body}$) which contains those of $Goal$. Then the success of $Goal$ by executing the above clause is represented by abstract substitution $Succ$ given by:

$$
\begin{aligned}
Succ\ &= extend(Call, Goal, Prime) \\
Prime\ &= exit2succ(project(Head, Exit), Goal, Head) \\
Exit\ &= entry2exit(Body, Entry) \\
Entry\ &= augment(F, call2entry(Proj, Goal, Head)) \\
Proj\ &= project(Goal, Call)
\end{aligned}
$$

where F is any term with the variables $\hat{Body} \setminus \hat{Head}$. Function *project* approximates the projection of a substitution on the variables of a given term. Function *augment* extends the domain of an abstract substitution to the variables of a given term, which are assumed to be new fresh variables. Function *entry2exit* is given by the framework, and basically traverses the body of a clause, analyzing each atom in turn. The other three domain-dependent abstract functions which are essential are:

- $call2entry(Proj, Goal, Head)$ yields a substitution on the variables of $Head$ which represents the effects of unification $Goal = Head$ in a context represented by substitution $Proj$ on the variables of $Goal$.
- $exit2succ(Exit', Goal, Head)$ yields a substitution on the variables of $Goal$ which represents the effects of unification $Goal = Head$ in a context represented by substitution $Exit'$ on the variables of $Head$.
- $extend(Call, Goal, Prime)$ yields a substitution for the success of $Goal$ when it is called in a context represented by substitution $Call$ on a set of variables which contains those of $Goal$, given that in such context the success of $Goal$ is already represented by substitution $Prime$ on the variables of $Goal$. The domain of the resulting substitution is the same as the domain of $Call$.

In fact, the first two can be defined from the abstract unification operation $amgu$. The third one, however, is specific to the top-down framework and needs to be defined specifically for a given domain.

Given an operation $amgu(x = t, ASub)$ of abstract unification for equation $x = t$, $x \in V$, $t \in Term$, and $ASub$ an abstract substitution (the domain of which contains variables $\hat{t} \cup \{x\}$), abstract unification for equation $t_1 = t_2$, $t_1 \in Term$, $t_2 \in Term$, is given by:

$$unify(ASub, t_1, t_2) = project(t_1, Amgu(solve(t_1 = t_2), augment(t_1, ASub)))$$

$$Amgu(Eq, ASub) = \begin{cases} ASub & \text{if } Eq = \emptyset \\ Amgu(Eq', amgu(x = t, ASub)) & \text{if } Eq = Eq' \cup \{x = t\} \end{cases}$$

Functions $call2entry$ and $exit2succ$ can defined as follows:

$$call2entry(ASub, Goal, Head) = unify(ASub, Head, Goal)$$
$$exit2succ(ASub, Goal, Head) = unify(ASub, Goal, Head)$$

However, $extend$, together with $project$, $augment$, and $amgu$ are all domain-dependent. In the Sharing domain, $extend$ [MH92], $project$, and $augment$ are defined as follows:

$$extend(Call, g, Prime) = \overline{Call_g} \cup \{ s \mid s \in Call_g^*, \ (s \cap \hat{g}) \in Prime \}$$
$$project(g, sh) = \{s \cap \hat{g} \mid s \in sh\} \setminus \{\emptyset\}$$
$$augment(g, sh) = sh \cup \{\{x\} \mid x \in \hat{g}\}$$

In the Shfr domain, these functions are defined as follows [MH91]:

$$project^f(g, (sh, f)) = (project(g, sh), f \cap \hat{g})$$
$$augment^f(g, (sh, f)) = (augment(g, sh), f \cup \hat{g})$$
$$extend^f((sh_1, f_1), g, (sh_2, f_2)) = (extend(sh_1, g, sh_2), f')$$
$$f' = f_2 \cup \{x \mid x \in (f_1 \setminus \hat{g}), ((\cup sh'_x) \cap \hat{g}) \subseteq f_2\}$$

3.1 Abstract Functions for Top-Down Analysis in the Clique-Domains

Functions $call2entry$ and $exit2succ$ have usually been defined in a way which is specific to the domain and for top-down analysis (see, e.g., [MH92] for a definition for set-sharing). We have chosen instead to present here a formalization of a way to use the *amgu* in top-down frameworks. Thus, the definitions of *call2entry* and *exit2succ* based on *amgu* given above. Our intuition in doing this is that the results should be (more) comparable to goal-dependent bottom-up analyses, where *amgu* is used directly.

Note, however, that such definitions imply a possible loss of precision. Using *amgu* in the way explained above does not allow to take advantage of the fact that all variables in the head of the clause being entered during analysis are free. Alternative definitions of *call2entry* can be obtained that improve precision from this observation.[2] The overall effect would be equivalent to using the *amgu* function for the Sharing domain coupled with freeness, with the head variables as free variables, and then throwing out the freeness component of the result. For example, for the Clique-Sharing domain a function $call2entry^s$ that takes advantage of freeness information can be defined as follows, where $unify^{sf}$ is the version of *unify* that uses $amgu^{sf}$:

$$call2entry^s(ASub, Goal, Head) = ASub'$$
$$\text{where} \qquad (ASub', Free) = unify^f((ASub, \emptyset), Head, Goal)$$

However, for the reasons mentioned above, we have used the definitions of *call2entry* and *exit2succ* based on *amgu*. The rest of the top-down functions are defined below. For the Clique-Sharing domain, let $g \in Term$, and $(cl, sh) \in SH^W$. Functions $project^s$ and $augment^s$ are defined as follows:

$$project^s(g, (cl, sh)) = (project(g, cl), project(g, sh))$$
$$augment^s(g, (cl, sh)) = (cl, augment(g, sh))$$

Function $extend^s(Call, g, Prime)$ is defined as follows. Let $Call = (cl_1, sh_1)$ and $Prime = (cl_2, sh_2)$. Let *normalize* be a function which normalizes a pair (cl, sh) so that no powersets occur in sh (all are "transferred" to cliques in cl; Section 4 presents a possible implementation of such a function). Let $Prime$ be already normalized, and:

$$(cl', sh') = normalize((cl_{1_g}^* \cup (cl_{1_g}^* \uplus sh_{1_g}^*)), sh_{1_g}^*)$$

The following two functions lift the classical *extend* [MH92] respectively to the cases of the two clique sets (clique groups of the *Call* allowed by the clique component of the *Prime*) and of the two sharing sets (sharing groups belonging to the *Call* allowed by the sharing part of the *Prime*):

$$extsh(sh_1, g, sh_2) = \overline{sh_{1_g}} \cup \{ s \mid s \in sh', (s \cap \hat{g}) \in sh_2 \}$$
$$extcl(cl_1, g, cl_2) = \overline{rel}(\hat{g}, cl_1) \cup \{ (s' \cap s) \cup (s' \setminus \hat{g}) \mid s' \in cl', s \in cl_2 \}$$

The following two functions account respectively for the sharing sets belonging to the clique component of the *Call* allowed by the sharing part of the *Prime*,

---

[2] For example, one such definition (developed independently) can be found in [AS05].

and the sharing sets of the sharing component of the *Call* allowed by the clique part of the *Prime*:

$$clsh(cl', g, sh_2) = \{\ s\ |\ s \subseteq c \in cl',\ (s \cap \hat{g}) \in sh_2\ \}$$
$$shcl(sh', g, cl_2) = \{\ s\ |\ s \in sh',\ (s \cap \hat{g}) \subseteq c \in cl_2\ \}$$

The *extend* function for the Clique-Sharing domain is thus:

$$extend^s((cl_1, sh_1), g, (cl_2, sh_2)) =$$
$$(\ extcl(cl_1, g, cl_2)$$
$$,\ extsh(sh_1, g, sh_2) \cup clsh(cl', g, sh_2) \cup shcl(sh', g, cl_2)\ )$$

Example 4. Let $Call = (cl_1, sh_1) = (\{xyz\}, \{u, v\})$, $Prime = (cl_2, sh_2) = (\{x\}, \{uv\})$, and $\hat{g} = \{x, u, v\}$. Then we have $(cl', sh') = (\{xyzuv\}, \emptyset)$. The $extend^s$ function is computed as follows:

$$extsh(sh_1, g, sh_2) = extsh(\{u, v\}, g, \{uv\}) = \emptyset$$
$$extcl(cl_1, g, cl_2) = extcl(\{xyz\}, g, \{x\}) = \{xyz, yz\}$$
$$clsh(cl', g, sh_2) = clsh(\{xyzuv\}, g, \{uv\}) = \{yzuv, yuv, zuv, uv\}$$
$$shcl(sh', g, cl_2) = shcl(\emptyset, g, \{x\}) = \emptyset$$

Thus, $extend^s(Call, g, Prime) = (\{xyz, yz\}, \{yzuv, yuv, zuv, uv\})$, which after regularization yields $(\{xyz\}, \{yzuv, yuv, zuv, uv\})$.

Note how the result is less precise than the exact result $(\{xyz\}, \{uv\})$. This is due to overestimation of sharing implied by the cliques; in particular, for the case of *extend*, overestimations stem mainly from the necessary worst-case assumption given by (cl', sh'), which is then "pruned" as much as possible by the functions defined above. The resulting operation, however, is correct: the sharing implied by $extend^s$ on two abstract substitutions *Call* and *Prime* is an over-approximation of that given by *extend* on the sharing set substitutions corresponding to *Call* and *Prime*.

Theorem 1. *Let* $Call \in SH^W$, $Prime \in SH^W$, *and* $g \in Term$, *such that the conditions for the extend function are satisfied. Let* $Call = (cl_1, sh_1)$, $Prime = (cl_2, sh_2)$, *and* $extend^s(Call, g, Prime) = (cl', sh')$. *Then*

$$(\Downarrow cl' \cup sh') \supseteq extend(\Downarrow cl_1 \cup sh_1, g, \Downarrow cl_2 \cup sh_2)\ .$$

For the Clique-Shfr domain, let $g \in Term$, and $s \in SHF^W$, $s = ((cl, sh), f)$. Functions $project^{sf}$ and $augment^{sf}$ are defined as follows:

$$project^{sf}(g, s) = (project^s(g, (cl, sh)), f \cap g)$$
$$augment^{sf}(g, s) = (augment^s(g, (cl, sh)), f \cup \hat{g})$$

Function $extend^{sf}(Call, g, Prime)$ is defined as follows. Let $Call = ((cl_1, sh_1), f_1)$ and $Prime = ((cl_2, sh_2), f_2)$, $extend^{sf}(Call, g, Prime) = ((cl', sh'), f')$, where:

$$(cl', sh') = extend^s((cl_1, sh_1), g, (cl_2, sh_2))$$
$$f' = f_2 \cup \{x\ |\ x \in (f_1 \setminus \hat{g}),\ ((\cup(sh'_x \cup cl'_x)) \cap \hat{g}) \subseteq f_2\}$$

Operation $extend^{sf}$ is correct: it gives safe approximations. The resulting sharing it implies when applied on two abstract substitutions $Call$ and $Prime$ is no less than that given by $extend^f$ on the sharing set substitutions corresponding to $Call$ and $Prime$; and the freeness is no more than what $extend^f$ would have computed.

Theorem 2. *Let $Call \in SHF^W$, $Prime \in SHF^W$, and $g \in Term$, such that the conditions for the extend function are satisfied. Let $Call = ((cl_1, sh_1), f_1)$, $Prime = ((cl_2, sh_2), f_2)$, and $extend^{sf}(Call, g, Prime) = ((cl', sh'), f')$. Let also $s_1 = \Downarrow cl_1 \cup sh_1$, $s_2 = \Downarrow cl_2 \cup sh_2$, and $extend^f((s_1, f_1), g, (s_2, f_2)) = (sh, f)$. Then $(\Downarrow cl' \cup sh') \supseteq sh$ and $f' \subseteq f$.*

4   Detecting Cliques

Obviously, to minimize the representation in SH^W it pays off to replace any set S of sharing groups which is the proper powerset of some set of variables C by including C as a clique. Once this is done, the set S can be eliminated from the sharing set, since the presence of C in the clique set makes S redundant. This is the normalization mentioned in Section 3.1 when defining $extend$ for the Clique-Sharing domain, and denoted there by a *normalize* function. In this section we present an algorithm for such a normalization.

Given an element $(cl, sh) \in SH^W$, sharing groups might occur in sh which are already implicit in cl. Such groups are redundant with respect to the sharing represented by the pair. We say that an element $(cl, sh) \in SH^W$ is *minimal* if $\Downarrow cl \cap sh = \emptyset$. An algorithm for minimization is straightforward: it should delete from sh all sharing groups which are a subset of an existing clique in cl. But normalization goes a step further by "moving sharing" from the sharing set of a pair to the clique set, thus forcing redundancy of some sharing groups (which can therefore be eliminated).

While normalizing, it turns out that powersets may exist which can be obtained from sharing groups in the sharing set plus sharing groups implied by existing cliques in the clique set. The representation can be minimized further if

1. Let $n = |sh|$; if $n < 3$, stop.
2. Compute the maximum m such that $n \geq 2^m - 1$.
3. Let $i = m$.
4. If $i = 1$, stop.
5. Let $C = \{s \mid s \in sh, |s| = i\}$.
6. If $C = \emptyset$ then decrement i and go to 4.
7. Take $S \in C$ and delete it from C.
8. Let $SS = \{s \mid s \in sh, s \subseteq S\}$.
9. Compute $[S]$.
10. If $|SS| = 2^i - 1 - [S]$ then:
    (a) Add S to cl (regularize cl).
    (b) Subtract SS from sh.
11. Go to 6.

Fig. 1. Algorithm for detecting cliques

such sharing groups are also "transferred" to the clique set by adding the adequate clique. We say that an element $(cl, sh) \in SH^W$ is *normalized* if whenever there is an $s \subseteq (\biguplus cl \cup sh)$ such that $s = \downarrow c$ for some set c then $s \cap sh = \emptyset$.

Our normalization algorithm is presented in Figure 1. It starts with an element $(cl, sh) \in SH^W$, which is already minimal, and obtains an equivalent element (w.r.t. the sharing represented) which is normalized and minimal. First, the number m is computed, which is the length of the longest possible clique. Then the sharing set sh is traversed to obtain candidate cliques of the greatest possible length i (which starts in m and is iteratively decremented). Existing subsets of a candidate clique S of length i are extracted from sh. If there are $2^i - 1 - [S]$ subsets of S in sh then S is a clique: it is added to cl and its subsets deleted from sh. Note that the test is performed on the number of existing subsets, and requires the computation of a number $[S]$, which is crucial for the correctness of the test.

The number $[S]$ stands for the number of subsets of S which may not appear in sh because they are already represented in cl (i.e., they are already subsets of an existing clique). In order to correctly compute this number it is essential that the input to the algorithm be already minimal; otherwise, redundant sharing groups might bias the calculation: the formula below may count as not present in sh a (redundant) group which is in fact present. The computation of $[S]$ is as follows. Let $I = \{S \cap C \mid C \in cl\} \setminus \{\emptyset\}$ and $A_i = \{\cap A \mid A \subseteq I, |A| = i\}$. Then:

$$[S] = \sum_{1 \leq i \leq |I|} (-1)^{i-1} \sum_{A \in A_i} (2^{|A|} - 1)$$

Note that the representation can be minimized further by eliminating cliques which are redundant with other cliques. This is the regularization mentioned in step 10 of the algorithm. We say that a clique set cl is *regular* if there are no two cliques $c_1 \in cl$, $c_2 \in cl$, such that $c_1 \subset c_2$. This can be tested while adding cliques in step 10 above.

Finally, there is a chance for further minimization by considering as cliques candidate sets of variables such that not all of their subsets exist in the given element of SH^W. Note that the algorithm preserves precision, since the sharing represented by the element of SH^W input to the algorithm is the same as that represented by the element which is output. However, we could set up a threshold for the number of subsets of the candidate clique that need be detected, and in this case the output element may in general represent more sharing. This might in fact be useful in practice in order to use the normalization algorithm as a widening operation. Note that, although the complexity of this algorithm is exponential since it is actually the problem of solving all the maximal cliques of an undirected graph (NP-complete), it is not a practical problem due to the small size of these graphs.

5   Widening Set-Sharing

A *widen* function for SH^W is based on a widening operator $\triangledown : SH^W \rightarrow SH^W$, which must guarantee that for each $clsh \in SH^W$, $\triangledown clsh \supseteq clsh$. The following theorem is necessary to establish the correctness of the widenings used:

Theorem 3. *Let* $clsh \in SH^W$ *and equation* $x = t$, $x \in V$, $t \in Term$, *we have*

$$amgu^s(\bigtriangledown clsh, x = t) \supseteq amgu^s(clsh, x = t)$$

For our experiments we start defining two widenings. The first of them, by [Fec96], is of an intermediate precision and it is as follows:

$$\bigtriangledown^F(cl, sh) = (cl \cup sh, \emptyset)$$

The second widening was defined in [ZBH99] as a cautious widening (because it did not introduce new sharing sets, although obviously information was lost as soon as the operations for the Clique-Sharing domain were used) and the idea was to define an undirected graph from an element $clsh \in SH^W$ and compute the maximal cliques of that graph:

$$\bigtriangledown^G(cl, sh) = (\{C_1, \dots, C_k\}, sh)$$

where $C_1, \dots, C_k$ are all the maximal cliques of the induced graph from (cl, sh). For the experimental evaluation in [ZBH99] a version of this cautious widening $\bigtriangledown^g$ was used which is equivalent to the previous one but disregarding the singletons. It is easy to see that our normalization process is totally equivalent to the computation of the maximal cliques of a graph and thus we will use the normalization process as a cautious widening $\bigtriangledown^N$. In the same way as [ZBH99], we use a more precise version of $\bigtriangledown^N$ which is based on disregarding the singletons called $\bigtriangledown^n$.

Since cliques should only be used when it is strictly necessary to keep the analysis from running out of memory, its application is guarded by a condition. We use the simplest possible condition based on cardinality of the sets in SH^W, imposing a threshold n on cardinality which triggers the widening. We have tuned the threshold in order to be able to achieve a reasonable trade-off between the objective of triggering widening only when strictly required and preventing running out of memory in all cases. For each widening, the triggering condition is defined as follows:

$$widen(cl, sh) = \begin{cases} \bigtriangledown(cl, sh) & \text{if } (\sum_{s \in sh} |s|) > n \\ (cl, sh) & \text{otherwise} \end{cases}$$

6   Experimental Results

We have measured experimentally the relative efficiency and precision obtained with the inclusion of cliques both as an alternative representation in the Sharing and Shfr domains and as a widening in the Shfr domain. Our first objective is to study the implications of the change in representation for analysis: although the introduction of cliques does not by itself imply a loss of precision, the abstract operations for cliques are not precise. We first want to measure such loss in practice. Second, to minimize precision loss, the clique representation should ideally be used only whenever necessary, i.e., when the classical representation cannot deal with the analysis of the program at hand. In this case, we will be using the clique representation as a widening to guarantee (smooth) termination of the analysis, i.e., that analysis does not abort because of running out of memory. It turns out that this is not a trivial task: it is not easy to determine beforehand when analysis will need more memory than is available.

Benchmarks are divided into three groups. Because of space limitations, for each group we only show a reduced number of the benchmarks actually used: those which are more representative. The first group, append (app in the tables) through serialize (serial), is a set of simple programs, used as a testbed for an analysis: they have only direct recursion and make a straightforward use of unification (basically, for input/output of arguments i.e., they are moded). The second group, aiakl through zebra, are more involved: they make use of mutual recursion and of elaborate aliasing between arguments to some extent; some of them are parts of "real" programs (aiakl is part of an analyzer of the AKL language; prolog_read (plread) and rdtok are Prolog parsers). The benchmarks in the third group are all (parts of) "real" programs: ann is the &-prolog parallelizer, peephole (peep) is the peephole optimizer of the SB-Prolog compiler, qplan is the core of the Chat-80 application, and witt is a conceptual clustering application.

Our results are shown in Tables 1 and 2. Columns labeled **T** show analysis times in milliseconds, on a medium-loaded Pentium IV Xeon 2.0Ghz with two processors, 4Gb of RAM memory, running Fedora Core 2.0, and averaging several runs after eliminating the best and worst values. Ciao version 1.11#326 and CiaoPP 1.0#2292 were used. Columns labeled **P** (precision) show the number of sharing groups in the information inferred and, between parenthesis, the number of sharing groups for the worst-case sharing. Columns labeled **#W** show the number of widenings performed and columns labeled **#C** show the number of clique groups. Since our top-down framework infers information at all program points (before and after calling each clause body atom), and also several variants for each program point, it is not trivial to provide a good absolute measure of precision: changes in precision may cause more variants during analysis, which in turn affect the precision measure. Instead, we have chosen to provide the accumulated number of sharing groups in all variants for all program points, in order to be able to compare results in different situations.

6.1   Cliques as Alternative Representation

Table 1 shows the results for Sharing, Clique-Sharing, Shfr, and Clique-Shfr, for the cases in which cliques are used as an alternative representation.

In order to understand the results it is important to note an existing synergy between normalization, efficiency, and precision when cliques are used as an alternative representation. If normalization causes no change in the sharing representation (i.e., sharing groups are not moved to cliques), usually because powersets do not really occur during analysis, then the clique part is empty. Analysis is the same as without cliques, but with the extra overhead due to the use of the normalization process. Then precision is the same but the time spent in analyzing the program is a little longer. This also occurs often if the use of normalization is kept to a minimum: only for correctness (in our implementation, normalization is required for correctness at least for the *extend* function and other functions used for comparing abstract substitutions). This should not be surprising, since the fact that powersets occur during analysis at a given time does not necessarily mean that they keep on occurring afterward: they can disappear because of groundness or other precision improvements during subsequent analysis (of, e.g., builtins).

Table 1. Precision and Time-efficiency

	Sh		SH^W			Shfr		SH^W fr		
	T	P	T	P	#C	T	P	T	P	#C
app	11	29 (60)	8	44 (60)	4	6	7 (30)	6	7 (30)	0
deriv	35	27 (546)	27	27 (546)	0	27	21 (546)	27	21 (546)	0
mmat	13	14 (694)	11	14 (694)	0	9	12 (694)	11	12 (694)	0
qsort	24	30 (1716)	25	30 (1716)	0	25	30 (1716)	27	30 (1716)	0
query	11	35 (501)	13	35 (501)	5	12	22 (501)	14	22 (501)	0
serial	306	1734 (10531)	90	2443 (10531)	88	61	545 (5264)	55	736 (5264)	41
aiakl	35	145 (13238)	42	145 (13238)	0	37	145 (13238)	43	145 (13238)	0
boyer	369	1688 (4631)	267	1997 (4631)	158	373	1739 (5036)	278	2074 (5036)	163
brow	30	69 (776)	29	69 (776)	0	29	69 (776)	31	69 (776)	0
plread	400	1080 (408755)	465	1080 (408755)	10	425	1050 (408634)	481	1050 (408634)	0
rdtok	325	1350 (11513)	344	1391 (11513)	182	335	1047 (11513)	357	1053 (11513)	2
wplan	3261	8207 (42089)	1430	8191 (26857)	420	1320	3068 (23501)	1264	5705 (25345)	209
zebra	25	280 ($67 \cdot 10^7$)	34	280 ($67 \cdot 10^7$)	0	41	280 ($67 \cdot 10^7$)	42	280 ($67 \cdot 10^7$)	0
ann	2382	10000 ($31 \cdot 10^4$)	802	19544 ($31 \cdot 10^4$)	700	1791	7811 ($40 \cdot 10^4$)	968	14108 ($39 \cdot 10^4$)	510
peep	831	2210 (12148)	435	2920 (12118)	171	508	1475 (9941)	403	2825 (12410)	135
qplan	-	-	860	$42 \cdot 10^4$ ($38 \cdot 10^5$)	747	-	-	2181	$23 \cdot 10^4$ ($31 \cdot 10^5$)	529
witt	405	858 ($45 \cdot 10^5$)	437	858 ($45 \cdot 10^5$)	25	484	813 ($45 \cdot 10^5$)	451	813 ($45 \cdot 10^5$)	0

When the normalization process is used more often (like for example at every call to *call2entry* as we have done), then sharing groups are moved more often to cliques. Thus, the use of the operations that compute on clique sets produces efficiency gains, and also precision losses, as it was expected. However, precision losses are not high. Finally, if normalization is used too often, then the analysis process suffers from heavy overhead, causing too high penalty in efficiency that it makes the analysis intractable. Therefore it is very clear that a thorough tuning of the use of the normalization process is crucial to lead analysis to good results in terms of both precision and efficiency.

As usual in top-down analysis, the *extend* function plays a crucial role. In our case, this function is a very important bottleneck for the use of normalization. As we have said, we use the normalization for correctness at the beginning of the *extend* function. Additionally, it would be convenient to use it also at the end of such function, since the number of sharing groups can grow too much. However, this is not possible in practice due to the *clsh* function, which can generate so many sharing groups that, at the limit, the normalization process itself cannot run. Alternative definitions of $clsh$ have been studied, but because of the precision losses incurred, they have been found impractical.

Table 1 shows that there are always programs whose analysis of which does not produce cliques. This occurs in some of the benchmarks (like all of the first group but serialize and some of the second one such as aiakl, browse (brow), prolog_read, and zebra). In this case, precision is maintained as expected but there is a small loss of efficiency due to the extra overhead discussed above. The same thing happens with benchmarks which produce cliques (append, query, prolog_read, and witt, in the case of Sharing without freeness), but this does not affect precision.

On the other hand, for those benchmarks which do generate cliques (like serialize, boyer, warplan (wplan), ann, and peephole) the gain in efficiency is considerable at the cost of a small precision loss. As usual, efficiency and precision correlate inversely: if precision increases then efficiency decreases and vice versa. A special case is, to some extent, that of rdtok, since precision losses are not coupled with efficiency gains. The reason is that for this benchmark there are extra success substitutions (which do not convey extra precision and, in fact, the result is less precise) that make the analysis times larger.

In general, the same effects are maintained with the addition of freeness, although the efficiency gains are lower whereas the precision gains are a little higher. The reason is that the $amgu^{sf}$ function is less efficient than $amgu^s$ (but more precise). Overall, however, the trade-off between precision and efficiency is beneficial. Moreover, the more compact representation of the clique domain makes possible to analyze benchmarks (e.g., qplan) which ran out of memory with the standard representation.

6.2   Widening Set-Sharing Via Cliques

As mentioned before, the intention of the widening operator is to limit the use of cliques only to the cases where it is necessary in order to avoid analysis running out of memory. This is not a trivial task, as explained below. Table 2 shows results from our experiments for Shfr, Clique-Shfr using widening. The widenings have been applied before each abstract unification and at the end of the *extend* function, and they are guarded by the condition discussed in Section 5.

The choice of a suitable value of the threshold is a key issue, since this threshold is responsible for triggering widening only for the cases where it is needed. In a top-down framework the choice of threshold is further complicated by the *extend* function. As commented above, this function and, in particular, the $clsh$ function defined in Section 3.1 can make the number of sharing groups grow excessively after every call, since that function generates powersets of the given cliques. In order to solve this problem we studied two different alternatives.

First, we tried a more efficient version of the $clsh$ function, which moved some extra sharing groups to cliques. This, however, resulted in excessive precision losses which reduced the usefulness of the analysis. Given this, we also developed a hybrid approach for the case of $\bigtriangledown^n$, where $\bigtriangledown^n$ is used in unifications but the more aggressive $\bigtriangledown^F$ is used after calling $clsh$. We call this version $\bigtriangledown^{nF}$.

As for practical thresholds, we have concluded experimentally that an appropriate value for the guard for the widenings in our test platform is 250. This is the highest value that prevents analysis from running out of memory. However, as we will see, it also triggers widening for a few cases where it is not needed. For the additional threshold used in the $\triangledown^{nF}$ operations (Section 4) we have determined that 40% is an appropriate value since, although low, it gives surprisingly good results. The results in Table 2 thus correspond to $\triangledown^{F}_{250}$ and $\triangledown^{nF}_{250-40}$.

Table 2. Precision and Time-efficiency with Widening

	Shfr		SH^{W} fr$+\triangledown^{F}_{250}$			SH^{W} fr$+\triangledown^{nF}_{250-40}$		
	T	P	T	P	#W	T	P	#W
app	6	7 (30)	11	7 (30)	0	10	7 (30)	0
deriv	27	21 (546)	48	21 (546)	0	35	21 (546)	0
mmat	9	12 (694)	16	12 (694)	0	16	12 (694)	0
qsort	25	30 (1716)	40	30 (1716)	0	43	30 (1716)	0
query	12	22 (501)	23	22 (501)	0	25	22 (501)	0
serial	61	545 (5264)	74	722 (5264)	6	70	703 (5264)	10
aiakl	37	145 (13238)	63	145 (13238)	6	61	145 (13238)	33
boyer	373	1739 (5036)	561	1744 (5036)	2	536	1743 (5036)	4
brow	29	69 (776)	44	69 (776)	0	42	69 (776)	0
plread	425	1050 (408634)	3419	24856 (1754310)	198	593	1050 (408634)	103
rdtok	335	1047 (11513)	472	1047 (11513)	0	466	1047 (11513)	0
wplan	1320	3068 (23501)	1878	5376 (21586)	42	1394	5121 (20894)	60
zebra	41	280 ($67 \cdot 10^{7}$)	42	280 ($67 \cdot 10^{7}$)	1	56	280 ($67 \cdot 10^{7}$)	48
ann	1791	7811 (401220)	751	16122 (394800)	17	726	16122 (394800)	34
peep	508	1475 (9941)	453	2827 (12410)	8	512	2815 (12410)	16
qplan	-	-	1722	238426 (3141556)	26	1897	233070 (3126973)	55
witt	484	813 (4545594)	2333	259366 (23378597)	110	736	813 (4545594)	140

As expected, the use of widening allows executing programs which the Shfr domain could not due to exceeded memory capacity. However, as mentioned in the discussion of the threshold, we do also widen for some benchmarks which the original domain could handle. Fortunately, the precision losses are limited.

Widening operator $\triangledown^{nF}_{250-40}$ results at least as precise as $\triangledown^{F}_{250}$ and, for most of the cases, better. In fact, the results obtained for prolog_read and witt using $\triangledown^{F}_{250}$ are remarkable since the information obtained is very poor.

The difference in time efficiency between $\triangledown^{F}_{250}$ and $\triangledown^{nF}_{250-40}$ is acceptable, and in fact for some programs $\triangledown^{nF}_{250-40}$ is more efficient than $\triangledown^{F}_{250}$. Note that for prolog_read and witt the difference is considerable in favor of $\triangledown^{nF}_{250-40}$. There appears to be a clear correspondence between number of widenings and efficiency gains. This holds even if the widening operations are expensive, such as with $\triangledown^{nF}_{250-40}$, because the widening expense is offset by efficiency gains in the abstract operations due to the reduction in the size of the abstract substitutions being processed.

7 Conclusions

We have studied the problem of efficient, scalable set-sharing analysis of logic programs using cliques both as alternative representation and as widenings. We have concentrated on the previously unexplored case of inferring set-sharing information in the context of top-down analyses. To this end, we have proposed all the operations required for top-down analyses for the cases of combining cliques with both Sharing and Sharing+Freeness. We have also proposed and studied several widenings, providing different levels of precision and efficiency tradeoff.

Our experimental evaluation supports the conclusion that, for inferring set-sharing, the use of cliques as an alternative representation results in limited precision losses (due to normalizations) while useful efficiency gains are obtained. We have also derives useful conclusions regarding the interactions between thresholds, precision, efficiency and cost of widening which have resulted in the proposal of a hybrid widening which resulted quite useful in practice. In fact, the new representations allowed analyzing some programs that exceeded memory capacity using classical sharing representations. Thus, we believe our results contribute to the practical application of top-down analysis of set sharing.

Acknowledgments

The authors would like to thank the anonymous referees for their useful comments. Manuel Hermenegildo and Jorge Navas are supported in part by the Prince of Asturias Chair in Information Science and Technology at UNM. This work was also funded in part by the EC Future and Emerging Technologies program IST-2001-38059 *ASAP* project and by the Spanish MEC TIC 2002-0055 *CUBICO* project.

References

[AS05]   Gianluca Amato and Francesca Scozzari. Optimality in goal-dependent analysis of sharing. Technical Report TR-05-06, Dipartimento di Informatica, Università di Pisa, 2005.

[BCM94]   M. Bruynooghe, M. Codish, and A. Mulkers. Abstract unification for a composite domain deriving sharing and freeness properties of program variables. In F.S. de Boer and M. Gabbrielli, editors, *Verification and Analysis of Logic Languages*, pages 213–230, 1994.

[BHZ02]   Roberto Bagnara, Patricia M. Hill, and Enea Zaffanella. Set-sharing is redundant for pair-sharing. *Theoretical Computer Science*, 277(1-2):3–46, 2002.

[BNH05]   F. Bueno, J. Navas, and M. Hermenegildo. Sharing, freeness, linearity, redundancy, widenings, and cliques. Technical Report CLIP5/2005.0, Technical University of Madrid (UPM), School of Computer Science, UPM, April 2005.

[CDFB96]   Michael Codish, Dennis Dams, Gilberto Filé, and Maurice Bruynooghe. On the design of a correct freeness analysis for logic programs. *The Journal of Logic Programming*, 28(3):181–206, 1996.

[CMB+93]   M. Codish, A. Mulkers, M. Bruynooghe, M. García de la Banda, and M. Hermenegildo. Improving Abstract Interpretations by Combining Domains. In *Proc. ACM SIGPLAN Symposium on Partial Evaluation and Semantics Based Program Manipulation*, pages 194–206. ACM, June 1993.

[Fec96]   Christian Fecht. An efficient and precise sharing domain for logic programs. In Herbert Kuchen and S. Doaitse Swierstra, editors, *PLILP*, volume 1140 of *Lecture Notes in Computer Science*, pages 469–470. Springer, 1996.

[Fil94]   G. Filé. Share x Free: Simple and correct. Technical Report 15, Dipartamento di Matematica, Universita di Padova, December 1994.

[HBPLG99]   M. Hermenegildo, F. Bueno, G. Puebla, and P. López-García. Program Analysis, Debugging and Optimization Using the Ciao System Preprocessor. In *1999 Int'l. Conference on Logic Programming*, pages 52–66, Cambridge, MA, November 1999. MIT Press.

[HPMS00]   M. Hermenegildo, G. Puebla, K. Marriott, and P. Stuckey. Incremental Analysis of Constraint Logic Programs. *ACM Transactions on Programming Languages and Systems*, 22(2):187–223, March 2000.

[HZB04]   P. M. Hill, E. Zaffanella, and R. Bagnara. A correct, precise and efficient integration of set-sharing, freeness and linearity for the analysis of finite and rational tree languages. *Theory and Practice of Logic Programming*, 4(3):289–323, 2004.

[JL92]   D. Jacobs and A. Langen. Static Analysis of Logic Programs for Independent And-Parallelism. *Journal of Logic Programming*, 13(2 and 3):291–314, July 1992.

[KS94]   A. King and P. Soper. Depth-k Sharing and Freeness. In *International Conference on Logic Programming*. MIT Press, June 1994.

[MH90]   K. Muthukumar and M. Hermenegildo. Deriving A Fixpoint Computation Algorithm for Top-down Abstract Interpretation of Logic Programs. Technical Report ACT-DC-153-90, Microelectronics and Computer Technology Corporation (MCC), Austin, TX 78759, April 1990.

[MH91]   K. Muthukumar and M. Hermenegildo. Combined Determination of Sharing and Freeness of Program Variables Through Abstract Interpretation. In *1991 International Conference on Logic Programming*, pages 49–63. MIT Press, June 1991.

[MH92]   K. Muthukumar and M. Hermenegildo. Compile-time Derivation of Variable Dependency Using Abstract Interpretation. *Journal of Logic Programming*, 13(2/3):315–347, July 1992.

[MSJB95]   A. Mulkers, W. Simoens, G. Janssens, and M. Bruynooghe. On the Practicality of Abstract Equation Systems. In *International Conference on Logic Programming*. MIT Press, June 1995.

[Zaf01]   Enea Zaffanella. *Correctness, Precision and Efficiency in the Sharing Analysis of Real Logic Languages*. PhD thesis, School of Computing, University of Leeds, Leeds, U.K., 2001.

[ZBH99]   E. Zaffanella, R. Bagnara, and P. M. Hill. Widening Sharing. In G. Nadathur, editor, *Principles and Practice of Declarative Programming*, volume 1702 of *Lecture Notes in Computer Science*, pages 414–431, Paris, France, 1999. Springer-Verlag, Berlin.

Querying Complex Graphs*

Yanhong A. Liu and Scott D. Stoller

Computer Science Department, State University of New York at Stony Brook,
Stony Brook, NY 11794
{liu, stoller}@cs.sunysb.edu

Abstract. This paper presents a powerful language for querying complex graphs and a method for generating efficient implementations that can answer queries with complexity guarantees. The graphs may have edge labels that may have parameters, and easily and naturally capture complex interrelated objects in object-oriented systems and XML data. The language is built on extended regular path expressions with variables and scoping, and can express queries more easily and clearly than previous query languages. The method for implementation first transforms queries into Datalog with limited extensions. It then extends a previous method to generate specialized algorithms and complexity formulas from Datalog with these extensions.

1 Introduction

Database applications must query complex interrelated objects, and thus languages that provide both the power and ease of querying complex graphs are highly desired. Such query languages are essential not only for traditional database applications and mining of semi-structured data, but also for analyzing large computer programs and systems.

Various forms of regular path queries are ways of declaratively expressing queries on graphs as regular-expression-like patterns that are matched against paths in the graph. Some have been used widely in querying semi-structured data (e.g., [1, 3, 7, 20]), including in particular tree structured data in XML, which is increasingly used for representing data, including knowledge as data and programs as data. Some more powerful kinds have provided general frameworks for analyzing computer programs and systems (e.g., [21, 11, 17]).

Regular-expression-like patterns are composed of simple and easy operations for sequencing, choice, repetition, skipping, negation, etc. Even though they are not as powerful as languages in more sophisticated frameworks, they are more perspicuous and convenient, and are sufficiently powerful to express common and important properties. The combined power and simplicity contribute to their wide use in computing, in database and web information retrieval, languages and compilers, operating systems and security, etc.

* This work was supported in part by ONR under grants N00014-04-1-0722 and N00014-02-1-0363 and NSF under grants CCR-0306399 and CCR-0311512.

While regular-expression-like patterns have been studied and used extensively in analysis of linear data and in recent years tree-structured data, many applications deal with much more complex interrelated objects. In regular path query frameworks, such information is captured as graphs, and the analyses are based on properties that hold on paths in the graph. In particular, parametric regular path queries [17] allow the use of variables, also called parameters, in queries so that additional information along paths can be captured and related.

Despite this progress, no previous regular path query framework supports easy, powerful, and efficient queries over a rich data model that naturally models all aspects of objects in object-oriented systems and XML data. Frameworks with rich data models exist for querying object-oriented databases [14] and for querying XML data [20], but the former does not support regular-expression like patterns, and the latter does not support queries on graphs. Languages that support regular-expression like patterns on graphs [10, 13] are studied heavily in terms of expressiveness and query containment, but not on improved ease of expressing queries or efficient implementation with precise complexity guarantees. The best of existing approaches must be combined and extended to support easy, powerful, and efficient queries of complex graphs.

This paper presents a powerful language for querying complex graphs and a method for generating efficient implementations that can answer queries with complexity guarantees. The graphs may have edge labels that may have parameters and easily and naturally capture complex interrelated objects in object-oriented systems and XML data. The language is built on parameterized regular path expressions with copings, and can express queries more easily and clearly than previous query languages. The method for implementation first transforms queries into Datalog with limited extensions. It then extends a previous method [18] to generate specialized algorithms and complexity formulas from Datalog with these extensions.

2   The Data Model

Complex graphs. We consider edge-labeled directed graphs where the labels may have parameters. We call such graphs *complex graphs*. A complex graph comprises a set of vertices and a set of edges. Each vertex has a unique id. Each edge has a source vertex, a target vertex, and a label.

A label captures information relating a source vertex and a target vertex. For example, in applications that manipulate computer programs, an edge may relate a program-point vertex to another program-point vertex with a label def that captures the assignment operation in between. In a supply chain application, an edge may relate a manufacturer vertex and a product vertex with a label supply. A label may have arguments that capture additional information about the relationship. For example, an assignment operation num := 5 may be represented using an edge label def(num) or def(num, 5). To represent the date and means of a supply relationship, a label such as supply(12/20/04, air) may be used. A special label can be used to indicate that no information about the relationship is of interest.

We refer to names, such as def and supply, that represent kinds of relationships, as *constructors*. We refer to names, such as num, 12/20/04, and vertex ids, that represent individuals, as *constants*. A *label* is a constructor applied to zero or more arguments, where each argument is a constant. We assume that the domains of constructors and constants are finite; this assumption always holds in any particular application.

Modeling objects and relationships.   Complex graphs can model objects and classes naturally and precisely. Objects are modeled as vertices, where vertex ids are object ids. Values of attributes are also modeled as vertices, consistent with them being objects in a pure object-oriented model. Classes are also modeled as vertices, consistent with classes being objects in a powerful object-oriented model.

Attributes and relationships are modeled as edges. An edge labeled with an attribute name connects an object to the value of that attribute of the object. An *instance-of* relationship connects an object to another object that is an instance of the first object. A *subclass* relationship connects an object to another object that represents a subclass of the first object.

Modeling XML data.   Complex graphs can model XML data easily and significantly better than using only trees. XML elements and attribute values are modeled as vertices. XML nested element relationship and attribute are modeled as edges relating an element to a child element of it and to the value of an attribute of it, respectively; these are the straightforward tree edges in XML documents. Relationships that can not be captured using tree edges are expressed directly as graph edges in our model but need to be encoded using IDREF and IDREFS in XML.

Paths.   A *path* in a complex graph is expressed as a sequence of vertices and edges of the form:

$$[v_0]\, l_1\, [v_1]\, l_2 \ldots [v_{n-1}]\, l_n\, [v_n] \tag{1}$$

where each v_i is a vertex, and each l_i is the label of an edge from v_{i-1} to v_i. In another word, the above expression asserts that there is an edge labeled l_i from vertex v_{i-1} to v_i. For example, the program point start followed by an operation prompt followed by the program point prelogin followed by an operation read(account.password) followed by the program point preauthentication may be represented as:

[start] prompt [prelogin] read(account, password) [preauthentication]

3   Path-Based Queries

For ease of presentation, in this section, we use x, y, and z possibly with subscripts for variables, and use other names besides keywords for constructors and constants.

Simple queries. One may query for vertices, labels, constructors, and arguments that satisfy certain properties based on paths. Simple queries are of the form:

$$x_1, ..., x_k : e \tag{2}$$

where $x_1, ..., x_k$ are variables, called *query variables*, and e is an expression, called a *path-properties expression*, and is constructed from paths that contain $x_1, ..., x_k$ and may contain other variables, wildcard _, and negation ¬; from combinations of paths using conjunction ∧, disjunction ∨, and negation ¬; and from constraints added to these that involve primitive arithmetic, comparison, and Boolean operations on variables in the paths. The query returns the set of tuples of values of $x_1, ..., x_k$ such that there exist values of the other variables, if any, for which the properties about paths asserted by the expression e hold.

Variables and wildcard may refer to, and negation may be applied to, vertices, labels, constructors, and arguments. Variables that refer to labels may not refer to vertices, constructors, or arguments. Multiple occurrences of a variable must be bound to the same value. A wildcard matches any value. A negation applied to an item matches any value other than what the item matches. For example, the following query returns the set containing each object that is a branch of acme and has a director whose salary is at least 150000:

$$x : [acme]\, branch\, [x]\, director\, [\_]\, salary\, [y] \land y >= 150000$$

We could easily query also the salary, by returning x, y. Each variable used in a constraint must also appear outside of the constraint, like y appears in salary $[y]$. Note that path-properties expression $[v_0]\, l_1\, [v_1]\, l_2\, [v_2]$ is equivalent to expression $[v_0]\, l_1\, [v_1] \land [v_1]\, l_2\, [v_2]$.

Extended regular expression based queries. One may also express the property that a path is formed by repeating a path segment 0 or more times. This is done by applying the repetition operator * to the repeated segment. For example, the following query returns the set of program points y that immediately follow a use of an uninitialized variable, i.e., there is a path from program point start on which a variable is not defined and is used right before y:

$$y : [start]\, (\neg def(x)[\_])^*\, use(x)\, [y] \tag{3}$$

One may return also the uninitialized variable by including x as another query variable.

Often, intermediate vertices in paths are not of interest, as in the example above. Thus we allow [_] to be omitted from a path; note that this also allows us to easily refer to the program point right before use(x) without unrolling the last iteration of the repetition. We also allow a shorthand |, instead of using ∨, to separate alternative paths. Queries that may use these notations are called *extended regular expression based queries*. For example, the following query returns the set of program point pairs z, y right before and after, respectively, the *first* use of an uninitialized variable:

$$z, y : [start]\, (\neg(def(x)|use(x)))^*\, [z]\, use(x)\, [y] \tag{4}$$

Extended regular expression based queries provide the full power and ease of using extended regular expressions in queries over parameterized edge labels, as in *parametric regular path queries* [17]. Parametric regular path queries do not support the use of vertex ids as the queries in this paper do. This support allows us to easily query vertices on cycles, i.e., a vertex is returned if some nonempty path from it goes back to it:

$$x : [x] \, \_^+ \, [x]$$

where s^+ is a short hand for $s \, s^*$.

Variable scoping and nested queries. Variables can be declared with a scope local to a subexpression. That is, a path-properties expression may be of the form:

$$\text{local } x_1, ..., x_k \; e \tag{5}$$

where the keyword `local` indicates that the scope of variables $x_1, ..., x_k$ is e. For example, in a model of a computer network, where `link` relates directly connected nodes, the following query returns all pairs of a client and a server such that the two are connected by a path containing nodes that do not block port 22:

$$x, y : [x] \, \text{type} \, [\text{client}] \land [y] \, \text{type} \, [\text{server}] \land$$
$$[x] \, (\text{local } z \, \text{link} \, [z] \land \neg([z] \, \text{block} \, [22]))^* \, \text{link} \, [y]$$

Note that when scoping is not inside a repetition, it is unnecessary and can be removed, by replacing each local variable with a fresh variable. Variables declared inside a repetition can not be replaced this way because such a variable is local to the repeated expression and may be bound to different values for different rounds in the repetition, but a non-local variable must be bound to the same value for all rounds of the repetition.

A query may also be nested inside [ ] to express the properties of the vertex in it, in the form of [x : e], and it is equivalent to conjuncting the expression e to the immediately enclosing expression. For example, the segment repeated in the example above can also be written as

$$\text{local } z \, \text{link} \, [z : \neg([z] \, \text{block} \, [22])]$$

This adds convenience and modularity using only the concepts and syntax already introduced.

Querying objects and XML data. Objects can be organized into classes, and methods can be defined in classes as usual for querying objects [14], except that extended regular expression based queries can now be used in the method body. The use of extended regular expressions is essential for querying graph structures of unbounded size, and it greatly increases the expressive power of the query language.

When a method m returns exactly one query variable, an invocation of m can have the same syntax and semantics as a short-cut edge, $[v_1]m(a_1, ..., a_k)[v_2]$, where the starting vertex v_1 is an object on which m is invoked, $a_1, ..., a_k$ are other arguments to m, and the ending vertex v_2 is an object returned by m. For simplicity, we may use the same name space for edge label constructors and method names, and may allow the same names to be used for both and give preference to one of them.

Objects can be created out of the end result of a query as usual, by viewing each returned tuple as an object, giving it a logical object id, and giving an attribute name to each component of the tuple [14]. Since these objects are created after query evaluation, all operations including repetitions in a query operate on finite data, and therefore we can guarantee that all queries terminate.

Querying XML data is easy using graph queries. Unbounded levels of element nesting poses a challenge to previous object query languages [14] but is easily expressed in our language using the repetition operator. Querying complicated graphs using our language is significantly easier than using XML query languages, such as XQuery, that employ explicit joins for relationships that are not nested elements or attributes.

Expressiveness. We think this query language has the same expressiveness as GraphLog [10], which is equivalent to stratified linear Datalog, first order logic with transitive closure, and non-deterministic logarithmic space. This is because our language supports all the kinds of graph edges and query operations that GraphLog does, and variable scoping and query nesting in our language can be translated into GraphLog.

Support for scoping, and textual flexibilities such as query nesting, make our language easier to use, either by itself or as part of another query language such as [15]. For example, the client-server example above, if expressed using GraphLog, needs two graphs, one for each of the following rules:

```
result(x,y) :- type(x,client), type(y,server),
               link_node_not_block_22*.link(x,y).
link_node_not_block_22(x,z) :- link(x,z), not block(z,22).
```

where each argument variable or constant corresponds to a vertex, and each label(vert1, vert2) corresponds to an edge from vert1 to vert2 and labeled label; the edge on the left of :- is called the distinguished edge of the graph, and is drawn as a thick line. So the first graph has 4 vertices and 4 edges, and the second has 3 vertices and 3 edges. Furthermore, if there are additional constraints involving z, x, and y, one can simply conjunct them with the segment repeated in our language, but one must add not only these constraints to the second rules, but also additional parameters to the label link_node_not_block_22 in both graphs to pass them between the graphs.

4   Transformation into Datalog with Limited Extensions

Datalog with limited extensions. A Datalog program is a finite set of relational rules of the form:

$$p_1(x_{11}, ..., x_{1a_1}) \wedge ... \wedge p_h(x_{h1}, ..., x_{ha_h}) \longrightarrow q(x_1, ..., x_a) \tag{6}$$

where h is a natural number, each p_i (respectively q) is a relation of a_i (respectively a) arguments, each x_{ij} and x_k is either a constant or a variable, and variables in x_k's must be a subset of the variables in x_{ij}'s. If $h = 0$, then there are no p_i's or x_{ij}'s, and x_k's must be constants, in which case $q(x_1, ..., x_a)$ is called a *fact*. For the rest of the paper, "rule" refers only to the case where $h \geq 1$, in which case each $p_i(x_{i1}, ..., x_{1a_i})$ is called a *hypothesis* of the rule, and $q(x_1, ..., x_a)$ is called the *conclusion* of the rule.

The meaning of a set of rules and a set of facts is the smallest set of facts that contains all the given facts and all the facts that can be inferred, directly or indirectly, using the rules. Note that variables occurring in exactly one hypothesis and not in the conclusion of a rule are equivalent to wildcards; their names do not affect the meaning of the rule and can be replaced with _.

Datalog is a database query language based on the logic programming paradigm [8, 2]. Recursion in Datalog allows queries that are not expressible in relational algebra or relational calculus but are essential for querying graph structures of unbounded size.

We consider Datalog with limited extensions—stratified negation, unsafe rules, and additional constraints—for capturing complex graph queries, including extended regular expression based queries. Stratified negation allows negated hypotheses, but they may not appear in cycles in recursive rules; it has much simpler meanings and more efficient implementations than arbitrary negation, by allowing all facts in a relation to be inferred before its negation is needed. Unsafe rules contain variables in the conclusion that are unbound, i.e., that do not appear in any hypothesis; such variables may be left in the arguments of inferred facts and be universally quantified. Additional constraints involve primitive arithmetic, comparison, and Boolean operations on variables that appear in the hypotheses or the conclusion of a rule; they are additional conditions on the values of those variables.

Transforming basic queries and extended regular expression based queries. Complex graph queries can be transformed into Datalog with stratified negation, unsafe rules, and additional constraints. Queries where variables, wildcard, and negation do not appear in constructors of edge labels are transformed as described below. Other queries can be transformed in the same way after each exceptional constructor is first transformed into a distinct new constructor that has an additional argument whose value ranges over possible constructors.

Each constructor c of an edge label corresponds to an *edge relation* c that relates source and target vertices and the arguments of the label. An edge from v_1 to v_2 with label $c(a_1, ..., a_k)$ corresponds to a fact $c(v_1, v_2, a_1, ..., a_k)$.

Operations in path-properties expressions correspond to rules that combine relations that capture sub-expressions into relations that capture larger expressions. Edge relations capture the smallest expressions. New relations are introduced to capture larger expressions; the arguments of a new relation are determined as described below. Finally, a special relation is introduced to capture the entire query; it projects the relation that captures the outermost path-properties expression onto the query variables.

Arguments of a new relation include all variables in the expression it captures that also appear in the rest of the query or, if the expression is a repetition or is inside a repetition, all variables except those that are local to the repeated expression and appear only in the expression captured; this takes care of variable scoping, and the requirement of appearance in the rest of the query avoids propagation of unneeded values. In particular, for an expression that represents a path segment, the starting vertex and ending vertex of the path segment are included as the first two arguments of the corresponding relation. For an expression that represents a path segment and whose starting or ending vertex is a wildcard or is not indicated explicitly, we introduce a fresh variable for such a vertex. The fresh variable is effectively a wildcard, so the semantics is preserved. When combining relations that capture smaller expressions into relations that capture larger expressions, shared variables are used to capture equality between the ending vertex of one path segment and the starting vertex of the next path segment.

Wildcards for, and negations applied to, vertices, arguments, and labels are transformed as follows. Wildcards for vertices and arguments are handled as described above by introducing fresh variables. All wildcards for labels are transformed into a special edge relation, $\mathtt{anylabel}(v_1, v_2)$ for source vertex v_1 and target vertex v_2, and a set of rules of the following form, one for each edge relation c:

$$c(v_1, v_2, a_1, ..., a_k) \rightarrow \mathtt{anylabel}(v_1, v_2) \tag{7}$$

Negation applied to a vertex or an argument is transformed into an inequality constraint attached to the relation that captures the enclosing path-properties expression and where the vertex or argument with negation is replaced by a fresh variable; the inequality constraint expresses that the fresh variable is not equal to the constant or variable to which the negation is applied, except that the constraint is omitted if the negation is applied to a variable not used in the rest of the query. Negation applied to a label is transformed into $\mathtt{anylabel}$ plus a negated hypothesis, where the hypothesis corresponds to the edge relation for the label without negation.

Combinations of paths using conjunction, disjunction, and negation are transformed as follows. Suppose $p_1(x_{11}, ..., x_{1k_1})$ captures $\mathtt{exp}_1$, and $p_2(x_{21}, ..., x_{2k_2})$ captures $\mathtt{exp}_2$. If $p(x_1, ..., x_k)$ captures $\mathtt{exp}_1 \wedge \mathtt{exp}_2$, then we introduce a rule:

$$p_1(x_{11}, ..., x_{1k_1}) \wedge p_2(x_{21}, ..., x_{2k_2}) \rightarrow p(x_1, ..., x_k) \tag{8}$$

Note that if $\mathtt{exp}_1$ and $\mathtt{exp}_2$ are consecutive path segments, then x_{12} and x_{21} are the same variable. If $p(x_1, ..., x_k)$ captures $\mathtt{exp}_1 \vee \mathtt{exp}_2$, then we introduce two rules:

$$\begin{aligned} p_1(x_{11}, ..., x_{1k_1}) &\rightarrow p(x_1, ..., x_k) \\ p_2(x_{21}, ..., x_{2k_2}) &\rightarrow p(x_1, ..., x_k) \end{aligned} \tag{9}$$

These rules may be unsafe, because any variable in $p(x_1, ..., x_k)$ that is not in a disjunct is unbound in the conclusion of the corresponding rule. More generally, a conjunction with k conjuncts is transformed into a rule with k hypotheses, and a disjunction with k disjuncts is transformed into k rules. Negation applied to a path-properties expression is simply transformed into a rule with a negated hypothesis; we show in the next section that these negations are stratified.

A repetition of an expression is transformed into a fact with variable arguments, for repeating zero times, and a rule involving recursion, for repeating non-zero times. If $p_1(x_1, x_2, x_3, ..., x_k)$ captures exp, and $p(x_1, x_2, x_3, ..., x_k)$ captures exp^*, then the fact is $p(x, x, x_3, ..., x_k)$, and the rule is

$$p(x_1, x_{12}, x_3, ..., x_k) \land p_1(x_{12}, x_2, x_3, ..., x_k) \rightarrow p(x_1, x_2, x_3, ..., x_k) \qquad (10)$$

The rule may also be written by exchanging p and p_1 in the hypotheses. They are both correct rules, but depending on the query, may lead to different asymptotic running times, as discussed below.

Constraints themselves do not require transformation. If all variables in a constraint are from the same scope after unnecessary scopings are removed, i.e., the constraint is not inside a repetition and involves both local variables and non-local variables of the repeated expression, then it is simply added as a hypothesis of the rule that combines all the subexpressions it constrains. Otherwise, the facts and rules for the repetition are rewritten when combining the repetition with the expression on the left or right that is constrained. For example, suppose (10) has, as an additional condition, a constraint $c(..., y)$ that is transformed from the same constraint in exp, where y is a variable not local to exp; $q(x_1, x_2, y)$ captures the expression to the left of the repetition; and $r(x_1, x_2, x_3, ..., x_k, y)$ captures the combined expression. Then, the fact $p(x, x, x_3, ..., x_k)$ and the rule (10) are rewritten into

$$q(x_1, x_2, y) \rightarrow r(x_1, x_2, x_3, ..., x_k, y)$$
$$r(x_1, x_{12}, x_3, ..., x_k, y) \land p_1(x_{12}, x_2, x_3, ..., x_k) \rightarrow r(x_1, x_2, x_3, ..., x_k, y)$$

Combining a repetition with the expression on the right that is constrained is similar. However, if a constraint involves non-local variables on both sides of the repetition, only one side can be combined using the rewrite above, and the non-local variables on the other side are not bound and must be enumerated during the execution of the resulting program. Therefore, one may choose to combine with the side that will minimize the enumeration.

The transformation into a set of facts and rules has a worst-case time complexity of $O(qvs)$, where q is the size of the query, v is the number of variables, and s is the maximum number of scopes that the variables in a constraint are in. This is because, if all variables in each constraint are from the same scope, then the transformation is linear in qv, since the transformation considers each construct in the query once, and in the worst case, each variable may be an argument in all the intermediate relations. Otherwise, to combine the repetition of each nested scope with an expression to the left or right of the repetition, we rewrite the fact and the rules for the repetition, which yields a factor of s in the complexity. In addition, if a constraint involves non-local variables on both sides of the repetition, and one chooses to combine with the side that minimizes the enumeration during execution, then trying all possible combinations to find the minimum will incur a factor exponential in s.

Handling methods and object creation. The definition of a method is transformed into a set of rules for the path-properties expression in the method body, as described above, except that the relation that captures the entire method is identified by the fully qualified method name, and is related to the class where the method is defined. That relation relates the arguments of the method, including this, to the return value, captured by the query variables of the method body. A method invocation is transformed into rules that conclude the relation corresponding to the invocation if the object on which the method is invoked is an instance of a class that defines the method or inherits the method from a class that defines it, and if the relation corresponding to the method holds for the arguments and return value of the invocation.

Objects are created from query results after query evaluation, so object creation does not need to be transformed into Datalog. While multiple logical object ids can be given to an object, for efficient search and equality comparison in subsequent queries and other processing, an object must have a unique physical id for indexing. To achieve this, whenever a new object is to be created and to which search and equality comparison might be applied, it is matched against existing objects, and if found, a reference to the existing object is used, as opposed to creating an identical copy of the existing object.

Example. For example, the query (3) is transformed into a fact $\texttt{notdefs}(x_1, x_1, x)$ and the following rules, where the query result is captured by the relation result:

$$
\begin{aligned}
\neg \texttt{def}(x_1, x_2, x) &\rightarrow \texttt{notdef}(x_1, x_2, x) \\
\texttt{notdefs}(x_1, x_2, x) \wedge \texttt{notdef}(x_2, x_3, x) &\rightarrow \texttt{notdefs}(x_1, x_3, x) \\
\texttt{notdefs}(x_1, x_2, x) \wedge \texttt{use}(x_2, x_3, x) &\rightarrow \texttt{notdefsuse}(x_1, x_3, x) \\
\texttt{notdefsuse}(\texttt{start}, y, x) &\rightarrow \texttt{result}(y)
\end{aligned}
\tag{11}
$$

The query (4) is transformed into the same rules except with $\neg \texttt{def}$ in (11) replaced by $\neg \texttt{deforuse}$ and with two additional rules:

$$
\begin{aligned}
\texttt{def}(x_1, x_2, x) &\rightarrow \texttt{deforuse}(x_1, x_2, x) \\
\texttt{use}(x_1, x_2, x) &\rightarrow \texttt{deforuse}(x_1, x_2, x)
\end{aligned}
$$

5   Generating Specialized Algorithms and Complexity Formulas

While Datalog programs can be executed in a Prolog system, recursion could cause nontermination or exponential running time, depending on the order of rules, due to failure to remember computations already attempted. Polynomial running time can be ensured by executing Datalog programs in a tabled logic programming system, such as XSB [24], but it could differ asymptotically, such as between linear and quadratic, depending on the order of hypotheses in individual rules. Also, analyzing the running time requires understanding the execution engine, including for XSB its sophisticated tabling mechanism, and is nontrivial even for experts. Additionally, a light-weight program that is specialized to do only the query at hand and can more easily be plugged into other applications is often preferable to a heavy-weight generic execution engine.

We summarize the method described in [18] for generating specialized algorithms and complexities from pure Datalog, and extend it here to handle stratified negation, unsafe rules, and additional constraints.

Generating algorithms and complexities from Datalog. A method for transforming any set of Datalog rules into an efficient, specialized program with time and space complexity guarantees has been studied [18]. The method breaks any given set of rules into rules that have one or two hypotheses and generates an efficient program that, given any set of facts, computes the meaning of the given rules and facts. The generated program embodies (1) an incremental algorithm to consider one fact at a time and (2) a combination of linked and indexed data structures for the sets of facts and indices used by the algorithm. Overall, each combination of instantiations of the hypotheses is considered exactly once and in constant time.

The method also produces formulas for the time and space complexity of the generated program in terms of data size. Let $\#p$ denote the number of facts that actually hold for relation p. A rule with one hypothesis about relation p is fired at most $\#p$ times; a rule with two hypotheses about relations p_1 and p_2 is fired at most

$$\min(\#p_1 \times \#p_2.\texttt{matched}, \#p_2 \times \#p_1.\texttt{matched}) \qquad (12)$$

times, where $\#p_2.\texttt{matched}$ denotes the maximum number of combinations of values of arguments of p_2 that are not shared with p_1 for each combination of values of arguments of p_2 that are shared with p_1, and vice versa for $\#p_1.\texttt{matched}$; if this number is not known from application domain knowledge, it is bounded by the product of the domain sizes of unshared arguments as well as by the size of the relation. The overall time complexity is the sum of the number of firing times for all rules.

The method applies to pure Datalog, and has been applied successfully to a number of applications, including regular path queries [19] and parametric regular path queries [17], grammar constraint simplifications [18], program pointer analysis [5], and parts of the ANSI standard for role-based access control [4]. A prototype has also been developed to support the applications and experiments.

Handling extensions. We extend the method above to handle variables as arguments in facts, additional constraints, and negations, as follows.

Unsafe rules and transformation of repetitions produce facts that contain variables as arguments. These variables are universally quantified, but we want to avoid enumerating all possible values of them. So we constrain these variables using equality during matching as much as possible, and leave them in the facts when they are not constrained. The complexity calculation is not affected by this optimization since the formulas are for the worst case.

For each constraint attached as an additional hypothesis in a rule where variables in the constraint are bound in other hypotheses, the constraint can simply be evaluated after all its variables are bound with definite values; constraints involving primitive arithmetic, comparison, and Boolean operations can be evaluated in constant time, so such a constraint does not contribute to the complexity formula. For any constraint that contains variables not bound in the other hypotheses, the domains of those variables are numerated. This increases the complexity by a factor linear in the size of the domain for each such variable, but this number will be minimized by the rewrite described in Section 4 for transforming constraints.

Negation applied to a vertex or argument produces an inequality constraint, which is handled as above. Negation applied to a label is transformed into anylabel plus a negation applied to an edge relation; the edge relation gives rise to a set of facts, so the negation, i.e., set complement, is easy to compute. Negation applied to an expression is transformed into a rule with a negated hypothesis, so we need to handle Datalog with negation, as described below.

Handling negation. We first show that negations in programs transformed from extended regular expression based queries are always stratified. Note that recursive definitions are only transformed from repetitions. For each relation that captures a repetition, the recursive occurrence of the relation in the hypothesis is not negated, even though the path-properties expression being repeated may be negated. Therefore, there is no negation in cycles formed by the dependency of conclusions on hypotheses in recursive rules.

For stratified negation, we generate a program that fully evaluates a relation before firing any rules that use the negation of the relation. For rules with one hypothesis, if the hypothesis is negative, the program enumerates all values of arguments of the corresponding relation excluding values for which the relation holds; the number of firings is changed from #p for a hypothesis about p to the product of the domain sizes of all arguments of p. For rules with two hypotheses, rather than considering only elements in a relation and elements that actually matched (corresponding to #p and #p.matched, respectively, in (12)), for a negated hypothesis, we instead consider all arguments of the relation and all unshared arguments, respectively; we pick the order of considering the two hypotheses to give the minimum of two products in a revised form of (12): the number of firings for each rule is the same as before except with relation size #p and matched size #p.matched replaced by the product of the domain sizes of all arguments and the product of the domain sizes of unshared arguments, respectively.

Example. For example, for the rules and fact in (11) for query (3), the time complexity is $O(\#\texttt{point}^3 \times \#\texttt{var})$, where #point is the domain size of the first two arguments of def and use, and #var is the domain size of the third argument. It is obtained from the following sum, one summand for each rule:

$$\#\texttt{point}^2 \times \#\texttt{var} + \#\texttt{point}^3 \times \#\texttt{var} + \#\texttt{use} \times \#\texttt{point} + \#\texttt{point} \times \#\texttt{var}$$

For the rules and fact for query (4), the time complexity formula is the same, except with two additional summands, #def and #use, for the two additional rules.

Additional optimizations and extensions are possible. The most important optimizations include on-demand, i.e., top-down, computation. In our prototype, we first apply magic set transformations [6] to the rules and the relation that captures the entire query, obtained from the previous section; we then implement the transformed program as described in this section. For query (3), the time complexity after the optimizations is $O((\#def + \#use) \times \#var)$. Details of the complexity analysis for on-demand computations using magic set transformations will be presented in a separate paper. We are currently experimenting with the prototype. Handling non-stratified negation is a subject for future study.

6   Related Work and Conclusion

A number of early studies relate graph analysis problems with regular expressions or regular-expression-like patterns. For example, Tarjan [28] showed that regular expressions provide a general approach for path analysis problems, and he gave efficient algorithms for constructing regular-expression patterns for several kinds of path problems [27]. Regular-expression-like patterns have also been used for static program analysis (e.g., [21]), traversing object graphs in developing adaptive software (e.g., [22, 16]), etc. Most of these works study specific domain problems, and none of them provides a generic and efficient framework for querying complex interrelated objects.

The idea of paths has played an essential role in querying object-oriented databases [14] and semi-structured data [1]. Object graphs may be cyclic but previous query languages do not support patterns that can match paths of unbounded length; this avoids nontermination. Query languages based on XPath [29] use some regular-expression-like features that allow path segments to be skipped but not repeated, and the data are treated as trees, not general graphs. Conditional XPath [20] extends XPath to allow path segments to be repeated, and is as expressive as first-order logic when interpreted on ordered trees, but it does not handle general graphs.

Various forms of regular path queries, allowing general regular-expression-like patterns over general graphs, have been proposed for querying databases and semi-structured data [30, 10, 1, 3, 13, 7]. These languages are studied heavily in terms of expressiveness and query containment, but not on improved ease of expressing queries or efficient implementations. The implementations are basically by transforming queries into logic programs and relying on logic programming engines, such as [23], for query evaluation, but such implementations do not provide precise complexity guarantees.

Regular path queries with parameters have been studied specially for program analysis and model checking [11, 17]. Parameters are essential for expressing correlations of information in different parts of the data, and are needed also in querying system logs for intrusion detection [26], and querying objects in general, as shown in this paper. Drape et al. [12] describe how to code parametric queries as extended logic programs. Liu et al. [17] give complete algorithms and data structures for directly and efficiently solving parametric queries with precise complexity analysis. However, these frameworks do not support a rich data model that can naturally model objects in object-oriented systems and XML data.

The language in this paper is built on parametric regular path queries [17] and a rich object model [14], extending the former with vertex ids, variable scoping, methods, etc., and extending the latter with powerful regular-expression like patterns. It has the same expressiveness as GraphLog [10], but the support of scoping, and textural flexibilities such as query nesting, make it easier to use, either by itself or as part of another query language such as [15]. The implementation is built on a powerful method for generating specialized implementation with precise complexity guarantees. The transformation to Datalog with limited extensions helps both in understanding the semantics and in implementation. We also extend the method in [18] to efficiently handle stratified negation, unsafe rules, and additional constraints.

Other related works include extensions to OCL path expressions [25] and trace-based program analysis that uses parameters to correlate information along paths [9], but they use more sophisticated heavy-weight mechanisms.

Further extensions and improvements to the query framework can be made. A possible extension is to support universal queries, where properties must hold on all paths in the graph and where a variable is bound to the same value on all paths. In terms of implementation, many optimizations can be explored, including on-demand computation, space reuse, and filtering with constraints. We are applying the query framework to existing and new problems in program analysis, model checking, and security policy analysis.

Acknowledgment. The authors thank Prof. Michael Kifer for references to related work in database research, for helpful explanations and discussions, and for their inspiring work on querying object-oriented and deductive databases.

References

1. S. Abiteboul. Querying semi-structured data. In *Proceedings of the International Conference on Database Theory*, pages 1–18, 1997.
2. S. Abiteboul, R. Hull, and V. Vianu. *Foundations of Databases.* Addison-Wesley, Reading, Mass., 1995.
3. S. Abiteboul and V. Vianu. Regular path queries with constraints. In *Proceedings of the 16th ACM Symposium on Principles of Database Systems*, pages 122–133, 1997.
4. American National Standards Institute, Inc. Role-Based Access Control. ANSI INCITS 359-2004. Approved Feb. 3, 2004. http://csrc.nist.gov/rbac.
5. L. O. Andersen. *Program Analysis and Specialization for the C Programming Language.* PhD thesis, DIKU, University of Copenhagen, May 1994.
6. C. Beeri and R. Ramakrishnan. On the power of magic. *Journal of Logic Programming*, 10(3-4):255–299, 1991.

7. D. Calvanese, G. D. Giacomo, M. Lenzerini, and M. Y. Vardi. Reasoning on regular path queries. *SIGMOD Record*, 32(4):83–92, 2003.

8. S. Ceri, G. Gottlob, and L. Tanca. *Logic Programming and Databases*. Springer-Verlag, 1990.

9. C. Colby and P. Lee. Trace-based program analysis. In *Conference Record of the 23rd Annual ACM Symposium on Principles of Programming Languages*, pages 195–207, 1996.

10. M. P. Consens and A. O. Mendelzon. Graphlog: a visual formalism for real life recursion. In *Proceedings of the 9th ACM SIGACT-SIGMOD-SIGART Symposium on Principles of database systems*, pages 404–416, 1990.

11. O. de Moor, D. Lacey, and E. V. Wyk. Universal regular path queries. *Higher-Order and Symbolic Computation*, 16(1-2), 2003.

12. S. Drape, O. de Moor, and G. Sittampalam. Transforming the .NET intermediate language using path logic programming. In *Proceedings of the 4th International Conference on Principles and Practice of Declarative Programming*, Oct. 2002.

13. D. Florescu, A. Levy, and D. Suciu. Query containment for conjunctive queries with regular expressions. In *Proceedings of the 17th ACM SIGACT-SIGMOD-SIGART Symposium on Principles of database systems*, pages 139–148, 1998.

14. M. Kifer, W. Kim, and Y. Sagiv. Querying object oriented databases. In *Proceedings of the ACM SIGMOD International Conference on Management of Data*, pages 393–402, June 1992.

15. M. Kifer, G. Lausen, and J. Wu. Logical foundations of object-oriented and frame-based languages. *Journal of ACM*, May 1995.

16. K. J. Lieberherr, B. Patt-Shamir, and D. Orleans. Traversals of object structures: Specification and efficient implementation. *ACM Trans. Program. Lang. Syst.*, 26(2):370–412, Mar. 2004.

17. Y. A. Liu, T. Rothamel, F. Yu, S. Stoller, and N. Hu. Parametric regular path queries. In *Proceedings of the ACM SIGPLAN 2004 Conference on Programming Language Design and Implementation*, pages 219–230, Washington, DC, June 2004.

18. Y. A. Liu and S. D. Stoller. From Datalog rules to efficient programs with time and space guarantees. In *Proceedings of the 5th ACM SIGPLAN International Conference on Principles and Practice of Declarative Programming*, pages 172–183, Aug. 2003.

19. Y. A. Liu and F. Yu. Solving regular path queries. In *Proceedings of the 6th International Conference on Mathematics of Program Construction*, volume 2386 of *LNCS*, pages 195–208. Springer-Verlag, Berlin, 2002.

20. M. Marx. Conditional XPath, the first order complete XPath dialect. In *Proceedings of the ACM 2004 Symposium on Principles of Database Systems*, 2004.

21. K. Olender and L. Osterweil. Cesar: a static sequencing constraint analyzer. In *Proceedings of the ACM SIGSOFT '89 3rd Symposium on software Testing, Analysis, and Verification*, pages 66–74, 1989.

22. J. Palsberg, C. Xiao, and K. Lieberherr. Efficient implementation of adaptive software. *ACM Trans. Program. Lang. Syst.*, 17(2):264–292, Mar. 1995.

23. R. Ramakrishnan, D. Srivastava, and S. Sudarshan. Coral—control, relations and logic. In *Proceedings of the 18th International Conference on Very Large Data Bases*, pages 238–250, San Francisco, CA, USA, 1992. Morgan Kaufmann Publishers Inc.

24. K. Sagonas, T. Swift, and D. S. Warren. XSB as a deductive database. In *Proceedings of the 5th ACM SIGACT-SIGMOD Symposium on Principles of Database Systems*, 1994.

25. A. Schürr. Adding graph transformation concepts to UML's constraint language OCL. In H. Ehrig, C. Ermel, and J. Padberg, editors, *Electronic Notes in Theoretical Computer Science*, volume 44. Elsevier, 2001.

26. R. Sekar and P. Uppuluri. Synthesizing fast intrusion prevention/detection systems from high-level specifications. In *Proceedings of the USENIX Security Symposium*, pages 63–78, 1999.

27. R. E. Tarjan. Fast algorithms for solving path problems. *J. ACM*, 28(3):594–614, July 1981.

28. R. E. Tarjan. A unified approach to path problems. *J. ACM*, 28(3):577–593, July 1981.

29. The World Wide Web Consortium. XML Path Language (XPath). http://www.w3.org/TR/xpath.

30. M. Yannakakis. Graph-theoretic methods in database theory. In *Proceedings of the ACM Symposium on Principles of Database Systems*, pages 230–242, 1990.

Incremental Evaluation of Tabled Prolog: Beyond Pure Logic Programs

Diptikalyan Saha and C.R. Ramakrishnan

Department of Computer Science,
State University of New York at Stony Brook,
Stony Brook, New York, 11794-4400, USA
{dsaha, cram}@cs.sunysb.edu

Abstract. Tabling, or memoization, enables incremental evaluation of logic programs. When the rules or facts of a program change, we need to recompute only those results that are affected by the changes. The current algorithms for incrementally maintaining memo tables treat insertion of facts/rules differently from their deletion. Hence these techniques cannot be directly applied for incremental evaluation of arbitrary tabled programs, especially those involving Prolog built-ins such as findall, other aggregation operations, or non-stratified negation. In this paper, we explore a simpler incremental evaluation algorithm that, based on the dynamic call graph, invalidates and re-evaluates entire calls. The algorithm is agnostic to whether a dependency adds or removes answers from tables, and hence can be applied uniformly to programs with negation, even when the negation is implicit (as is the case with certain aggregation operations). We find that the call-based algorithm is very effective in examples where the call dependencies are largely acyclic (e.g. dynamic programming examples) and is moderately effective when the dependencies contain independent cyclic components (e.g. data flow analysis problems). This is the first practical algorithm to handle all legal tabled logic programs for which incremental evaluation is meaningful.

1 Introduction

Tabled resolution for logic programs [6, 27] alleviates some of the well-known problems of Prolog, including susceptibility to looping, repeated subcomputations, and unsatisfactory semantics for negation. Tabled resolution-based systems evaluate programs by memoizing subgoals (referred to as *calls*) and their provable instances (referred to as *answers*) in a set of tables. When resolving a subgoal, if it is present in the call table, then it is resolved against the answers recorded in the corresponding answer table; otherwise the subgoal is entered in the call table, and its answers, computed by resolving the subgoal against program clauses, are also entered in the answer table. Implementations of tabling [9, 20, 28, 30, e.g.] have become stable and efficient and practical applications can be developed by encoding them as high-level logic programs [7, 18].

Tabling enables *incremental* evaluation: when some facts or rules in a program change, we can recompute only the results affected by the changes, instead of re-evaluating the program from scratch. The crucial questions for incremental evaluation are how to detect which table entries need to change, and how to compute the changes.

P. Van Hentenryck (Ed.): PADL 2006, LNCS 3819, pp. 215–229, 2006.

Based on earlier works on view maintenance in databases [10, e.g.], we have developed time- and space-efficient techniques for incremental evaluation of tabled logic programs [21, 22, 24]. These techniques, based on maintaining dependencies between answers, use separate algorithms for handling additions and deletions incrementally. These techniques have been highly effective for incremental evaluation of large definite logic programs (e.g. points-to analysis for C programs), and have been integrated into experimental versions[1] of the XSB logic programming system [28]. See Section 4 for detailed discussion on earlier works.

However, these techniques cannot be readily applied to arbitrary tabled logic programs, especially those that use aggregation and other Prolog built-ins, or have non-stratified negation. In the presence of non-monotonic operators, it is often difficult to determine whether the addition of an answer to a table results in addition or deletion of an answer to another table.

In this paper, we present an incremental evaluation algorithm that is based on *call* dependencies instead of answer dependencies, and process insertions as well as deletions using a single method. At a high level, the technique works as follows. When facts or rules of a program change, we first mark all calls in tables whose answers may be affected by this change. In the next step we re-evaluate the marked calls. Naive re-evaluation is often inefficient since the call dependencies are too coarse. Our algorithm chooses calls to be re-evaluated optimally, and sequences the re-evaluations judiciously to minimize the number of wasteful computations (see Section 2).

The salient advantages of this technique are:

- The technique can be used on any tabled program, regardless of the use of intermediate non-tabled predicates and Prolog built-ins.
- The technique is agnostic to the sign of a dependency—— i.e. whether a call depends negatively or positively on another—— and hence can be used without change on general logic programs: *even those with non-stratified negation.*
- The re-evaluation phase issues calls in an optimal order, re-evaluating calls only when needed, and resulting in good performance in practice.
- Call graphs are generally small, and hence the technique scales to large examples.

We also present an extensive experimental evaluation of this new technique (see Section 3). We present the results for evaluating a wide variety of programs: dynamic programming examples, points-to analysis for C programs, data flow analysis of C programs, and validation of XML documents with respect to DTDs. We survey the closely related prior work in Section 4 and conclude with a discussion on the extensions to the new incremental evaluation techniques (Section 5).

2   Incremental Evaluation Based on Call Dependencies

Our technical development is based on the SLG resolution [6]; however the definitions as well as the results of this paper can be ported to other tabled evaluation schemes as well [9, 30, e.g.]. Although SLG resolution is usually described using pure logic

---

[1] See http://www.lmc.cs.sunysb.edu/~dsaha/symspt/

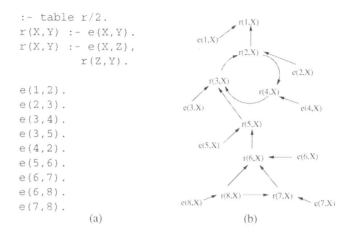

```
:- table r/2.
r(X,Y) :- e(X,Y).
r(X,Y) :- e(X,Z),
          r(Z,Y).

e(1,2).
e(2,3).
e(3,4).
e(3,5).
e(4,2).
e(5,6).
e(6,7).
e(6,8).
e(7,8).
```

(a)   (b)

Fig. 1. Example program (a); and called-by graph (b) for evaluating r(1,X)

programs, it has been integrated into Prolog-based systems such as [20, 28] seamlessly enough to permit programs to mix tabled and non-tabled predicates, use aggregate and other Prolog builtins, and even use cuts over nontabled predicates. Analogously, the concepts formally developed below based on SLG resolution can be extended to the more general class of tabled Prolog programs.

Given a program P and an initial query q, the set of call tables constructed by SLG resolution is denoted by $calls(q, P)$. The set of answers computed for a subgoal q over program P is denoted by $ans(q, P)$. The set of all answer tables constructed during evaluation of a query q, denoted by $answer\_tables(q, P)$ is given by the collection $\{ans(q', P) \mid q' \in calls(q, P)\}$. In SLG resolution derivations are captured as a SLG *forest*, where each tree corresponds to a single call and its associated answer table. Our incremental algorithm makes a non-trivial change to only one of the operations used to build the SLG forest: namely, the *completion check* operation, which determines whether any more answers can be added to an answer table. The other operations are either unchanged or are changed trivially to record call dependency information.

We consider incremental evaluation of tabled programs, where facts or rules may be added or deleted after query evaluation is completed. Each complete query evaluation is called a *run*. Between each run, a set of rules in the program may change. We denote this set by C and partition C into two sets C^+ and C^- that contain the added and deleted rules respectively. Given a program P, the changed program P' obtained by applying the changes in C is given by $P' = P \cup C^+ - C^-$. Note that our technical development is general and considers changes to a program's *rules*. Facts, which are rules with empty bodies, naturally become a special case.

Our algorithm is based on tracking dependencies between the calls during query evaluation. The smallest set of calls that need to be re-examined after a change, defined formally below, are those whose answer tables are modified by the change.

Definition 1 (Changed Calls). *Let P be a program, $C = C^+ \cup C^-$ be the set of rules that are changed, and $P' = P \cup C^+ - C^-$ be the changed program. Let Q be the set* *of calls due to evaluation of some query over P. The set of changed calls, denoted by changed(P, C) is the set of all calls in Q such that ans$(q, P) \not\equiv$ ans(q, P').*

We assume that all predicates whose definitions are subject to change between runs are marked as *volatile*. For instance, in the program in Figure 1(a), edge/2 is a volatile predicate. In general a volatile predicate may be defined by rules, and may even be tabled.

Our call-dependency-based incremental evaluation technique is based on a data structure known as *called-by* graph, defined below.

Definition 2 (Called-By Graph). *The called-by graph due to the evaluation of query q over program P is a directed graph (V, E) such that (i) $V = V_t \cup V_f$ where V_t is the set of tabled subgoals that occur as roots of trees in the SLG forest, and V_f is the set of selected literals in the SLG forest that unify with the head of some volatile rule; and (ii) $(c_1, c_2) \in E$ if and only if c_1 is a selected subgoal in a tree with c_2 as the root (i.e. c_1 is called by c_2).*

The called-by graph after evaluation of query r(1,X) over the program in Figure 1(a) is given in Figure 1(b). The graph captures the dependencies between tabled calls and calls to volatile predicates. It is first generated in the initial (non-incremental) run, and maintained over subsequent incremental runs. Note that it is the transpose of the subgoal dependency graph [5] extended with edges from calls to volatile predicates.

The incremental algorithm has two phases. The first is the *invalidation* phase, where calls that may be affected by the change are marked as *affected*.

Definition 3 (Initially Changed Calls). *Given a called-by graph $G = (V, E)$ and a non-empty set $C = C^+ \cup C^-$ of rules that were changed (inserted or deleted) since the last run, the set of initially changed calls, denoted by init(G, C) are those $v \in V$ such that v unifies with the head of some rule in C.*

Definition 4 (Affected Calls). *Given a called-by graph $G = (V, E)$ and a non-empty set $C = C^+ \cup C^-$ of rules that were changed (inserted or deleted) since the last run, the set of affected calls, denoted by affected(G, C), is the smallest set such that $v \in$ affected(C, G) if*

  – *$v \in$ init(G, C), or*
  – *$\exists v' \in$ affected(G, C) such that $(v', v) \in E$.*

The set of affected calls (based on the above definition) can be found by simply traversing the called-by graph starting from the vertices that unify with changed rule heads (case (i) above). Note that the direction of edges in the called-by graph is from callee to caller which enables us to compute the affected calls by traversing the called-by graph.

The idea behind the invalidation phase is calls that are not deemed affected are unchanged by the modification, as formally stated below:

Theorem 1. *Let P be an initial program, $C = C^+ \cup C^-$ be the set of changed rules, and $P' = P \cup C^+ - C^-$ be the changed program. Let $G = (V, E)$ be the called-by graph for some query over P. Then, every changed call is affected; i.e. changed$(P, C) \subseteq$ affected(G, C).*

Naive Re-evaluation: Theorem 1 means that when some program rules change, it is sufficient to re-evaluate the set of affected calls. Our naive strategy is remove all table entries corresponding to the affected calls (i.e. their entries in the call table, as well as their answer tables) in the invalidation phase. In the second phase, called re-evaluation phase, we re-do all the affected calls. Note that *all* affected calls are deleted to ensure that any answer derived for an affected call is based only on valid information: either rederived answers of another affected call, or existing answers of an unaffected call. While deleting the table entries for an affected call, we also remove the corresponding vertex and the edges incident on it from the called-by graph. Note that the re-evaluation may generate new vertices and edges in the called-by graph. Thus the called-by graph itself is (incrementally) modified when processing incremental changes.

For example, consider the deletion of the fact $e(3,5)$ from the program in Figure 1(a). The invalidation phase identifies the calls $e(3,X)$, $r(3,X)$, $r(2,X)$, $r(4,X)$ and $r(1,X)$ as affected. Since these calls will be re-evaluated, the edges incident on these vertices, i.e. $e(3,X) \rightarrow r(3,X)$, $r(5,X) \rightarrow r(3,X)$, $e(4,X) \rightarrow r(4,X)$, $r(4,X) \rightarrow r(3,X)$, $e(2,X) \rightarrow r(2,X)$, $r(2,X) \rightarrow r(4,X)$, $e(1,X) \rightarrow r(1,X)$, and $r(2,X) \rightarrow r(1,X)$, are deleted from the called-by graph. In the re-evaluation phase, the call $r(1,X)$ gives rise to calls $r(2,X)$, $r(3,X)$, and $r(4,X)$, and their answers are subsequently computed. These calls and the corresponding edges are added (back) to the called-by graph. Note that, answers to unaffected calls can be found directly from the tables. For example, the call $r(3,X)$ uses already existing answers for $e(3,X)$ and $r(5,X)$; calls such as $r(5,X)$ are unaffected by the deletion and are not re-evaluated, thereby saving expensive program clause resolution steps.

Optimized Re-evaluation: The set of affected calls over-approximates the set of changed calls. In many cases, the approximation may be severe and the naive re-evaluation strategy wastefully re-evaluates unchanged calls. Consider the deletion of fact $e(7,8)$ from the program Figure 1(a). The invalidation phase identifies the calls $e(7,X)$, $r(7,X)$, $r(6,X)$, $r(5,X)$, $r(3,X)$, $r(2,X)$, $r(4,X)$, and $r(1,X)$ as affected. However, the set of changed calls is only $e(7,X)$ and $r(7,X)$, but the naive strategy also re-evaluates all other affected calls.

We obtain a better approximation of the changed set, called as the recomputed set defined as follows.

Definition 5 (Recomputed Set). *Let P be a program, $C = C^+ \cup C^-$ be the set of changed rules, and $P' = P \cup C^+ - C^-$ be the changed program. Let $G = (V, E)$ be the called-by graph for some query q over P. Then, the set of recomputed calls, denoted by recomputed(G, C), is the smallest set such that $c \in$ recomputed(G, C) if*

1. *$c \in init(G, C)$, or*
2. *there is some c' such that $(c', c) \in E$ and $c' \in changed(P, C)$, or*
3. *there is some c' such that c and c' are in the same strongly connected component of G, and $c' \in recomputed(G, C)$.*

The recomputed set represents the smallest set of calls that need to be re-evaluated. The intuition behind this definition follows from the following observations:

1. Every changed call needs to be re-evaluated.
2. Every call that immediately depends on a changed call needs to be re-evaluated (even if it itself is not changed). Note that the called-by graph contains no qualitative information on *how* the change of a call affects another. Only the program has this information embedded in it, and hence the only way to determine whether or not such a call changes is to re-evaluate it.
3. If a re-evaluated call is in a SCC, then all calls in that SCC need to be re-evaluated. For instance, when e(3,5) is deleted from the program in Figure 1(a), e(3,X) is changed, and hence r(3,X) is recomputed. Note that we cannot simply delete r(3,X)'s tables are re-evaluate it: since r(4,X) currently contains the answer X=5, and e(3,4) holds, we will then (incorrectly) conclude that r(3,5) still holds. Hence, we have to re-evaluate all mutually dependent calls simultaneously (r(3,X), r(4,X) and r(2,X), in this case).

It follows from the definition that every changed call is also in the recomputed set. It can also be readily shown that every call in the recomputed set is affected. Formally,

Proposition 2. *Let P be a program, $C = C^+ \cup C^-$ be the set of changed rules, and $P' = P \cup C^+ - C^-$ be the changed program. Let $G = (V, E)$ be the called-by graph for some query q over P. Then changed$(P, C) \subseteq$ recomputed$(G, C) \subseteq$ affected(G, C).*

In optimized re-evaluation we redo the calls in the *recomputed set*. We need two basic mechanisms to accomplish this: (a) determine whether a re-evaluated call is changed or not, and (b) determine SCCs in the called-by graph.

a. Marking Changed Calls: First of all, instead of deleting all the affected tables in the invalidation phase, we only mark the answers of a recomputed call as (currently) invalid just before the call is re-evaluated. We do not mark the answers of the affected calls which are not scheduled for re-evaluation. Invalid answers are ignored when doing answer clause resolution. With each such recomputed call, we also keep the number of invalid answers (in a counter called *invalid_count*), initialized to the total number of answers at the beginning of the re-evaluation phase. Finally, we keep a flag with each recomputed call (called *addl_answer*) to indicate whether a new answer was added to this call's answer table in the re-evaluation phase. During re-evaluation, whenever an answer is added to a table, if the answer already exists but is invalid, we remove the invalid mark and decrement *invalid_count* for the table. If the answer did not exist before, we add the answer and set *addl_answer* of the call to true. When a call is completely re-evaluated (at the Completion operation of SLG), we can determine that the call is *changed* iff *addl_answer* is true or *invalid_count* is non-zero.

b. Evaluating SCCs: Finding SCCs in the called-by graph is fundamental to evaluating the *recomputed* set. Apart from the explicit use of SCC information in its definition, note that we determine whether or not a call is *changed* only after completion. Consequently we need to evaluate the calls "bottom-up" through the called-by graph, and triggering re-evaluations at higher levels only after confirming that the lower-level calls have changed. This strategy, when applied to acyclic graphs has been shown to be optimal [19] (see Section 4).

Algorithms for finding SCCs typically need an additional pass over the graph. We now describe a technique to find SCCs without making this additional pass, by slightly modifying the traversal used in the invalidation phase. This technique is based on Kosaraju and Sharir's SCC computation algorithm [25], which works as follows. To find SCCs in a graph G, we first traverse G and give post-order numbers to the vertices in G. We then traverse G^T, the transpose of G, starting from the vertex with the highest post-order number; this traversal builds a spanning tree for one SCC of G. Whenever the traversal ends, we begin a new traversal from the unvisited vertex with the highest post-order number, thereby building a spanning tree for another SCC. This process continues until all vertices have been visited, enumerating all SCCs of G. The order in which SCCs are found by the Kosaraju-Sharir algorithm is a topological order in the SCC-reduced graph of G: if (v_1, v_2) is an edge in E, then the SCC containing v_1 is found at least as early as the one containing v_2.

The Re-Evaluation Algorithm: We now describe a re-evaluation algorithm that implicitly finds SCCs. In the invalidation phase, we traverse the called-by graph and assign a post-order number to each affected call. With each affected call we keep a flag *processed* which is initialized to false.

In the re-evaluation phase, shown in Figure 2, we maintain a sequence of calls to be re-evaluated in a global data structure known as the *working sequence* (variable *ws* in the algorithm). This sequence is maintained using a heap data structure, keeping the calls in the descending order of their post-order numbers. During re-evaluation, we pick the call with the highest post-order number from *ws* and invoke the call. Re-evaluation continues until the working sequence becomes empty. When the re-evaluation of a call c is complete, if c has changed, we add all its immediate successors in the called-by graph to the working sequence.

```
re_eval(G, C)
1.    ws := init(G, C);
2.    while (ws is not empty)
3.       remove c, the call with the
                  highest PO number from ws;
4.       call(c);

In SLG's Completion Op. for call c:
1.    if (c.addl_answer) or
                  (c.invalid_count > 0)
2.       foreach c' such that (c, c') ∈ E
3.          if not c'.processed
4.             add c' to ws
5.             c'.processed := true
```

Fig. 2. Optimized Re-Evaluation Algorithm

Note that, during re-evaluation, if c_2 calls c_1 then corresponding edge in the called by graph is (c_1, c_2). *Thus re-evaluation implicitly traverses the transpose of the called-by graph.* If c_1's table is either unaffected or has been recomputed completely, then c_2 can use the answers from that table. Otherwise, c_1 will also be re-evaluated. This ensures that all calls in an SCC of the called-by graph will be evaluated simultaneously.

The correctness of the algorithm, stated in the following theorem, can be established following the properties of the Kosaraju-Sharir algorithm and the definition of *recomputed* set.

Theorem 3. *The set of calls picked by the re-evaluation algorithm (line 3 of re_eval in Figure 2) is the same as the recomputed set.*

In the example, when e(7,8) is deleted, the reverse postorder of affected calls is given by the sequence e(7,X), r(7,X), r(6,X), r(5,X), r(3,X), r(4,X), r(2,X), r(1,X). The set of initially changed calls is {e(7,X)}. When e(7,X) is re-evaluated, its answer e(7,8) is removed, and hence we deem the call to have changed. This causes r(7,X) to be added to the working sequence. When this call is re-evaluated, it too is deemed to have changed (answer r(7,8) is no longer derivable). Hence we add r(6,X) to the working sequence. Re-evaluating r(6,X), we find that it has not changed. The working sequence is now empty and the re-evaluation is complete. Thus, among the 8 affected calls, we re-evaluated only 3.

3   Experimental Results

Below we present preliminary results on the performance of the naive and optimized algorithms on various classes of tabled logic programs. The algorithms were implemented by extending XSB logic programming system [28] (v2.7.1). All measurements were taken on a PC with 3GHz Pentium 4 processor with 2GB of physical memory running Linux (RedHat) version 2.6.9. Our implementation, benchmarks, additional experimental results on simple reachability analysis and push down model checking are available in [23].

Dynamic Programming: We measured the performance of our algorithms on a set of familiar dynamic programming problems. Support graph based incremental techniques [24] cannot be directly used to capture the answer dependencies in these problems due to the use of aggregation operations (min, max etc.). Figure 3 summarizes the relative time performance of incremental evaluation (w.r.t. from-scratch evaluation time) averaged over several possible changes for different dynamic programming problems: longest common subsequence (LCS), minimum edit distance (EDD), and matrix chain multiplication (MM).

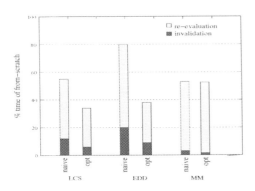

Fig. 3. Performance on Dynamic Programming problems

LCS: We evaluated the performance of incremental evaluation on LCS by changing the character at some position in one of the strings. On average, 50% calls are affected, and 11% of are changed and 15% are recomputed. Although only 15% of the calls are re-evaluated by our optimized incremental algorithm, the time taken for re-evaluation is close 30%. This is due to the overhead of answer clause resolution that our current implementation performs (from the top-level) even for calls that are not recomputed. Incremental evaluation of LCS is sensitive to positions of characters in the string that were changed, as shown by Figure 4.

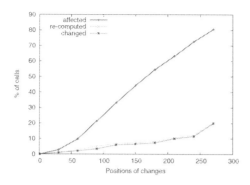

Fig. 4. The effectiveness of the optimized algorithm on LCS

EDD: The solution to EDD is very similar to that of LCS. The two problems differ in the number of dependent calls for each call. Every call in EDD evaluation is connected to 3 calls in the call-by graph whereas in LCS each call is connected to at most 2 calls. Hence the number of affected calls in higher in EDD, resulting in higher invalidation time.

MM: For matrix chain multiplication, we deleted one matrix from the chain and measured the incremental and from-scratch time. For such a change, all affected calls are recomputed. Hence the optimized algorithm performs no better than the naive one.

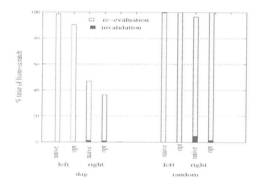

Fig. 5. Performance on All-Pair Shortest Path

All-Pair Shortest Path: We experimented with encodings of the all-pair shortest path problem on a directed acyclic graph having 50K nodes and randomly generated graph having 50K edges and 250 nodes (close to complete graph). We performed separate experiments with two different logic program encodings (with left and right recursion, resp.). For the almost-complete graph, incremental evaluation algorithms are not effective since almost all calls are recomputed. For DAGs, the right-recursive version shows better incremental performance due to the availability of nontrivial call dependency information.

Data Flow Analysis: Reaching definition analysis for imperative programs is a well-known data flow analysis which determines, for each program point, the set of variable definitions (assignments) that may reach that point [2]. We extended the intra-procedural analysis to an inter-procedural setting using the classical approach of replacing procedure calls with jumps: from the call site to the entry point of the callee, and from the exit point of the callee to the statement following the call site. The experiments were performed on various large C programs and for each benchmark 100 random statements (one per incremental run) were chosen for replacement with a skip statement. The logic programming formulation of data flow analysis uses stratified negation, and the techniques based on answer dependency [24] cannot be readily used in this case.

Table 1 shows that incremental algorithms takes on average 50% of from-scratch time although number of affected calls is close to 30%. In all the experiments the in-

Table 1. Data flow analysis; One statement replaced with skip; Time is seconds

Benchmark	Non Incr.	Non-opt. Incr.		Opt. Incr.		% of calls affected	% of aff. calls	
		Re-eval	%	Re-eval	%		recomputed	changed
assembler	5.95	3.60	60.6	3.64	61.2	23.5	85	1
diff	4.55	2.23	49.0	2.24	49.2	30.9	97	1
dixie	1.73	0.96	55.6	0.94	54.4	26.8	95	7
gnugo	4.41	2.38	53.9	2.42	54.8	30.6	99	1
learn	1.29	0.53	40.7	0.54	41.4	26.6	93	9
smail	5.50	2.89	52.4	2.85	51.7	25.4	98	2

validation times were negligible. Closer inspection reveal that for these examples 90% of the call nodes belong to a few non-trivial SCCs in the called-by graph. The formation of such large SCCs is due the inter-procedural jumps which introduce cycles even when the original program had no recursion. Due to the large SCCs, most affected calls are also recomputed. For example in benchmark learn 93% of the affected calls are recomputed but only 9% of the affected calls are changed.

Pointer Analysis: We used the call-graph based techniques for the incremental evaluation of Anderson's Points-to analysis [3] encoded as a tabled logic program [22]. We measured the performance of the analyzer on programs taken from C benchmarks available with PAF [15] compiler suite and SPEC95 benchmarks. The largest of these, vortex, has more than 65K lines of code.

Table 2 shows the relative performance of naive and optimized incremental algorithms after removal of one (source-level) statement from the benchmark programs, compared to the from-scratch time. Deleting one source level assignment statement may delete multiple primitive assignments statements and hence multiple facts. The results were averaged over 100 randomly chosen deletion of source statements.

Table 2. Performance of naive and optimized algorithms on pointer analysis; Time is seconds

Benchmark	Non Incr.	Naive Incremental			Opt. Incremental			% of calls affected	% of aff. calls	
		Invalid	Re-eval	%	Invalid	Re-eval	%		recomputed	changed
m88ksim	0.39	0.00	0.04	10.1	0.00	0.03	6.8	1.1	56.4	25.2
vpr	0.65	0.01	0.19	30.8	0.01	0.17	27.8	4.0	57.9	6.1
smail	1.65	0.01	1.18	72.2	0.01	1.19	72.3	6.0	90.3	25.8
twmc	2.22	0.01	0.93	42.5	0.00	0.92	41.7	2.9	85.7	6.0
nethack	0.98	0.01	0.80	82.8	0.00	0.80	82.2	5.6	67.2	12.8
vortex	12.44	0.04	12.10	97.5	0.02	11.35	91.3	5.5	68.3	6.6

Observe that the incremental times for large benchmarks are close to the non-incremental times. We investigated the vortex program to explain its behavior. Pointer analysis of vortex makes 68K calls in total of which on average 4K calls are affected. Close inspection of affected calls revealed the existence of large SCC (consisting 2.7K nodes) in the call graph. Also about 90% of the time taken by pointer analysis is attributed to the calls in the large SCC. Since the nodes in the SCC are part of the affected set, re-evaluation takes almost same time as from-scratch analysis. The calls in the SCC are also in the recomputed set and hence we do not observe any appreciable difference in the performance of the optimized algorithm relative to its naive counterpart.

The presence of large SCCs limits the performance of call-graph-based algorithms. In contrast, techniques based on the finer-grained answer dependencies perform very well for this program. For instance, the time for incremental evaluation after one source statement deletion from the vortex benchmark is 0.1%, 15% and 0.5% using techniques in [21], [22] and [24] resp. Hence it would be useful to incorporate these specialized techniques into the more general call dependency based algorithm.

XML Validation: We investigated incremental validation of XML documents with respect to Document Type Definitions (DTD) [4]. The basic validation problem checks whether a string belongs to a regular language or not.

Table 3 shows the result of applying the naive algorithm for incremental validation of XML documents for different number of elements (first column). The example XML documents and DTD describe a library catalog which contains zero or more number of books. Each book contains zero of more number of authors followed by title. Each author has a name, zero or more emails and an address. We generated XML documents having 1K–50K books, with up to 3 authors per book and up to 3 email addresses per author. Each update consists of deletion of one book element from the chain of book elements of the library. The number of affected calls is less than 0.01% of total number of calls. The savings due to incremental evaluation arise from reusing the prior validation of each book element. Since the number of books is large, it results in considerable savings due to incremental evaluation. We encoded the validator using left recursion. Since this results in only one call, we do not see any additional benefits due to the optimized algorithm.

Table 3. XML Validation; deletion of one element; Time is seconds

No. of Elements	Non-Incr	Naive Re-eval.	
		Re-eval	%
12K	0.18	0.00	1.25
120K	1.89	0.03	1.55
240K	3.79	0.06	1.59
360K	5.67	0.09	1.64
480K	7.63	0.12	1.62
600K	9.60	0.16	1.64

Space Overhead. We measured the space needed for keeping the called-by graph for sample applications. Note that although the number of nodes in the called-by graph is bounded by the number of tabled calls, the number of edges can be large. Observe from Table 4 that space needed for the called-by graph is about 30% of the table space for most of the applications. For matrix chain multiplication with chain length n, the number of calls is $O(n^2)$ but the number of called-by graph edges is $O(n^3)$. This contributes to the large size of the called-by graph compared to its table space. For such applications, it will be better to not materialize the graph, as described in Section 5.

4 Related Work

The problem of incremental evaluation has been addressed in various fields of research, viz. view maintenance in databases, model checking, program analysis, logic programming, functional programming, attribute grammar evaluation and AI.

Table 4. Space usage (in MB) of the incremental algorithm

Application	Table Space	Called-by Graph Space
Pointer Analysis (vortex)	51.0	13.6
Pointer Analysis (twmc)	18.3	3.5
Matrix Multiplication (chain 200)	4.0	75.0
Longest Common Subsequence (strlen 1000)	168.7	50.1
Minimum Edit Distance (strlen 600)	63.3	21.6
Reaching Definition (diff)	211.0	39.3
XML validation (60K elements)	107.0	13.0

The materialized view maintenance problem has been extensively researched (see, e.g. [10, 14] for surveys). Most of the works in recursive views maintenance generate rules that are similar in spirit to those of DRed [11] and are subsumed by DRed (as compared in [10]). DRed computes the dependencies between answers using rules derived from the original program and does not maintain any dependency structure. The MCI algorithm [26] for incremental model checking maintains a dependency graph analogous to support graph [21] which keeps track of dependency between answers. Both MCI and DRed mark an answer in deletion phase if at least one derivation of answer depends on the deleted fact. In the rederivation phase both algorithms rederive an answer if it can be derived based on unmarked answers and facts. The DRed-like strategy is also used in incremental program analysis techniques: e.g. Yur et. al.'s algorithm to update points-to analysis information [29] and Pollock and Soffa's incremental iterative algorithm using change classification and reinitialization for bitvector problems [16]. They employ a two phase solution where the *exaggerate* and *adjust* phases correspond to DRed's delete and rederive phases respectively. Our primary-support-based algorithm [21] improved on the DRed strategy by significantly reducing the need to propagate deletions. In [22] we generalize the idea of primary support, identifying multiple acyclic supports for an answer, all of which should be deleted before the answer can be marked, and also gave an algorithm that uses only partial support information to bound space overheads. In [24] we presented a data structure to store full support graphs symbolically, making the technique scalable in terms of both time and space to large applications.

In contrast to the algorithm presented in this paper, the above techniques cannot be readily applied to arbitrary tabled logic programs, especially those that use aggregation and other Prolog built-ins, or have non-stratified negation. However, when applicable, the fine-grained dependency information (i.e. between answers) used by these algorithms will enable them to outperform the call-graph based algorithms.

The idea of recording the evaluation process as a graph and using a topological order to guide incremental change propagation has been used in various fields of attribute grammar, functional programming and logic programming. The dependency graphs used in [19] for attribute grammar evaluation is *static* and whereas the augmented dependency graph (ADG) used in [1] for recording dependencies between input and output values in the execution of pure functional programs is *dynamic*. In both algorithms the graphs are *acyclic*, which restricts their use in logic programming.

Incremental algorithms for the re-analysis of constraint logic programs [12, 13, 17] are perhaps closest to our work. These algorithms, intended for program analysis, use call dependencies to propagate changes in the analysis information due to insertion and deletion of rules. A bottom-up deletion algorithm using a static predicate dependency graph was presented in [13]. A SCC-reduced dynamic call graph based algorithm was presented in [12] to handle arbitrary changes. Our algorithm is very similar to these in terms of using call graphs for change propagation. Notable differences are as follows. Firstly, through the use of post-order numbers, we perform re-evaluation without explicitly computing the SCCs whereas they use a separate SCC maintenance phase. Secondly, we use full-fledged tabled resolution to recompute answers and hence can handle prolog builtins, aggregates and non-stratified negation. In contrast, the other algorithms keep track of the direction of a change (i.e. insert or delete) and hence are difficult to generalize for arbitrary programs (e.g. those with findall). Processing of insertion of rules was improved in [17] by making the non-incremental algorithm SCC-preserving without explicitly computing the SCCs by using a specialized event scheduling strategy. We obtain the same effect by using XSB's local scheduling [8].

5   Discussion

In this section we discuss possible extensions to the algorithms presented in Section 2.

Lazy re-evaluation: The algorithms presented in Section 2 refreshes all answer tables such that after each incremental phase the set of answers is sound and complete with respect to the changed program. Certain applications (e.g. ontology management systems), access tables through a graphical user interface, and access some or all of the answers only when required. In such cases, it will be better to re-evaluate a call only on demand. This can be done by keeping a subgoal dependency graph to propagate demand top-down, while keeping the called-by graph to perform re-evaluations bottom-up. Since the invalidation phase takes very little time, it can still be done eagerly. That will ensure that the optimized algorithm can still be used in order to re-evaluate only those calls in the *recomputed* set that are also demanded.

Insertion for Definite Logic Programs: The algorithm presented here re-evaluates a call by generating all its answers using program clause resolution. When the direction of the change (i.e. whether it is an addition, deletion or both) is known, we can do better. If the change made is an addition and the program has no negation, we can derive a new program that computes these changes efficiently. The rules of the new program are called "delta rules" and are derived by finite-differencing the original definite program [11, 21]. This has a potential to significantly improve incremental evaluation times. For example, a single statement insertion using delta rules takes on average 8% of from-scratch time for pointer analysis in vortex benchmark whereas it takes 90% of from-scratch time when the affected calls are completely re-evaluated. While it is relatively straightforward to use the "delta rules" program for incrementally processing additions for predicates without negation, light-weight re-evaluation techniques for other kinds of changes and for general logic programs remains an open problem.

Mixed Strategy: In [24] we described a space efficient technique for storing answer dependencies in the form of symbolic support graph. Symbolic support graph based deletion algorithm is extremely efficient in practice— taking less than 5% of from-scratch time in all the applications we have tested. We can combine these two techniques, keeping call dependencies in general but keeping symbolic support graphs whenever possible to efficiently process deletions.

Non-materialized called-by graph: Although the call dependencies are typically smaller than answer dependencies, and the number of calls is bounded by table space, the called-by graph itself may take more space than the tables (e.g. the matrix chain multiplication example in Section 3). It is hence worth exploring whether we can avoid storing the edges of the called-by graph, and instead compute them on the fly. It is relatively easy to derive the called-by relation for a given definite logic program. For instance, from every rule of the form $p :- q_1, q_2, \ldots, q_n$ we can derive "called-by" rules such as $called\_by(q_i, p) :- q_1, q_2, \ldots, q_{i-1}$. While the computed called-by relation is a space-efficient alternative to storing large called-by graphs, it is not clear whether such rules can be derived for arbitrary logic programs (especially those employing impure constructs such as cuts).

Summary: We presented an incremental evaluation algorithm based on call dependencies that can handle tabled logic programs with negation, aggregation and Prolog builtins. Experiments show that the general algorithm is useful although not as effective as the (more restricted) answer-dependency-based techniques. The algorithm identifies a small set of calls to be re-evaluated and invokes them in a particular order to ensure optimality. The actual re-evaluation itself is performed rather naively, by (effectively) removing all answers from a table to be re-evaluated and using program clause resolution to restore the answer table. More sophisticated techniques that optimize the re-evaluation itself are of significant interest. Our experience with this algorithm shows that programs written for efficient tabled evaluation may not be most suited for efficient incremental evaluation too. Developing a methodology to write efficient incremental programs (analogous to recursion transformations and supplementary tabling for tabled programs) is an important avenue of future research.

Acknowledgements

This research was supported in part by NSF grants CCR-0205376, and CCR-0311512. We thank David Warren for many useful discussions on the call graph based incremental algorithm. We also thank the anonymous referees for their helpful comments on the earlier version of the paper.

References

1. U. A. Acar, G. E. Blelloch, and R. Harper. Adaptive functional programming. In *POPL*, pages 247–259. ACM Press, 2002.
2. A. V. Aho, R. Sethi, and J. D. Ullman. *Compilers: principles, techniques, and tools*, pages 585–718. Addison-Wesley, 1986.
3. L. O. Anderson. *Program Analysis and Specialization for the C Programming Language*. PhD thesis, DIKU, Unversity of Copenhagen, 1994.
4. A. Balmin, Y. Papakonstantinou, and V. Vianu. Incremental validation of xml documents. *ACM Trans. Database Syst.*, 29(4):710–751, 2004.
5. W. Chen, T. Swift, and D. S. Warren. Efficient implementation of general logical queries. *JLP*, 1995.

6. W. Chen and D. S. Warren. Tabled evaluation with delaying for general logic programs. *JACM*, 43(1):20–74, 1996.
7. S. Dawson, C. R. Ramakrishnan, and D. S. Warren. Practical program analysis using general purpose logic programming systems — a case study. In *ACM PLDI*, pages 117–126, 1996.
8. J. Freire, T. Swift, and D. S. Warren. Beyond depth-first: Improving tabled logic programs through alternative scheduling strategies. In *PLILP*, pages 243–258, 1996.
9. H. Guo and G. Gupta. A simple scheme for implementing tabled logic programming systems based on dynamic reordering of alternatives. In *ICLP*, pages 181–196. Springer, 2001.
10. A. Gupta and I. Mumick. Maintenance of materialized views: Problems, techniques, and applications. *IEEE Data Engineering Bulletin*, 18(2):3–18, 1995.
11. A. Gupta, I. S. Mumick, and V. S. Subrahmanian. Maintaining views incrementally. In *SIGMOD*, pages 157–166, 1993.
12. M. Hermenegildo, G. Puebla, K. Marriott, and P. J. Stuckey. Incremental analysis of constraint logic programs. *ACM Trans. Program. Lang. Syst.*, 22(2):187–223, 2000.
13. M. V. Hermenegildo, G. Puebla, K. Marriott, and P. J. Stuckey. Incremental evaluation of tabled logic programs. In *ICLP*, MIT Press, pages 797–811, 1995.
14. E. Mayol and E. Teniente. A survey of current methods for integrity constraint maintenance and view updating. In *ER Workshops*, pages 62–73, 1999.
15. PAF. Prolangs analysis framework. Available at http://www.prolangs.rutgers.edu/public.html.
16. L. L. Pollock and M. L. Soffa. An incremental version of iterative data flow analysis. *IEEE Trans. Softw. Eng.*, 15(12):1537–1549, 1989.
17. G. Puebla and M. V. Hermenegildo. Optimized algorithms for incremental analysis of logic programs. In *SAS*, pages 270–284, 1996.
18. C. R. Ramakrishnan et al. XMC: A logic-programming-based verification toolset. In *CAV*, number 1855 in LNCS, pages 576–580, 2000.
19. T. Reps, T. Teitelbaum, and A. Demers. Incremental context-dependent analysis for language-based editors. *TOPLAS*, 5(3):449–477, 1983.
20. R. Rocha, F. Silva, and V. S. Costa. YapTab: A Tabling Engine Designed to Support Parallelism. In *Workshop on Tabling in Parsing and Deduction*, 2000.
21. D. Saha and C. R. Ramakrishnan. Incremental evaluation of tabled logic programs. In *ICLP*, volume 2916 of *LNCS*, pages 389–406, 2003.
22. D. Saha and C. R. Ramakrishnan. Incremental and demand-driven points-to analysis using logic programming. In *Principles and Practice of Declarative Programming*, 2005.
23. D. Saha and C. R. Ramakrishnan. A practical framework for incremental evaluation, 2005. Available at http://www.lmc.cs.sunysb.edu/~dsaha/callg.
24. D. Saha and C. R. Ramakrishnan. Symbolic support graph: A space efficient data structure for incremental tabled evaluation. In *ICLP*, volume 3668 of *LNCS*, pages 235–249, 2005.
25. M. Sharir. A strong connectivity algorithm and its application in data flow analysis. *Computer and Mathemetics with Applications*, 7(1):67–72, 1981.
26. O. V. Sokolsky and S. A. Smolka. Incremental model checking in the modal mu-calculus. In *CAV*, volume 818 of *LNCS*, pages 351–363, 1994.
27. H. Tamaki and T. Sato. OLDT resolution with tabulation. In *ICLP*, pages 84–98, 1986.
28. XSB. The XSB logic programming system. Available at http://xsb.sourceforge.net.
29. J. Yur, B. G. Ryder, and W. Landi. An incremental flow- and context-sensitive pointer aliasing analysis. In *ICSE*, pages 442–451, 1999.
30. N. Zhou, Y. Shen, L. Yuan, and J. You. Implementation of a linear tabling mechanism. *Journal of Functional and Logic Programming*, 2001(10), October 2001.

Author Index

Lecture Notes in Computer Science

For information about Vols. 1–3738

please contact your bookseller or Springer

Vol. 3788: B. Roy (Ed.), Advances in Cryptology - ASI-ACRYPT 2005. XIV, 703 pages. 2005.

Vol. 3785: K.-K. Lau, R. Banach (Eds.), Formal Methods and Software Engineering. XIV, 496 pages. 2005.

Vol. 3784: J. Tao, T. Tan, R.W. Picard (Eds.), Affective Computing and Intelligent Interaction. XIX, 1008 pages. 2005.

Vol. 3783: S. Qing, W. Mao, J. Lopez, G. Wang (Eds.), Information and Communications Security. XIV, 492 pages. 2005.

Vol. 3781: S.Z. Li, Z. Sun, T. Tan, S. Pankanti, G. Chollet, D. Zhang (Eds.), Advances in Biometric Person Authentication. XI, 250 pages. 2005.

Vol. 3780: K. Yi (Ed.), Programming Languages and Systems. XI, 435 pages. 2005.

Vol. 3779: H. Jin, D. Reed, W. Jiang (Eds.), Network and Parallel Computing. XV, 513 pages. 2005.

Vol. 3778: C. Atkinson, C. Bunse, H.-G. Gross, C. Peper (Eds.), Component-Based Software Development for Embedded Systems. VIII, 345 pages. 2005.

Vol. 3777: O.B. Lupanov, O.M. Kasim-Zade, A.V. Chaskin, K. Steinhöfel (Eds.), Stochastic Algorithms: Foundations and Applications. VIII, 239 pages. 2005.

Vol. 3776: S.K. Pal, S. Bandyopadhyay, S. Biswas (Eds.), Pattern Recognition and Machine Intelligence. XXIV, 808 pages. 2005.

Vol. 3775: J. Schönwälder, J. Serrat (Eds.), Ambient Networks. XIII, 281 pages. 2005.

Vol. 3774: G. Bierman, C. Koch (Eds.), Database Programming Languages. X, 295 pages. 2005.

Vol. 3773: A. Sanfeliu, M.L. Cortés (Eds.), Progress in Pattern Recognition, Image Analysis and Applications. XX, 1094 pages. 2005.

Vol. 3772: M. Consens, G. Navarro (Eds.), String Processing and Information Retrieval. XIV, 406 pages. 2005.

Vol. 3771: J.M.T. Romijn, G.P. Smith, J. van de Pol (Eds.), Integrated Formal Methods. XI, 407 pages. 2005.

Vol. 3770: J. Akoka, S.W. Liddle, I.-Y. Song, M. Bertolotto, I. Comyn-Wattiau, W.-J. van den Heuvel, M. Kolp, J. Trujillo, C. Kop, H.C. Mayr (Eds.), Perspectives in Conceptual Modeling. XXII, 476 pages. 2005.

Vol. 3769: D.A. Bader, M. Parashar, V. Sridhar, V.K. Prasanna (Eds.), High Performance Computing – HiPC 2005. XXVIII, 550 pages. 2005.

Vol. 3768: Y.-S. Ho, H.J. Kim (Eds.), Advances in Multimedia Information Processing - PCM 2005, Part II. XXVIII, 1088 pages. 2005.

Vol. 3767: Y.-S. Ho, H.J. Kim (Eds.), Advances in Multimedia Information Processing - PCM 2005, Part I. XXVIII, 1022 pages. 2005.

Vol. 3766: N. Sebe, M.S. Lew, T.S. Huang (Eds.), Computer Vision in Human-Computer Interaction. X, 231 pages. 2005.

Vol. 3765: Y. Liu, T. Jiang, C. Zhang (Eds.), Computer Vision for Biomedical Image Applications. X, 563 pages. 2005.

Vol. 3764: S. Tixeuil, T. Herman (Eds.), Self-Stabilizing Systems. VIII, 229 pages. 2005.

Vol. 3762: R. Meersman, Z. Tari, P. Herrero (Eds.), On the Move to Meaningful Internet Systems 2005: OTM 2005 Workshops. XXXI, 1228 pages. 2005.

Vol. 3761: R. Meersman, Z. Tari (Eds.), On the Move to Meaningful Internet Systems 2005: CoopIS, DOA, and ODBASE, Part II. XXVII, 653 pages. 2005.

Vol. 3760: R. Meersman, Z. Tari (Eds.), On the Move to Meaningful Internet Systems 2005: CoopIS, DOA, and ODBASE, Part I. XXVII, 921 pages. 2005.

Vol. 3759: G. Chen, Y. Pan, M. Guo, J. Lu (Eds.), Parallel and Distributed Processing and Applications - ISPA 2005 Workshops. XIII, 669 pages. 2005.

Vol. 3758: Y. Pan, D.-x. Chen, M. Guo, J. Cao, J.J. Dongarra (Eds.), Parallel and Distributed Processing and Applications. XXIII, 1162 pages. 2005.

Vol. 3757: A. Rangarajan, B. Vemuri, A.L. Yuille (Eds.), Energy Minimization Methods in Computer Vision and Pattern Recognition. XII, 666 pages. 2005.

Vol. 3756: J. Cao, W. Nejdl, M. Xu (Eds.), Advanced Parallel Processing Technologies. XIV, 526 pages. 2005.

Vol. 3754: J. Dalmau Royo, G. Hasegawa (Eds.), Management of Multimedia Networks and Services. XII, 384 pages. 2005.

Vol. 3753: O.F. Olsen, L.M.J. Florack, A. Kuijper (Eds.), Deep Structure, Singularities, and Computer Vision. X, 259 pages. 2005.

Vol. 3752: N. Paragios, O. Faugeras, T. Chan, C. Schnörr (Eds.), Variational, Geometric, and Level Set Methods in Computer Vision. XI, 369 pages. 2005.

Vol. 3751: T. Magedanz, E.R. M. Madeira, P. Dini (Eds.), Operations and Management in IP-Based Networks. X, 213 pages. 2005.

Vol. 3750: J.S. Duncan, G. Gerig (Eds.), Medical Image Computing and Computer-Assisted Intervention – MICCAI 2005, Part II. XL, 1018 pages. 2005.

Vol. 3749: J.S. Duncan, G. Gerig (Eds.), Medical Image Computing and Computer-Assisted Intervention – MICCAI 2005, Part I. XXXIX, 942 pages. 2005.

Vol. 3748: A. Hartman, D. Kreische (Eds.), Model Driven Architecture – Foundations and Applications. IX, 349 pages. 2005.

Vol. 3747: C.A. Maziero, J.G. Silva, A.M.S. Andrade, F.M.d. Assis Silva (Eds.), Dependable Computing. XV, 267 pages. 2005.

Vol. 3746: P. Bozanis, E.N. Houstis (Eds.), Advances in Informatics. XIX, 879 pages. 2005.

Vol. 3745: J.L. Oliveira, V. Maojo, F. Martín-Sánchez, A.S. Pereira (Eds.), Biological and Medical Data Analysis. XII, 422 pages. 2005. (Subseries LNBI).

Vol. 3744: T. Magedanz, A. Karmouch, S. Pierre, I. Venieris (Eds.), Mobility Aware Technologies and Applications. XIV, 418 pages. 2005.

Vol. 3742: J. Akiyama, M. Kano, X. Tan (Eds.), Discrete and Computational Geometry. VIII, 213 pages. 2005.

Vol. 3740: T. Srikanthan, J. Xue, C.-H. Chang (Eds.), Advances in Computer Systems Architecture. XVII, 833 pages. 2005.

Vol. 3739: W. Fan, Z. Wu, J. Yang (Eds.), Advances in Web-Age Information Management. XXIV, 930 pages. 2005.